Writing Her Own Life

Literature of the American West
William Kittredge, General Editor

Other books by Mary Clearman Blew

Lambing Out and Other Stories (Columbia, 1977; paperback, Norman, 2001)

All but the Waltz: Essays on a Montana Family (New York, 1991; paperback, Norman, 2001)

Balsamroot: A Memoir (New York, 1994; paperback, Norman, 2001)

Runaway (Lewiston, Idaho, 1990)

Bone Deep in Landscape: Writing, Reading, and Place (Norman, 1999)

Sister Coyote (New York, 2000)

(ed.) *When Montana and I Were Young*, by Margaret Bell (Lincoln, 2002)

(ed.) *Circle of Women: An Anthology of Contemporary Western Women Writers,* with Kim Barnes (New York, 1994; paperback, Norman, 2001)

(ed.) *Written on Water: Essays on Idaho Rivers* (New York, 2000)

Writing Her Own Life

Imogene Welch,
Western Rural Schoolteacher

Mary Clearman Blew

UNIVERSITY OF OKLAHOMA PRESS : NORMAN

Library of Congress Cataloging-in-Publication Data

Blew, Mary Clearman, 1939–
    Writing her own life : Imogene Welch, Western rural schoolteacher / Mary
Clearman Blew.
        p.   cm. — (Literature of the American West ; v. 14)
    A narrative built around entries from the diaries of Imogene Welch.
    Includes bibliographical references.
    ISBN 0-8061-3581-6 (alk. paper)
        1. Welch, Imogene. 2. Teachers—West (U.S.)—Biography. 3. Women
teachers—West (U.S.)—Biography. 4. Autobiography—Women authors.
    5. World War, 1939–1945—Social aspects—West (U.S.) I. Welch, Imogene.
    II. Title III. Series

LA2317.W373B54 2004
371.1'0092—dc22
[B]
                                                                    2003060169

Writing Her Own Life: Imogene Welch, Western Rural Schoolteacher is Volume 14 in the
Literature of the American West series.

1   2   3   4   5   6   7   8   9   10

For
Doris, my mother
Sylva, my aunt
and Florence, my aunt by marriage

CONTENTS

ILLUSTRATIONS

following page 136

Photographs are from Mary Clearman Blew's family collection

ACKNOWLEDGMENTS

I have many to thank for their assistance: my daughter Rachel Blew, who traveled with me along Imogene's route through Washington State and then spent a summer cooking and keeping house to free me for writing; Susanne George Bloomfield for her friendship and the hours we've spent together, discussing writing; Yvonne Demestre of the Tenino, Washington, branch of the Timberland Regional Library; Steve Fisher of Timberland Virtual Reference; Melody Graulich for her helpful suggestions at a late stage in the manuscript; Bill Lang, for sharing his encyclopedic knowledge of southwest Washington history; Sylva Noel for all the years she has loved and encouraged me; Barb Rieger of the *Tenino Independent*; Ann Ronald, for twice reading drafts of the manuscript with sympathy and helpful criticism; Daniel Simon, formerly of the University of Oklahoma Press, for his enthusiasm for this book; James R. Warren, for his insights into the war years in Washington State; Florence Welch for her long and generous letters of reminiscence; Imogene Welch for the amazing legacy of her life; and Karen Wieder of the University of Oklahoma Press, who has guided the book at last to completion.

Writing Her Own Life

INTRODUCTION

January 8, 1934. Got only a C in Algebra—a D in History. Bot a type writer.

My aunt, Imogene Welch, began keeping a diary on January 1, 1934. A homestead child, born and raised on the Montana prairie during the worst of the drought and depression years, in 1934 she was just twenty-four years old. After two years of normal school in Montana and a few years of teaching in rural schools, she was attending the University of Minnesota and hoping to improve her lot by earning a bachelor's degree, but she was finding herself woefully unprepared for a university curriculum. In that first diary, a small brown leather book with her name and *A Line A Day: Five Year Diary* stamped in gold on the cover, she noted her homesickness and her academic difficulties and set herself a pattern that would continue for the next fifty-odd years. She went on to teach school until she retired, and she filled a dozen such small volumes, seldom writing more than a line or two a day, but hardly ever missing a day.

Although Imogene and I had been a very close aunt and niece, I had had no idea of her diaries' existence until, clearing out her possessions after she was disabled by a series of strokes, I came across the little cache of leather-bound books.

"You get in the habit," a woman of my aunt's generation told me, a few years later. "That line or two in your diary, first thing in the morning over coffee. Or maybe the last thing at night. You get to where you can't go on with your day without writing your line or two," and apparently this was the case with Imogene, whose line or two a day chronicle the whole of her adult life.

It is hard to imagine a narrative form more linear than these inexorable daily jottings over weeks and months and years, in which faces appear and disappear without explanation, scenes are left unfinished, and plot and form flow as unceasing as the current of a river. Entries are written in past tense, but without reflection, composing a kind of continuous present. Time is the only constant and immediacy is the mode, in which the writer cannot look ahead, as I can. The diarist has no way of knowing what the future holds. She can only read down the lines that remind her of her previous hopes or fears, written last year or the year before, or the year before that, one space below another on a page of her five-year diary.

But if much of what Imogene mentions in those daily jottings is the weather or the muddy Montana roads or the behavior of her pupils, she is also keeping an implicit record of her own growth. Although she doesn't know it, she is about to be catapulted by a combination of near-fatal accident and national catastrophe into a life that she never could have imagined. From my vantage point, living in the future that the diaries cannot foresee, I know that the gathering storm of World War II will interrupt the dismal pattern of her days and send her into the unimaginable. She will be separated from family and friends, she will be faced with challenges undreamed of, she will redirect her life and transform herself into the independent professional woman that I knew.

She won't be alone in this transformation. Because of World War II, count-less young men and women will find themselves crossing a divide between the known and the unknown. For many, the tumult and the horrors will be much more shocking than the upheaval and social change that Imogene will experience. But like many others, she will make her way on new and shaky ground. All that is familiar to her—her family, her friends, the dusty slow-moving ranch communities of depression-era Montana—will fade into the hazy landscape of the past. Possibility waits in an equally hazy future.

In the spring of 1934, having lost her battle with algebra and trigonometry, homesick and broke, Imogene left Minneapolis and went back to Montana, where she would teach in rural schools for the next eight years. She was a healthy young woman—touchingly young—with huge brown eyes, a ready laugh, and a tendency to plumpness that would distress her all of her life. Her first teaching position after returning to Montana was a summer term in a school with eight pupils somewhere in the badlands near the Missouri River, miles from nowhere over dirt roads. She was paid seventy-five dollars a month. In her diary, she writes about knitting or doing chores during lonely evenings in the teacherage. Hoping a neighbor will drop off her groceries and mail on his way home from town. Longing for a new book to read or a battery radio to keep her company. Driven by boredom, she caused a neighborhood scandal that summer by walking a few miles to a sheep camp in the evenings to play cards and gossip.

The risks for country schoolteachers were not always as trivial as neigh-borhood gossip. A few years later, at another school, she will sit alone in the dark, holding a jammed .22 rifle and listening to young men of the neighbor-hood argue about breaking in and raping *that damned schoolteacher*—"But hey, she's got a gun," one of them says, and at last they leave.

For the next five years her diaries reflect her frustration with low pay. Seventy-five dollars a month, and then, as times get harder, forty-five dollars a month. She knows that school boards routinely let their teachers go after one or two years so that they won't have to give them tenure, she worries about getting her contract renewed, and every fall it's the same fear: will she find a school? Will she have a job at all? And even with a job, on forty-five dollars a month, can she manage to save any money? Oh, how she would like to earn enough money to buy pretty clothes! But if only she could save enough to buy a car! Oh, for the freedom her own car would give her!

As I read Imogene's diaries, I find myself wondering what a rural schoolteacher in her twenties had to look forward to beyond hard work, isolation, hand-to-mouth living, and a lack of job security. What kept her going? What were her dreams?

One factor that kept Imogene going was her lack of options. During those years just before the outbreak of World War II, her father was showing early signs of the dementia that eventually would incapacitate him. Her mother was struggling to make ends meet on her own pitiful pay as a rural schoolteacher and couldn't be asked to feed another mouth. And what other jobs, in depression-era Montana, could a young woman find? At one point in her diary Imogene records that, in desperation because it is late summer and she has not yet found a school to teach, she has inquired at a local laundry and learned that they pay their women ten cents an hour. Eighty cents a day, four or five dollars a week, compared with even the forty-five dollars a month she can earn by teaching?

Imogene also clung to the hope of finding a teaching job at better pay, under better conditions, in Washington State. Her older sister, Sylva, had married and moved to Bremerton, Washington, with her husband, Ervin, who finally had found work in the ship lofts after following a scanty succession of depression-era jobs across the Pacific Northwest. In June of 1939, Imogene paid Sylva and Ervin a visit, and she notes in her diary that Sylva has tried to line her up for some interviews—*Interviewed Supt. Peterson for a job or trace of one. He referrred me to an agency and a Co. Supt.*

But teaching positions in the Puget Sound area were as scarce as they were in Montana, and the interviews came to nothing.

Imogene had another dream. Maybe she could rescue herself from oblivion by writing. During the evenings, exhausted after a day of teaching and finishing her lesson plans and doing her chores (cleaning the school house, carrying water, hauling wood), she sat by the light of a kerosene lamp and forced herself to write short story after short story which she submitted to, and invariably had rejected by, *The Saturday Evening Post, The American,* or *The Ladies Home Journal.*

Writing was not a dream that Imogene ever relinquished; in her seventies and retired from teaching in Port Angeles, Washington, she attended an evening creative writing class, started writing fiction again, and at last saw a story of hers in print. But in her twenties, as she jots her nightly line or two in her diary, she cannot skip ahead through the pages as I can and read her future. *Now* is when she so desperately needs money and encouragement, and she gets neither.

Finally, Imogene dreamed of marriage. Both of her sisters had married after a year or two of teaching, Sylva to my uncle Ervin and Doris, my mother, to a young rancher named Jack Hogeland. In her diary, Imogene details her hopes: to live on a ranch like Doris's, to have children, to raise her own flowers and vegetables and chickens. She embroiders pillowcases for a hope chest, she starts a quilt. And she falls in love, but alas, with the wrong man.

Lud Lange was the son of central European immigrant homesteaders. *Bohunks,* their white Protestant neighbors sneered, lumping the Bohemians with the Czechoslovakians and Croatians and even the Swiss, mistrusting their old-country language and their Catholic religion. Imogene's family opposed her friendship with Lud, who was one of eleven children and who probably went no further in school than eighth grade. He owned a few horses and the clothes he wore. But throughout the worst of the drought and depression years of the 1930s, he courted Imogene, wrote to her while she was at the University of Minnesota, and visited her at her far-flung country schools whenever he could. Imogene records his small gifts of candy and flowers, his letters, and her own loneliness when she doesn't see him for days or weeks.

Gradually Imogene and Lud both must have realized that they would never have the money to marry. She had her precarious teaching career, but Lud had nothing: a dollar a day for ranch work when he could find it and long stretches of days when he couldn't. Perhaps he lost heart. His name turns up less frequently in Imogene's diaries. And then a bombshell. Lud and another young man are arrested for the theft of a neighbor's saddle, tried, and sentenced to the Montana State Prison at Deer Lodge. Imogene was heartsick and ashamed. Lud's thievery had violated the ethics of her rigid, hard-working family, and, although she never forgot him, even during the dementia of her last years, she was never able to forgive him. Nor was she able to love any other man. In her diaries, she records brief interests that never bloom. Even in her forties she tells herself that she hopes to marry. But in fact, she remained single for the rest of her life.

So much for dreams. Now for the real future.

Advice from the title page of Imogene's first five-year diary:

THE MIND is a wonderful machine. It needs but to be just refreshed and incidents can again be revived in their former clarity. A LINE each day, whether it be of the weather or of more important substances, will in time to come bring back those vague memories, worth remembering, to almost actual reality.

In the beginning, as I tried to understand my aunt's life, and through her life to understand my own, I read between her lines and supplied my own memories and research to bring back "those vague memories" that Imogene's brief entries might have brought back to her. In doing so, I was on the same trail as any shaper of story. I studied Imogene's diaries and described a life for her in the light of my own experiences. Whether or not "incidents can again be revived in their former clarity," or "vague memories" can be restored to "almost actual reality," whatever that might be, I thought that I could trace Imogene's road through heartbreak and disappointment to independence and acceptance, and that I could convince myself that I was following the same road. I also hoped that, by bringing to light Imogene's experiences in her quiet rural backwaters during World War II, I could make a modest contribution to the ongoing recovery of ordinary women's stories during an important historical event.

The question behind such an approach would have been whether Imogene's life is a template for these pages, or whether the writing itself is a template into which I try to fit her life and mine. And perhaps that question is still valid. But the act of writing, for me, has always been less about reaching conclusions than about meditation and recovery. What strange artifacts are these that rise out of the dark well of the mind, perhaps a warped and blackened nail from a house fire so long ago that the stories about it are fragmentary and stripped of significance? Two women and a baby died in that fire. It was somebody's fault; it was nobody's fault. By the time I was old enough to play where the house had stood, nothing remained by a few nails, brittle from undergoing fire. By the time I am old enough to write about them, even the nails are gone. From memory I resurrect the roughened texture of those nails, the way the tiny scales of burnt metal flaked away in the child's curious fingers, and I hammer together a shelter, however fragile, against the swirling winds of no meaning at all.

In assembling such unstable material into coherence, what tools to use? The usual way of framing this question is to ask whether we're writing fiction or nonfiction. Not, of course, that there is universal agreement on the difference between fiction and nonfiction, much less the rules for writing one or the other. On the contrary, reviewers and panelists and workshop participants continue to argue the unanswerable: if fiction and nonfiction are to be distinguished by freedom of invention on the one hand and adherence to literal truth—"what really happened"—on the other; and if, further, we know that absolute literal truth is, at best, a shifting story, depending on what the writer decides to tell or to withhold, where can we draw a line to distinguish between the two genres? If we recognize the impossibility of absolute literal truth, to what extent do we allow composite characters, compressed timelines, altered details, approximated dialogue, and invented scenes before we decide that we're writing fiction, not nonfiction?

"What are the rules?" implored a student in a graduate writing class recently, and was not reassured to be told that, yes, the journalists have rules, the historians have rules, but the writers of personal essay and memoir during the last decade have been blurring the lines traditionally drawn between the genres.

Just because a question is unanswerable doesn't mean that we shouldn't try to answer it, and in fact nearly every writer of nonfiction tries, and so do some fiction writers. In his introduction to *Mountain Blood*, a collection of what the jacket copy calls *tales*, Will Baker writes that "readers have a right to know what kind of book they are up against, in a general way," but then admits "the overall slant of [*Mountain Blood*] is definitely toward truth—a certain kind of truth—but I don't claim scrupulous accuracy, and terms like yarn or essay or memoir or meditation would help only a little, even though there are elements of all these approaches in what follows." With no-nonsense brevity, Norman Maclean subtitled *A River Runs Through It,* which many would call memoir, *And Other Stories*. Other writers draw their own subjective lines in shifting sands. Noting the oft-cited example of Annie Dillard's cat—rather, the cat that turned out not to be Annie Dillard's—"I've always thought the distinction between truth and lies was clear, but during the past few years I've collected examples of differing views on the issue of how much truth a reader can expect in a book labeled 'nonfiction,'" Linda Hasselstrom writes in the introduction to her recent book, *Between Grass and Sky*. So have we all.

What I have discovered, however, in the course of my meditation upon Imogene's diaries, has been a more useful question: not, what is the difference between fiction and nonfiction, nor, how far from literal "truth" can nonfiction wander before it turns into fiction, but, why do I choose to write fiction or to write nonfiction? What are my advantages and disadvantages in choosing fiction, in choosing nonfiction? While mindful of Will Baker's caution, can I write simultaneously in both forms as a way of patching together my recovered artifacts, dreams and speculations into the structure that I seek? It is in part to test these questions that this book has come into being. In larger part, the book is what it began as: the recovered artifacts of memory, voices, documents, and scribbled notations, fetched up from the dark and hammered together into a shape as exact and sturdy as I can make it.

Many of the entries in Imogene's diaries record the weather or tick off her small repetitive chores, and I have transcribed only enough of these to suggest the flavor of her days and to test certain concepts developed by recent scholars of alternative texts. I have made no corrections (although I occasionally have changed names), just as I have made no corrections in the family letters from which I quote. In asides I identify family members and neighbors and, where I can, I clarify the more cryptic of her entries. The excerpts that I have chosen will reflect the changes brought to Imogene's life through technology, like electricity and automobile ownership, the increasing tension she feels as America approaches World War II, and her growing awareness of her own transition between the familiar Montana landscape and an uncertain future. This approach is not without its risks. Choosing another set of excerpts, it might be argued, might shape a different story, or an infinite number of stories, like infinite parallel universes which Imogene might have inhabited. On the other hand, it might be argued that, in omitting portions of Imogene's diaries, I have co-opted her work and imposed my concept of story upon a text that does not contain story. Even my concentrating on the diaries Imogene kept during World War II might be seen as a distortion of a text created over fifty years in a dozen volumes.

All writing is collaborative, however—collaboration between the writer and her tradition of story; collaboration between the writer and her reader; collaboration between the writer and the thin edge where her daily lines press into the future. And drawing as it does upon letters, memories, and family stories, this book is, at the very least, multi-authored.

Before her mind dissolved into dementia, Imogene had been hand-piecing the blocks for a Stars and Flowers quilt. I found the blocks in a drawer after her death. Each about the size of the palm of my hand, the "stars" blocks were six-pointed, in a rainbow of pastel solids, while the "flowers" blocks were six-petaled pastel prints with yellow hexagon centers. I've never seen a Stars and Flowers quilt outside my own family, although my mother and Imogene each made several and showed me how. It's a good pattern for using the smallest scraps of fabric, the kinds of scraps that women used to trade with each other, and my mother and Imogene always "set up" theirs—that is, they pieced together their star and flower blocks—with little diamonds in another pastel fabric. Finishing another woman's quilt left unfinished after her death is a traditional task that many have undertaken, but pastels are not for me. I chose a midnight blue cotton—actually went out and bought it, with my mother's voice hammering at me for my extravagance when the whole point of quilting is economy—and I snipped the dark blue fabric into tiny diamonds and began to set up Imogene's quilt by hand. It took several months, while my mind traveled many roads, and then I chose a scarlet backing fabric and quilted it, again by hand.

"She must have been watching over your shoulder," said my sister when she saw the finished quilt.

The Montana Years

September 1940–
August 1942

1

/ / /

After all, memory occupies no space. Memory lives in its own small realm of bone and brain, and it worries, not about some measureless past which somehow exists behind us, but about the frayed edges of a dimensionless map whose markings of roads and rivers and events are overlaid, like a series of transparencies, upon the shifting present. Memory starts nowhere, starts anywhere, radiates perhaps from some asterisked city of the mind. Explores and abandons its trails. Writes down lies in indelible ink. Erases the truth. A diary may correspond to a timeline, days following days, but memory toes nobody's line.

Still, a narrative must impose some order, narrative must find a beginning. "The Montana Years" sounds so good, so definite a beginning, so precise a division to account for a life begun in remote dryland Montana but transplanted to the Olympic Peninsula of Washington State. "The Montana Years," "The Washington Years." Before the war, after the war.

And yet already I'm telling a lie, or at least an incomplete truth. My quest for "almost actual reality," as my aunt's first diary calls it, begins not with the official outbreak of war in Europe in 1939, or even with my aunt's next-to-last year of rural teaching in Montana, in 1940, but with another beginning; because one of those asterisked cities of the mind is not a city at all, but a small white frame schoolhouse set upon a knoll among wheat-fields, waiting for me to start my own first day of school in September of 1948.

Even this beginning is a false one, for how did I arrive at that first day of school, if not along another of those half-erased trails from an asterisk in the mind, which in this case stars the beautiful old Fergus County Courthouse in Lewistown, Montana? Therefore I begin with the courthouse and with myself, appropriately enough, since it's within my undependable synapses that the story exists—within my memory and, of course, within my aunt's diaries, which also exist as artifacts in the present tense, in this precarious new century we're all entering.

The Fergus County Courthouse also is an artifact; that is, it still exists, although shabby in comparison with my first memory of its expansive Spanish-style architecture and watered lawns. The courthouse was an example of another form of myth-making, and already about fifty years old when I first remember it (practically new, I realize, when I look back now), but timeless, of course, from the point of view of that child of dust and sagebrush who wondered less at those broad steps and porches and cornices and domed clock tower than at the novelty of water sprinklers on clipped grass and *trees*, beautiful trees, beautiful weeping willow trees that drooped their deep green fronds across paved walks.

Why did the willows weep, I asked my aunt, and cannot remember her answer, because the map of memory has become a different kind of transparency for me, has become a film which begins at the courthouse steps, enters the cool marble-floored corridors, and finds a somber door of dark varnished wood, with gold lettering, *County Superintendent of Schools.*

The time was late summer, and the leaves of the weeping willows brushed the windows and shadowed the bookshelves in the office of the superintendent of county schools. I was eight years old. I had been brought (although I didn't seem to know it at the time, or perhaps I didn't think it was important) to be tested, to determine my grade level when I started school for the first time in the fall. Up until now I had been taught at home, at a time when home-schooling had little to do with political or religious conviction or doubts about the public schools, and everything to do with life on remote ranches. In 1948 the rural west was still a region of wood stoves and kerosene lights and dirt roads and distances. In 1948, although we weren't aware of it, we in Montana were on the cusp of change, even in Fergus County. The war was over and consumer goods were becoming available again, and electrification was coming, and bringing marvels like refrigeration, and roads were going to be paved, and distances would suddenly shrink to accommodate school bus routes and school consolidations. How could we have known that refrigeration and paved roads would so drastically change our lives, when we thought only that we were getting back to normal after the war?

In 1948 the rural west was still scattered with one-room country schools. Fergus County alone contained over a hundred rural schools, each school equipped with one teacher and anywhere from three to thirty students. Most of those schools had been built during the homestead era, less than forty years earlier, when the idea of a rural school district was to provide eight grades of education within walking or buggy-driving or horseback-riding distance for every child. (And why in the world would amenities like paved roads and school buses help bring an end to such an established institution as the rural school system? Who could have supposed such an outcome?)

Despite the good intentions behind the planning of the rural school districts, it happened that the school which should have been within walking or horseback-riding distance from my parents' ranch was situated on the far side of the Judith River. There was no bridge across that stretch of the Judith at that time (still isn't). It was the lack of a bridge that accounted for my

home-schooling. But by 1948, when I was eight and my sister was five, nego-
tiations were underway to enroll us in an out-of-district school, the Warm
Spring Creek school, a mere seven miles distant over gumbo mud and gravel.
My sister would be a first-grader, and I would be, well, whatever grade the
county superintendent's test indicated I was ready for.

Back to the film, back to the dubious transparency. Back to the courthouse, to that varnished dark door with its gold lettering, which slowly opens
on a room filled with dappled sunlight and the flickering shadows of leaves
upon shelves and shelves of books.

Books! Without knowing it, I have opened the door to the county library.
From these shelves, the superintendent of schools will load boxes into the
back seat of her car to distribute and redistribute to the farflung rural schools
during her periodic visits of inspection. Smiling, rosy-faced Mrs. Barsness will
break the monotony of our school year. She'll assist the teacher for an afternoon, she'll ask us what we like to read, what we've read so far, and what
we'd like her to bring us next time. She'll reassure us that we're part of a
complete and encompassing world, though we sit in our oak and iron desks
in our little white frame outpost on the knoll in the midst of wheatfields.

For me, however, the pleasure of Mrs. Barsness's visits lies in the future.
For now, I am beside myself. Books! Along these shelves, a child can wander
until she loses herself among all these titles, all these unread pages.

Not that I had no books. My grandmother and my aunt brought me the
outdated textbooks from the schools that they taught, and I also possessed, or
had access to, the books that had been my father's when he was a child. Some
of these books, survivors of my mother's forays against household clutter—
books!—I still possess. No, no, don't encourage me to digress, don't let me
pause to describe the tattered 1902 edition of *Just So Stories*, illustrated by the
author, a concept which fascinated me because I loved to write and draw. Or
the ancient copy of *America First: One Hundred Stories from Our History*, with my
father's name still written on the flyleaf beside my drawing of a Pilgrim girl
with a smile and a dot for a nose. I won't wander into the delights of these

books, or even into the wealth that the county library held, a wealth that at the age of eight I had never imagined. I couldn't decide where to start, which treasure to pull down from the shelves first; and before I could even begin, Mrs. Barsness's hand on my shoulder was guiding me away, guiding me back to the task at hand in much the same way that I now must keep myself on task as I write. I was in the county library to be tested, not to read.

I knew Mrs. Barsness, because she was a friend of my grandmother's, and I loved her, as I think all the children of her far-flung domain loved her, and that morning I willingly let her lead me to a long oak conference table, where she seated me opposite a boy perhaps a year or two older than myself, who also was being given the placement test. The boy was told my name, and I was told his, which may have been Tom. He had an open, unsuspicious face, and he wore a striped T shirt, which reminded me of the clothing worn by the boys in my outdated school readers and seemed quite dashing, compared with my own home-sewn clothes. But I had no time to get to know Tom, or inquire about his T shirt, because, in that lovely dappled light of memory, Mrs. Barsness is giving us each a test booklet and a pencil and explaining how to mark our answers.

The first part of the test is arithmetic, which is no fun, so I skim along as fast as I can, adding and subtracting and multiplying; but then I reach the point in the test where a crooked little symbol begins to dominate the problems. I know that my mother has explained the crooked symbol, but its function eludes me. The number on one side of the curious little hook is supposed to "go into" the number on the other side of the hook, I remember that much, but how? What does "go into" mean? I entertain myself for a few minutes, imagining little mobile numbers, like mice, "going into" a room, before I lose interest and skip all the division problems and draw pictures on the margins of my test booklet while I wait for Tom to finish. At last he does, and we go on to the reading portion of the test, and suddenly I'm entranced, because what I'm being asked to do is read stories and mark answers about the stories.

As soon as I've marked all the answers, I can go on to the next story. I tear through story after story, marking answers, completely absorbed, until I come to the end of the text, surface, and find myself at the oak table in the dappled light.

Across the table from me, Tom is crying.

Mrs. Barsness has gone to Tom and put her arms around him. For me, the moment is embedded forever, although of course I don't know it; at the time I only realize that somehow I am responsible for Tom's tears, and I stare with unabashed curiosity as Mrs. Barsness tries to comfort him—"Don't cry. Everybody doesn't have to be good at all the same things. Don't feel bad because she can read faster than you can."

A forewarning. Reading is not necessarily a safe thing to be doing. The girl with her nose in a book may be too absorbed to notice, but her reading is affecting the people around her in unpredictable ways.

September, 1940. Only eight years before the late summer of 1948, when I made Tom cry. How can that be, when my aunt's story always seemed like ancient history to me? Even now I feel a jolt at the strange elasticity of time that stretches forever for the child and snaps back to nothing, a mere breath, for the adult.

In the late summer and fall of 1940, when I am not yet a year old, my aunt's diaries begin to reflect her growing desperation at having no school to teach, with the school year approaching so fast.

August 27: No mail, so [Ma and I] went to Lewistown. . . . Saw Jack & Doris [Imogene's sister and brother-in-law; my parents]. They said # 72 [a nearby rural school] wanted to hire Ma. Doris wanted me to ask for it so I did, & spent the evening bawling about it.

August 28: Cried at night & most all morning. . . . Heard the [school] board could not get together. Helped Jack get his truck home then Doris & I went to town, saw Snapp [chairman of another rural school board]—got nowhere.

*August 31:... heard there were 3 $70 jobs in Fergus & the Spring Creek
teacher might not come. Thot it worth checking up on.*

Then, on September 3: *I started for Lewistown. Stopped at Spring Creek School.
The teacher did not come so I got the job—started school—$80 & a room with
electric lights.*

As I read the diary entries, scenes unfold out of the past. What I have experienced blossoms into what I imagine. There sits the white-painted schoolhouse at the top of its little rise, deep in the rustling gold grass of a Montana fall, with its long row of blank-eyed north windows and its clanging set of swings. The time is late morning, perhaps ten or eleven o'clock, but the dozen or so kids are playing some game or other in the schoolyard, running and trampling down the grass that has overgrown the gravel during the summer. I can almost hear their voices, piping in the brisk air as they enjoy their unexpected respite from the start of school, and I can see the anxious face that peers out from one of the schoolhouse windows, watching the road. It's the Clerk of the School, waiting to see if the teacher will show up and set these kids to work at their lessons.

Now a column of dust rises in the distance, as a small black car chuffs along the gravel highway toward Lewistown at thirty miles an hour. The Clerk watches hopefully as the driver approaches the turn-off to the school, hesitates, then brakes and comes chuffing up the little side road. Can this be the teacher?

No, but it's *a* teacher, thank heaven. The young woman getting out of the car has all the earmarks. The decent print dress, the dark hair worn in braids severely pinned around her head, the eyes that are filled with the resigned experience of a seasoned cattle dog.

"The teacher we hired hasn't shown up. Can you start right now?"

"This morning?" says Imogene, taken aback only for a moment. "Well—all right."

Tomorrow she will be thirty years old, and her life, as she sees it, is over. All that lies ahead are more days of same old, same old. But at least this job pays better than the last, and she's glad to get it. She hangs up her jacket in the dusty cloakroom, finds the hand bell in the clutter on the teacher's desk. Goes to the back door and rings the bell, sees the children pause in their game and turn and walk reluctantly in her direction.

But she can't see the future from the back steps of the Warm Spring Creek school as she rings the bell in the crisp morning air of September 3, 1940. What she sees is a school that hasn't been cleaned, supplies that haven't been ordered, an empty teacherage, and a new bunch of kids who are running around the schoolroom, throwing erasers and spitwads and fighting over the desks that best accommodate their summer's growth of legs.

She turns to settle them down. Closes the door.

The next day, September 4, she writes, *My birthday—30—how I hate to see it come. Husband & ranch prospects all gone now.*

2

/ / /

State Highway 81 is paved now, and has been since the early 1950s. It branches from another state highway just south of Square Butte, winds more or less east through the tiny wheat ranching communities of Coffee Creek and Denton, where my grandparents homesteaded, crosses the Judith River, and passes the knoll where the Warm Spring Creek school used to sit before it intersects with Highway 191 and drops south to Lewistown. I dislike driving this road, I dislike seeing the empty space on the knoll, and I feel drained by the demands of the ghosts who ride in the back seat of my car and scold me for not remembering more.

The Warm Spring Creek school was always a landmark, from a distance, and, after snowmelt, a permanent white speck on a low rise in the middle of the wheatfields. Like so many of the rural school buildings, it eventually was purchased from the county and hauled off for a granary. My sister and I visited it on its new site a few years ago and found that its hardwood floor had held it together pretty well, although sadly canted, with a spill of old textbooks and faded papers among the chaff. There can't be many who still remember when it was a community bastion, with its tall row of windows to the north, its barbed wire fence and set of chain-link swings.

Although some rural schools were provided with separate little houses as teacherages, the Warm Spring Creek teacherage was a single room behind the schoolroom where the teacher could sleep and cook for herself and keep her things. Outdoors and well behind the school were the flanking pair of white toilets, one for the boys and one for the girls, at the regulation 150 feet apart. At the far side of the schoolyard sagged a board barn, which in its day had stabled a dozen or more horses during any given school year. One of those horses had been my father's, when he used to ride several miles around the base of the South Moccasin mountains to school at Warm Spring Creek in 1925. But the school-aged population had dwindled, even in 1948, from its heyday during homestead days, and what kids were left were being driven to school in jeeps and Ford pickups. By the time I started school at Warm Spring Creek, the horses were down to the sorrel and the pinto that the Walton girls rode back and forth from their ranch a couple of miles to the north.

The unused front door of the school looked out over the highway, which we kids all called the Road to Town. Lewistown had a population of about 3,000 at that time, and the most pavement and neon than most of us had ever seen, but it was an hour's drive on the gravel. The school was our center, and beyond the boundary of the schoolyard's barbed-wire fence were the wheat-fields and the distant blue shoulders of the South Moccasins, which sloped down to brushy pastures where, summer and fall, white-faced cattle grazed or dozed in the shade of the willows and quaking aspen, chokecherries, and hawthorns that grew along the slow convoluted flow of Warm Spring Creek on its way to the Judith River. One of the springs was the main source of drinking water for the school, carried by us kids, who took turns crossing the road in pairs, climbing the stile over the barbed-wire fence, hiking down the cattle trail to the spring, and lugging back the cold, slopping pail between us, to be poured into the big Red Wing ceramic cooler and drunk in driblets through the day in cone-shaped paper cups.

Nothing seemed more permanent to us than the school, nothing promised more continuity than the inevitable ringing of the hand bell at eight o'clock and at the end of morning and afternoon recesses, the stampede of our feet out of blank sunlight and through the cloakroom to the smell of chalk dust and real ink in wells on every desk. In the room where my father had been a pupil and my aunt had taught, I dipped a steel pen in ink and practiced penmanship on special lined paper. Strokes and ovals! Then a line of vowels in cursive. Don't use your fingers to write, because your hand will cramp. Rest your forearm on your desk and let it do the moving. Press harder with the pen on the upstroke so the letters will be shaded.

I didn't know then that Montana had always had a strong commitment to public education, that its earliest schools had been established during the gold rush days, and that its first territorial legislature, in 1864, had authorized the county commissioners to fund public education by levying property taxes. I didn't know that the Enlarged Homestead Act of 1909, with its lure of free land, had doubled the number of Montana farms and ranches and quadrupled its population, or that Montana had had 2,500 rural schools when my father attended the Warm Spring Creek school in the 1920s. (Not as many as it seems; with an area of over 145,000 square miles, that's about a school for every 58 square miles.) But the terrible drought years of the 1920s and 1930s had eroded the rural population of Montana, and then the war came, and the number of rural schools statewide was reduced to 1,300. Today, paved highways and sixty-mile school bus routes take ranch kids to consolidated schools in town, and just about the only remaining rural schools are the ones on Hutterite colonies, where, like my father, the Hutterites can try to keep their children safe from the influences of the world.

What I did know was that school was important, because to get my little sister and me to Warm Spring Creek, it sometimes took my father an hour or more to make the seven-mile drive up through the river bluffs when he had to shovel through frozen snowdrifts in the winter or, with chains on all four wheels of his truck, gouge new ruts through wet gumbo mud during the spring thaw. I knew that my grandmother on my mother's side had fed her family by going out to teach during the drought years when their homestead dried up and their crops blew away, that she had been one of the first married women to teach in Montana, and that in the early 1950s she was still teaching in the rural schools, a year here and a year there in districts reluctant to keep a teacher long enough for her to earn tenure. My mother had taught school briefly, before her marriage, and so had my aunt Sylva. My aunt Imogene still taught in a faraway place called Port Angeles, Washington, and someday I, too, would teach.

Being a teacher when I grew up was fine with me. I thought of teaching not as my grandmother and mother and aunt had—that it was the one respectable paying job that a ranch girl could get close to home—but as a way to explore a world beyond the low blue mountains of central Montana through the books that I loved. School itself contained its own mystique for me. Because of the distance and bad roads, my mother had home-schooled me until I was eight, and I had dreamed over the illustrations in my readers of a limitless sequence of classrooms with shining desks and friends—friends beyond the imagination of an isolated ranch child—and books, books, and more books.

That first September in 1948, my little sister and I arrived at school in new gingham dresses my mother had sewn for us, and our hair was braided, and we were carrying a lunch box with sandwiches and a thermos of milk to share for our lunch, and we each had pencils and crayons and scissors and a pulp tablet with a cowboy movie star on the cover. With six other ranch kids of varying ages we ran blinking into the schoolroom, which smelled of wax and window-cleaner and fresh chalk, because the Clerk of the School had brought her own bucket and rags the week before and swept out the road dust from summer and polished the floor and washed the blackboards.

My sister and I had no idea what to expect. We were the new kids, the out-of-district kids. The others already knew each other and, after the summer's lonely hiatus on their ranches, were wild to resume their games. Games I had never heard of, games I haven't heard of since. Steal Sticks. Pump-pump-pull-away. Last Couple Out. Games that could be played with any number of children with no equipment that we couldn't drag out of the woodpile for ourselves. But for me, once I had staked a claim to one of the ancient desks with oak lids and wrought-iron legs—sold now in antique shops, but at that time defaced with generations of initials in spite of the Clerk's best efforts, and screwed together in rows so that you didn't want to be dipping your pen in the inkwell just as somebody in the row ahead of you sat down with a jolt—the real excitement was new tablets and pencils, new boxes of crayons that ached to be opened, and three whole shelves of unread library books! Who could ask for a wider window into the world?

The teacher's desk stood in front of the unused front door between the forty-eight star American flag and the dark blue Montana state flag. Portraits of George Washington and Abraham Lincoln hung above the wainscoting. Our teacher that first year was a redheaded woman who lived during the school week with her beagle puppy in the little room behind the schoolroom, mysterious and forbidden to us, where she had been provided with a bed and a marble-topped dresser and a cast-iron stove for cooking. For water she had the sweating Red Wing cooler in the main schoolroom, filled with water from the spring in the cow pasture, and for necessity she had the girls' toilet, out behind the school.

We were lucky to have the redheaded woman. Parents in the ranch communities were all hearing worried talk about how hard it was to find and keep a teacher. None of the rural schools paid more than sixty or seventy dollars a month, and some were closing because they couldn't find a teacher who would put up with the drudgery and the isolation. School boards hired whomever they could find, the barely qualified and the cranky and the peculiar. At the Ware school, where one of my cousins was a first-grader, the board hired a gentleman in his eighties who dropped dead one day in front of his pupils.

Some might have predicted that the rural teacher shortage was a harbinger of a future where ranch kids, bused to consolidated schools, would play basketball and listen to rock and roll and otherwise lose their innocence by hanging around with kids from town—*them damn town kids*, as my father called them. But my parents thought a teacher shortage meant that I would be sure to get a school near home to teach after I had finished high school and gone away for the mandatory five quarters of normal school it had taken, in my mother's day, to get a teaching certificate.

As for the redheaded woman, I supposed that she liked school as much as I did. Why else would she be teaching? No one, of course, had told me about her miscarriage the previous year, or her current pregnancy, or her failing marriage, or that she resented my little sister and me because we came from outside the district and meant more work for her. In particular, I drove her crazy. The placement tests Mrs. Barsness had given me indicated that I was doing arithmetic on the third-grade level (that peculiar little symbol for division that I couldn't remember), reading on the twelfth-grade level, and therefore (wonderful word, *therefore*, with its assurance of logic behind it and logic to come), *therefore* it made sense to start me in the fourth grade with the three other fourth-graders instead of a grade all by myself, which would have made more work for the teacher. And, after all, I was only eight.

Still, the redheaded woman could not keep me busy.

"Teacher, I want something to do."

"Read your chapter."

"I did."

"Read it again."

I read it again, sighed, raised my hand. "Teacher, I want something to do."

She startled me by coming up behind me and pummeling my shoulders with her fists—"You didn't read that whole chapter again! I watched your eyes! They weren't moving back and forth with the sentences. Don't try to tell me you can read that fast!"

Already subversive at the age of eight, I became a practiced daydreamer and sketcher on margins as I waited for the other fourth-graders to catch up. But lest anyone feel overly nostalgic for the passing of the rural schools, consider the plight of my little sister, who was only five years old and really too young for school in the first place. When the redheaded woman screamed at her for not learning to read, she threw up. That was the end of reading lessons for my sister. It wasn't until she started town school several years later that anyone found out that she never had learned to read.

Fall in Montana is often the shortest season, and winter can set in without warning. Snowfall in October is not unusual, and temperatures can drop in an hour to thirty degrees below zero. During the fall of 1948 and the early winter of 1949, my father and the other ranchers fought the roads to get their kids to school in trucks that roared and bucked through solid white drifts. It was too cold for the Walton girls to ride their horses to school, so they stopped attending. The rest of us huddled by the oil stove and finished our workbooks in the eerie white light that fell through the tall windows and reminded us of the vast snowfields that surrounded us. Although the only peace and quiet the redheaded woman got during the day were our fifteen-minute recesses, she allowed us to stay indoors and play Hangman or Tic-tac-toe on the blackboard. By four o'clock the sun was a stain on the horizon, the snow had turned dark blue, and headlights announced the arrival of parents come to fetch us home.

One morning my father was the first to drive into the schoolyard, crunching tracks through the fresh snow and pulling up in a blast of exhaust. The heater in the pickup was having no effect on the thick frost on the windshield, but my father had scraped a patch to drive by, and through that patch we could see the redheaded woman watching through the schoolhouse window. Then she was out the door and running toward us through the knee-deep snow in her boots and mackinaw and a heavy wool scarf.

My father cranked down the window to an arctic blast.

"I've had all that I can take!" the redheaded woman shouted. Her face was glowing with rage and cold. "I can't keep the school warm enough to teach in. The water was frozen in my dog's dish this morning. Take your kids home! The school board can stuff my contract. Until you insulate that school and buy a better stove, I'm moving back to town!"

Later, when my father told my mother why he had brought my sister and me home with him, he was still laughing. "She was one mad redhead!"

But her tantrum brought a change. The men on the school board might not have stirred themselves if she hadn't threatened to quit, but they must have thought she meant it, because they found the money to fix the stove and pay for insulation. For a week, while we kids were shut at home with nothing to do, my father and the other fathers met at the school and tore out the old wainscoting, lined the joists with big silver-coated rolls of insulation, and nailed the wainscoting back up. They were men who were used to working alone, in prairie isolation, and, judging from the stories my father brought home to tell at supper, the insulation project gave them a fine, companionable time of it.

3

/ / /

My grandmother, Mary Welch, had been determined that her daughters would get a good education, which to her meant a teaching certificate and a chance for marginal independence. Back in Iowa, she had had to battle her own father to finish high school, which he thought wasted on a girl. After all, he pointed out, not only would her schooling cost money, but there would be the loss of money she didn't earn while she was going to school. But my grandmother scrubbed floors to pay her own way, and she taught school in Iowa until she married my grandfather and moved to Montana. When their homestead failed and she was desperate for a way to feed her children, she took correspondence courses to renew her teaching certificate; and she taught continuously in rural schools from 1922 to 1952, supporting her children and sending the daughters to normal school, paying her husband's nursing home bills during his years of dementia, and, eventually, lending her granddaughters the money to go to college. Three daughters and four granddaughters, all teachers.

Imogene was born in 1910, the second of five children and the first born in Montana after my grandparents filed on their dryland homestead. She was a beautiful little girl, with a bubbling laugh and brown eyes and long brown ringlets, until her mother cut her hair short to keep her from getting vain. *Beauty is only skin deep! Pretty is as Pretty does!* Imogene was raised to the tune of all the old edicts, as was I, but she kept her laugh until the last.

For a child, life on an isolated homestead required an imagination. Imogene and her older sister, Sylva, tamed and named litters of wild kittens, hunted gophers with a .22, and learned to read from back issues of *The Youth's Companion* sent by their schoolteaching aunts in Iowa. When they were old enough, they walked a trail through the coulees to the Baulley Dome school, where their mother later taught and where Imogene herself would teach.

Sylva was a quiet, shy girl who preferred to withdraw at recess with a book (that bad habit that seems to skip through our family, wreaking its own havoc), but Imogene was a swashbuckler. Years later she told me how, as a ten-year-old, she had beaten up every kid in school except for Sylva and one older boy, who had promised Imogene that she could play with his gopher trap at recess and then promised another girl the same gopher trap.

"He did it on purpose," Imogene said, "just to watch the fight. I swung the gopher trap and sent all the little kids bawling back to the schoolhouse, and then I pitched into the other big girl and bloodied her nose. Sylva was the only one who stayed out of it."

Where was the teacher while the fight went on?

"Oh, she was just a little young girl herself, just out of high school. She didn't know much more than we did. I remember that we read part of *The Odyssey* in the eighth grade, and she pronounced Penelope's name as Pennylope, just the way we did."

To get to high school in the little wheat-ranching community of Denton, in northern Fergus County, Sylva and Imogene and later my mother, Doris, drove a horse and buggy from the homestead in good weather or lived in a rented room in town during bad weather. They played basketball in bloomers, and they saved and scrimped to get their hair cut and marcelled, and they yearned for the clothes they could not afford. But—"Don't worry about your appearance!" my grandmother warned them all. "Beauty is only skin deep! When you go away to normal school, you'll see that it's the girls in the simple skirts and middy blouses who earn the best grades."

At first the only normal college in Montana, later to be called Western Montana College, was at Dillon. Another normal college would open in Billings in time for my mother to attend it, and still another would come to be called Northern Montana College, in Havre, as the drought-stricken counties of Montana competed for state institutions to shore up their local economies. But in the mid-twenties, when Sylva and Imogene graduated from high school, their only option was the long train ride across the prairie to the mountains of western Montana, where trees grew, for a two-year training program that would qualify them to follow in their mother's footsteps in the rural schools. Imogene, who had skipped grades, was only sixteen when she took that train ride.

My parents expected me to follow the same path. They did not know (although I did, because I had been told so at a high school career night,) that two-year lifetime teaching certificates had been phased out after World War II, and that by the late 1950s it took four years of college to teach even in the elementary schools. Subversive as ever, I kept this knowledge to myself while my mother worried aloud. "If you can just get so you can teach," she would promise me and promise herself, during my last year of high school. "It only took me five quarters. I couldn't see wasting any more of Ma's money with another quarter when I found out I could get a school right away. Ma will help you with money, and so will Imogene, until you can just get so you can teach."

For my mother, college classes had been an obstacle course, a series of uneven hurdles between her and self-sufficiency. She had been the prettiest of the three Welch sisters, with a verve and a smile that radiates from the old snapshots, and she didn't care a snap for books or study. Her few years of teaching had been no pleasure for her, and then she had had to home-school me, which I think was a burden to her. But she subscribed to the family litany: *get the girl enough education so she can support herself if she has to.*

Get her to college long enough for her to get her teaching certificate. After all, teaching is respectable. It pays better than clerking in the five and ten or working in the bank, and a teacher has her summers off, so she can help with branding and haying. Oh, she'll probably marry, but you never know. Imogene never married. And sometimes even a married woman has to fall back on teaching. Look at Ma. Look at the redheaded woman, for that matter, who teaches, so the rumor goes, to pay her husband's gambling debts. Look at how it gets harder and harder to make a living on the ranch. Somebody had better be able to bring in some cash money.

Jobs will be available in your future that have not been dreamed of today, reads a university's recent promotional material for prospective students, and even though my eyes slide over the copy in the brochure as though it's been glazed, I know that it's not just rhetoric, I know that it's true. I cannot even dream of the kind of work that my twenty-year-old daughters may be doing in another twenty years, any more than my parents could have imagined the work I do today. They came of age at a time when the world seemed, at least, to promise continuity, along with more drought, more debts, and more hard work. If the girl can just get her teaching certificate and get a school near home! Well. We can hope for that, at least. And that way, there'll at least be cash money coming in for the ranch.

Because at that time she had not begun to keep diaries, what I know about the two years Imogene spent at the normal school in Dillon is gleaned from her college yearbooks and from half-remembered stories she later told. In a formal portrait taken of her at that time, she looks like the sixteen-year-old she is, in a droopy crepe dress with a string of beads and a silk flower tacked to one shoulder. Her hair is bobbed but subdued, and she has plastered one curl across her forehead as, what, a gesture toward flapper mode, perhaps.

But her child's face shines through her attempt at fashion. The round, unblemished cheeks, the unsuspecting eyes, the slight, sweet smile—or is there something set about that smile? Perhaps a withholding of judgment, perhaps a foreknowledge of how ridiculous the dress, the hair-do will look in a few years?

Still, she enjoyed college; she played on the field hockey team, and she loved swimming and hiking. And she had an independent streak.

"The dean called us girls together and warned us, 'Whatever you do, don't read a book called *The Well of Loneliness*, by Radclyffe Hall.' So of course I ran right out and bought it."

"Do you still have it?" I asked her.

"Yes, it's right over there on the shelf. But I warn you, it isn't very interesting."

I read it, and it wasn't.

Because Imogene had graduated so young from high school, when she finished at Dillon in 1928 and came home to the prairies of central Montana to teach, she was only eighteen. What she faced sounds more daunting to me than it probably did to her, because she had lived so much of her life in country teacherages. And of course, she had her mother's example.

"Ma gave me advice that I never heard in normal school," she told me years later. "Like, *Always go out to the barn after school and stay there until the last kid has saddled up or hitched up and headed for home.*"

A teacher as young as Imogene usually boarded with a local family rather than stay alone in one of the remote teacherages. It was safer for those girls, sometimes as young as sixteen, often homesick and ill-educated, who had been sent out to do respectable work and bring home their pay warrants. Imogene, like all rural teachers, was expected to arrive at the school ahead of her pupils, on horseback or by buggy in scorching weather or in blizzards, to feed and stable her own horse and shovel out the trails to the outhouses, build a fire in the stove, light the lamps she had washed and filled with kerosene the night before, plan lessons for as many as eight grades with no more supplies than a blackboard and chalk and a dictionary, supervise the stabling of her pupils' horses, join in their games at recess, and deal with emergencies.

(As always, my grandmother had set the family standard. When her youngest child, my uncle Dave, was kicked in the head by a horse and lay unconscious while the other pupils ran to her, screaming, she took the opportunity to lecture them on the proper treatment of head injuries while she administered first aid to her son. Uncle Dave lived to be eighty, but this incident may explain my grandmother's policy of staying in the barn until the kids were done saddling their horses and were headed for home.)

So that was that for Imogene, or should have been. She taught in rural schools for the next twelve years, interrupted only by her year at the University of Minnesota and enlivened, if that's the word, by falling in love with the wrong man. But that's all behind her now, she's thirty years old, and she thinks her life is over. It's 1940, and she's just gotten a last-minute job at the Warm Spring Creek school, which at least has electric light in the school room. But as far as she knows, the next twelve years will hold just as much drudgery and uncertainty as the last twelve.

4

/ / /

September 3, 1940: I started out for Lewistown. Stopped at Spring Creek School. The teacher did not come so I got the job—started school—$80 a month & a room with electric lights.

September 6: Fri. over & now home to see how goes the ranch. Must stop & pick up harness for Dad at Jack's. Got most of my supplies this morning. Must check on a few tomorrow.

September 7: What a day—saw the girl who got raped last May. Visited Ruth—Carolyn—Pauline—Muriel.

September 9: Have lots of letters to write & unpacking to do. Had to clean the spring on top of everything else. Good thing I'd lots of practice.

As I read between the lines of these brief entries, I remember that Imogene had been staying that summer with her parents on the homestead north of

Denton and trying unsuccessfully to find a school to teach for the coming year, until on the third of September, she pulled off the gravel highway at the Warm Spring Creek school and found that anxious clerk, and now she's starting a familiar routine of organizing her classroom of seven grades, ordering supplies, getting herself moved into the teacherage, and attending the fall teachers' meetings in Lewistown. She's had a chance to visit with other young teachers, and she's also found the time to run family errands, like borrowing a workhorse harness from her brother-in-law for her father to use (after all, she's the one with a car, and she feels obligated).

But—*$80 a month & a room with electric lights*—what a relief! The bonus of electricity means she will not have to wash and trim kerosene lamps to light her pupils through long dark winter afternoons, although she will have to hike through the neighbor's cattle pasture to the spring and clean out its summer accumulation of leaves and twigs. Hired at the last minute, she hasn't had a chance to order school supplies, but she'll make do. That's what a rural schoolteacher does: she makes do.

The previous May, Imogene had finally talked herself into buying that car, worrying all the while because she couldn't really afford it. By now, she knows that car ownership is a mixed blessing. She doesn't have to depend upon others for transportation over the distances between schools, but she's learning about the cost and inconvenience of breakdowns, not to speak of all those errands she has to run for her family. This September, she will be living in the Warm Spring Creek teacherage during the week and driving twenty miles over gravel and dirt roads to spend weekends with my grandfather, who is living by himself on the homestead while my grandmother teaches at some remote rural school. My parents, Doris and Jack, are living on a ranch on the Judith River, just off the highway on Imogene's way to the homestead, so she visits often and helps out with child care and ranch chores. After the shock of Lud's going to prison, Imogene has turned more and more to her mother and sisters for emotional support, and being so close to her family is one reason she's so glad to get the Warm Spring Creek school.

In later years, she often will describe the fall teachers' meetings as boring, but at the end of this first full week of school, she's glad for the chance to see friends and count heads and reassure herself that everybody's got work for one more school year. On May 13, 1940, she had written in her diary, *Miss Patton [the county superintendent of schools] was out [to visit the two-room school where Imogene was teaching]. . . . She told Ruth [the other teacher] about a rape that happened last night. Poor teacher.*

September 10: Dave is in Calif. this year. He sees country any way. With 7 grades my day goes quickly. One blessing. Have my register nearly done.

A sign of the times. Dave, her younger brother, is following military construction work as it becomes increasingly likely that the United States will go to war. By the following January he will write a letter to Imogene that has survived among her papers in its faded blue-and-red edged airmail envelope, to let her know, in a tone innocent of events to come, that he is on Midway Island:

Jan 9, 1941

Dear Imogene,

I left Honolulu on the 4th of Jan. Got here on the 7th.

I thought you might like to have the envelope as a suvineer. On the envelope is a picture of the boat we came to Midway on. It is called a crusar. It is faster than a battle ship but it doesn't have as heavy armor plating as a battle ship. In case you don't know, it is very unusual for a civilian to ride on a navy crusar . . .

Well I sure am a long way from nowhere out here. It is about 4000 mi from Frisco. . . . I have been inside the Tropic of Cancer so now I can say I have been in the tropics.

I wish you could see the ocean out here. It is the blueist water I have ever seen.

All there is on this island is Albatross. There is sure a lot of them. They are quite tame. . . . The weather is warm here. I don't even wear a coat at all. . . .

Your brother

Dave

But in September of 1940, Imogene is too busy to worry about Dave, although he will be much on her mind during the coming months.

September 11: 7 grades keep me busy—am tired at night—but by the end of this week my odd jobs should be well under control.

September 13: Stopped to see Doris & Mary & promised to come down for dinner on Sunday. Pa seems lonesome & glad to see me.

In September of 1940, I am nine months old, and Imogene is enchanted with me. The previous May she had written, *Mary is sure the sweetest baby ever. What a smile,* and her diaries for the next two years are filled with references to me. Perhaps her overwhelming love for her first little niece was another symptom of her emotional shock over losing Lud Lange, but it was the beginning of the closeness between us that lasted for the rest of her life.

September 16: A hard day—Gloria rude—such a nervous child—so excitable it is too bad. Seem to have lots to do. Wish I could settle down to write.

Gloria Walton—and I've changed her name—is a first-grader in 1940. I knew her as a seventeen-year-old eighth-grader when I went to the Warm Spring Creek school. She and her sisters were wild-haired girls who rode horseback from a ranch primitive even by the standards of the 1940s. A succession of teachers considered them unteachable. Their mother was said to have died of a self-induced abortion, and their father and grandmother raised the girls until the grandmother died and the work fell on the shoulders of Gloria, then about sixteen. A rumor went around the community about an incestuous relationship between Gloria and her father, but was silenced by those who believed that such depravity could not possibly be taking place in decent Montana. Imogene's diary entry implies more than she is willing to commit to writing, but what she thinks is "too bad' is impossible to say.

September 19: Got the pictures of Mary. Must start an album soon. Got three pages done on my story in an hour. I have to drive myself to work. Really should be able to get lots done.

September 24: No mail—very little else of note happening all day. Will be glad when I get a story off to the editors. Heard of one story I'd like to read.

September 25: Tonight I got 5 pages done. It does not take long if I can drive myself to do it. Hope I can write saleable stories.

September 26: Got my story half done and it is beginning to be more fun to write & more interesting. I believe I can manage to do 5 pages a night which means 4 nights to a 5,000 word story.

None of the stories which Imogene forced herself to type on her old manual typewriter after a full day of teaching has survived. I never knew that she dreamed of writing until years later, although I remember my mother telling me that Imogene had once published a poem, about a cowboy and a horse. Perhaps her stories were romantic westerns, like the undated sonnet, typed on her old blotchy manual typewriter, that I found among her papers:

Scent of Wild Roses

The roses by the river, do you not
Remember them, as they bloomed there in June?

Can't you see them in the late afternoon?
And can't you just smell the dust and the hot
Sweet, stifling scent of the roses you got,
As the river slipped by, singing a tune
Of the wild rose blossoms that die so soon,
In the dusty air so heavy and hot?
I wonder if we will ever ride together,
There by the Judith when the shadows fall,
And halt again beneath that old gnarled tree,
Lis'n'ing to the river, and the leather
Of the saddles, creaking, and hear a bird's call,
And smelling those dear roses, you and me.

At the time that Imogene was forcing herself to write her five pages a night, after teaching all day, I was embarking on my own writing career. Having been taught to print letters in capitals, I printed up a pageful and took my story to Imogene to have it read aloud to me. "But honey, it doesn't say anything," she kept saying. "I don't know what you want me to do." I remember my intense disappointment and frustration. There were, I decided, difficulties in the writing process that I had not yet imagined, and then too there was the risk of ridicule; early on, family laughter had taught me not to tell my stories aloud to myself, but to keep them in my head.

Is that why Imogene kept her stories and poems a secret?

September 27: Sure pulled out from school fast. Got to Doris early. Mary came to me right off & seemed glad to see me. Pa was waiting. No bread— no water.

September 28: A coyote got one of his [Pa's] last two turkeys.

September 29: Baked bread, cake & beans & left Pa about one. Hated to go & leave him but Sunday afternoon is my only chance to visit Doris.

My grandfather had led a lonely life for years, all by himself on the home-stead while my grandmother taught from one end of Fergus County to the other and lived in teacherages. He was a dreamer, a man of vast ambitions and no resources. My aunts have told me that they believe he suffered from depression for years before his final breakdown. By 1940, as Imogene's diary indicates, his behavior has become increasingly erratic. He can't seem to pull himself together, can't get a day's work done, takes less and less care of himself. Imogene's diary entry shows that she has tried to prepare enough food to keep him through the week in the unrefrigerated homestead house.

Another dilemma for her—as the one unmarried daughter, will her father's care eventually fall to her?

October 2: This day was a beaner—started early, worked hard and late. Kids fight—big ones mix in—had a salesman call—& he wanted a date. Hope to get a map set tho.

For a woman who laments that she will never marry, Imogene certainly brushes off any man who shows an interest in her. Perhaps her disastrous romance with Lud had left her so bruised that she never again allowed herself to be hurt. Then too, though she laments being single, she is gradually learning that she can take care of herself and to value her independence.

October 3: A very rainy day. Things went well & I got lots done. Was ready to get supper shortly after 5 o'clock. My poor budget is sadly skrimped. I don't know what to do if I can't sell stories.

October 6: Pa came down & hit me up for money but I couldn't let him have it due to my L. In. & car payments.

October 8: Exams & report cards again this week. Guess I'll take them home to do Sat. evening. Never have enuf to do then. Guess I'll try to remember a gingerbread receipt too.

October 14: Monday & report cards out. Guess Polly did not like hers too well. Fortunes came up to see me. Had a nice visit. But I am afraid they may feel I do not understand Faye & Jeane.

October 15: Miss Patton visited today. Kids behaved good.

Miss Patton, the superintendent of county schools, visits every rural school on a rotating basis, just as Mrs. Barsness will do while I am a pupil at the Warm Spring Creek school. All the teachers want Miss Patton's visits to be a success, because she hears about all the vacancies, and an early word from her can mean a job for the next year. In fact, a tip from Miss Patton was why Imogene pulled off the road at the Warm Spring Creek school back in September and stopped to see if they needed a teacher.

Dear Mrs. Barsness! We kids always greeted her with glad shouts, but our redheaded teacher probably shared Imogene's nervousness and hoped we would behave ourselves.

October 16: Went to Brooks for gro[ceries]. Registering of men going on apace. School board had a meeting—agreed on the maps—sweeping compound, & a clock.

Another sign of the times. The men of Fergus County are registering for the draft.

Brooks was, still is, a windswept little community a few miles from the Warm Spring Creek school, set on the prairie against a magnificent backdrop of the Judith Mountains. Over the years it has shrunk, like many other little prairie towns, to a handful of frame houses where retired wheat ranchers live, but in the 1940s it boasted grain elevators, a post office, grocery store, a church, and a school with *two rooms* and *two teachers*.

Imogene often drove the few miles to Brooks to buy staples like flour and yeast without making the really long twenty-mile drive into Lewistown.

However, she sniffed in her diary that the Brooks grocery store "wasn't much."

October 28: Went pheasant hunting with one of Polly's brothers. I wish I had the conscription list. I'd like to count the men I know.

November 1: Friday again. Tomorrow I want to wash & go to town so tonight I put my towels to soak. Have so much to do—got a card from Jack reminding me of the dance Sat.

Her mention of the postcard from Jack stops me, after all these years. How to imagine a world where a reminder of a dance arrives by postcard from a brother-in-law living less than ten miles away?

Be quiet, ghosts. I'm doing the best that I can.

During the winters, dances were held monthly in the various community halls around Fergus County, and everybody showed up. A hat would be passed to pay for the music—a piano and perhaps a guitar or a fiddle—and supper would be served at midnight, followed by dancing until three or four in the morning. My mother says that, as a young married couple, she and my father would drive home from the dances at dawn, milk the cows and feed the livestock, and go to bed. They took me along to a few of those dances when I was small, but my memories are sparse and have to do with yawning through the odor of resin scattered on the dance floor, trying to stay awake, and being wrapped in a blanket and carried out to the pickup to sleep on the seat of the cab, where strange sensations sometimes roused me—a jolt against the side of the cab, a glimpse of shadows staggering off between the rows of parked trucks, husky male laughter—alcohol was forbidden at the dances, but there were always the stashed bottles.

Although Imogene continues to note the salesmen and young ranchers who stop by the school to visit with her, she invariably chooses to attend the community social events with her sister and brother-in-law.

November 3: We had quite some time at the dance, took our own lunch—saved $1.50—enuf to buy a thermos. Took Pa's grub up to him today. It looks stormy so I headed back at 5:00.

November 5: Went to Denton to vote. Got some groceries. Stayed with Doris all night. Baby [Mary] sure ran to me. Told Doris she could have the car the rest of the week if she'd bring me to school.

November 10: Went to −14 degrees last night. After dinner Jack started work on my car & got it going.

That troublesome car again! How to keep it running! She's thankful for her brother-in-law. Although Jack is a far better hand with horses than he is with a combustible engine, he'll do his best for her, and in return she'll make the car available to him and Doris whenever she can. That's the homestead spirit: give help where you can, because you're eventually going to need help, yourself. And particularly it's our family spirit. Imogene's the one with the cash income, she's the one who has a car, she's expected to help out.

November 18: It was a cold, grey, snowy world this morning. Hated to see the snow this week. Hate to see winter begin.

November 22: Had to wait for my warrent. Got lots done in town but sure could use more money.

The school districts paid their teachers with warrants, which were often delayed because the chairman of the school board had been too busy rounding up cattle or doing other ranch work to get the warrant signed, or—more ominously—because the district was running short of money. During the hard years of the 1920s and 1930s, many teachers simply didn't get paid, but by the 1940s, they usually got their warrants eventually.

November 25: Vaneks stopped tonight. Said the desks were lost & a tracer had been sent. I have my reports to do yet & must write my play. Hot lunches make more towel washing too.

In this entry, Imogene gives several clues why "so much to do" is such a constant refrain in her diaries, and also a clue to her constant anxiety. Mr. Vanek, a neighboring rancher, is on the school board, which has the power not only to hire and fire teachers, but also to purchase or decide not to purchase basic equipment like the maps and the clock Imogene was so glad to get in October.

The play she is writing is for the school Christmas program. Like the community dances, the Christmas programs at the rural schools were important social events before television came to Montana and everyone started staying home to watch it. When my sister and I attended the Warm Spring Creek school, we would be asked to bring bedsheets from home, which the teacher would transform into stage curtains by stringing them on wires with safety pins. For the next three weeks, we would rehearse our play, songs, and recitations under the teacher's direction. Such excitement, such importance! On the great night, the school would be crammed with relatives and neighbors, standing room only, come to admire our talents and compare us with the pupils of the two or three other school districts whose programs they would be attending. After the program, there would be a Christmas tree and that same Mr. Vanek in a Santa suit with treats for everyone, and then a chance for everybody to visit.

Also in this entry, Imogene refers for the first time to the hot lunch program that has been inaugurated in the rural schools. At first the lunches will be cooked from supplies brought by the pupils from home. Later they will be augmented by a federal commodities program. Naturally, the lunches are cooked by the teacher. Although the Warm Spring Creek school has electricity, all cooking and baking is done on the wood stove in the teacherage, and the washing up with water carried from the spring and heated on the stove. Imogene is now cooking lunch for a dozen children, five days a week. Teaches them, does her lesson planning, grades their work. Cleans the school, carries more water from the spring. On weekends she goes home and cooks and bakes enough to get her father through another week, also on a wood stove and without refrigeration or running water. Then she forces herself to write short stories during the evenings. No wonder she's tired.

November 26: Baked potatoes for hot lunch—easy to fix. The oven was just full. Practiced sq. dances for the program the last period.

November 27: The kids brot in a slug of supplies for hot lunch. We have enuf meat for next week. We also got some blanks to fill for commodities. Wish we'd get them soon so the kids would not have to bring so much.

And evidence of hard times in her Christmas planning:

December 2: Well, the bills will pour in now for a few days. Must spend a little time on my accounts. Traded my radio to Doris & Jack for $10 & some chains. They will give theirs to Pa for Xmas.

December 10: Mary's birthday. Doris & I found some candles in my scrap box in the attic. Vaneks brot the commodities for school lunch. We were shocked at the way they pass them out.

I wonder what she found so shocking about the way the commodities were distributed? Whether she thought the government was being lavish and wasteful? Or stingy? Or careless? I'll never know, although I suspect that the lavishness of free food from the government was painful from the point of view of people who rummaged for candles for a child's birthday and swapped radios to give as Christmas presents.

December 11: Made commodity cookies. Will serve peaches & cocoa & cookies tomorrow.

December 12: Made donuts for the kids. Will give them potato soup &
prunes.

December 17: The men put up the stage & tree. I baked cookies, finished
my cards, & here came a guy I didn't know—asked if I was Doris, said he was
Robert Lahr. Had to talk to him. Another evening gone.

Again, Imogene describes an available man as someone who interrupts her
peaceful evening after a hard day of teaching, cooking, getting ready for a
Christmas program, working her Christmas cards, writing her secret stories.

December 19: Vaneks & Mrs. Norton came down & helped pack the treats
& I made a pile of donuts for the kids.

December 20: Had a nice crowd. Got thru pretty well. Mary gave me a
wooden spoon. Got 7 handkerchiefs. 4 lbs. candy. Santa was a great success.
Had fun taking the little kids to him.

December 31: End of 1940 & this book. Must get a new one as soon as I
get to town. We plan to take in a dance to ring out the old, ring in the new.

The end of the last peaceful year, she must have thought, later on. Or
maybe, the end of the last dull year. The next eighteen months will find her
life altered beyond anything she could have predicted from the unchanging
wheat fields and pastures of Fergus County.

Meanwhile, unknowing, she sits late over her typewriter, dreaming a
writer's dreams. If only somebody will buy this story. Or the next. What the
money would mean. What the validation would mean. If only, if only.

And she buys her new diary and begins recording 1941.

5

January 6, 1941: Not locating the key, I went in thru the window &
opened the front door last night. Had the fire going by 5 this morning. I was
horrified at my weight & measurements.

January 11: Finished my coyote story—wrote 2 letters, did my wash—
had to carry 6 pails of water from the spring—then Polly came—we went
for commodities, & baked over 100 cookies.

January 15: Started exams. I knew the 7th grade was fooling around. High-
est grade was 60. Made up my mind Gloria has to learn her combinations.

January 22: Went to Danvers tonight, got 8 gals of gas for $1.08. Also
some groceries. Finished my reports. Made dream bars. Ate 4.

January 27: Start what I hope is a 3 day fast-course-weight. Hope I make
it. Gave up. Ate before I went to bed.

February 3: Got my story returned—letter from the editor—said it showed promise—had a headache, went to bed—got nothing done at all.

Anyone driving late on the highway, passing by the Warm Spring Creek school and seeing light from the row of tall north windows casting oblongs across the snow might have wondered what on earth the schoolteacher was doing, all by herself at such an hour. Sitting in an empty schoolroom under a bare electric lightbulb, tapping away at her typewriter was what she was doing.

What kept her, what keeps any writer writing?

The letter from the editor who says the story shows promise. The dream that maybe next time the story will sell.

Or maybe she, too, writes to silence the ghosts.

February 14: Had a Valentine Party—went off quite well. Mrs. Huffine brot her boy & Buddy Vanek came also. I melted snow to wash my hair & clothes with.

Like the Christmas programs, school parties were considered entertainment for the community, and all the little preschool brothers and sisters were welcome. The boy that Mrs. Huffine brought was probably the Buzzie Huffine who was a seventh grader when I started at the Warm Spring Creek school.

March 21: First day of Spring—we played baseball.

March 26: Gloria brot the first spring flowers—3 purple crocus. It rained & snowed both. Such a life.

Yes, such a life, and still so normal.

On the eleventh of March, her brother Dave had written from Midway Island:

Dear Imogene,

. . . There isn't much to do here to have fun. I haven't been swimming yet as I haven't had time. Men don't come out here to have fun they come here to make all the money they can. . . . When all a man does is work eat and sleep he sure gets hard to get along with. Most of the men stay only 4 to 6 months. This is the longest place I have ever been in.

I saw a school of perpoise following a tug boat the other day. They sometimes follow a ship at sea for days. . .

As ever

Dave

On March 20 he wrote again:

I got a nice letter from Florence. I gess she felt sorry for me and wrote.

Florence, my other laughing aunt, who sang songs to me and taught me how to paint my fingernails! Almost exactly 58 years after Dave mentioned her name in a letter to his sister, Florence wrote to me to fill in the background of a story that had become family legend. I quote from her letter partly for the pleasure of hearing her voice, but mainly to cast a prosaic light on the legend, which held that Florence had saved Dave from being captured or killed by the Japanese when they invaded Midway (after all, if he left Midway in June of 1941 to come home and marry Florence, he had several months leeway before the Japanese got there).

Florence's letter also provides a glimpse into the working life of a young woman who did *not* become a teacher. "We've got a whole family of schoolteachers and one renegade beautician!" she once told me, laughing.

3-17-1999

Dear Mary,

Dave & I went together a year in hi school in Denton MT. & he kept drinking & I told him finally if he got drunk one more time I was quitting him. So he did & I did . . .so he just left the country. He rode around on freight trains for a few years worked at Fort Peck Grand Coulee & Shasta Dam. Then he went to Midway Island. When he was at Midway I had graduated from hi school & fooled around working for people in harvest & cleaning house & for people having babies (a revolting job). I did ironing cooking & taking care of kids. Then I went to beauty school 1939–1940.

So one day Dad was going to town & A.P [Dave's father] . . . wanted a ride to Denton so on the way he told Dad that Dave was at Midway Island working & he was very lonesome. I told Dad "Gee if I had Dave's address I'd write to him." So next time Dad picked up A.P. Dad got [Dave']s address. I had just graduated from Acme Beauty College in Billings & wasn't going with any boy friend just then. So we wrote about 3 or 4 letters & he said he was coming home . . . he quit his job just to come see me. We hadn't written about any thing only our jobs & the weather. I was working at Ina's Beauty Shoppe in the Montana Building in Lewistown at that time. So when he got to MT. He came right up to the Beauty Shoppe to see me. We went together 13 days & got married on Friday the 13 of June 1941. We hadn't seen each other for 7 years. He told me he had quit drinking. I think he just quit that day but Dave was always the most honest person in the whole world & he never took another drink in the 55 $^1/_2$ years we were married.

Meanwhile Imogene's school year at Warm Spring Creek was winding down.

March 31: The kids sure fought at noon. I went to Danvers. Had a swell vacancy notice from Wash. Vaneks & Mr. Norton came and put the new desks up.

April 5: Young Chuck Huffine got the 3 yr. Term. But Vanek & Gremaux tied for the two yr. Term which means Miss Patton will appoint that member. I wonder who.

Imogene refers here to a recent school board election, which of course she has followed with interest. "Young Chuck Huffine" was still on the school board when the redheaded woman threatened to quit if they didn't insulate the school, and it was Chuck who headed up the work party that my father enjoyed so much. He was the father of Buzzie, who attended the Valentine's Day party and later went to school with me. The Huffines were heirs to the vast Huffine-Lincoln cattle outfit, for which my grandfather had ridden rep, and which had dwindled in a generation from old west romance to the gritty day-to-day in which we all lived.

April 7: Jitters! Got a letter from Washington asking for an interview in Spokane. Went down to talk it over with Doris. She advises for it.

How Imogene had longed for this chance to teach in Washington state, at a better salary and under better conditions! And yet, how chilling it must have felt to think of living in a city as big as Spokane, so far from her family.

April 9: Went down to see Vaneks & got Friday off scot free. Went to town & blew myself for a new hat & dress—hope it turns the trick.

April 11: Left at 7:00 & got as far as Superior. It rained all day from Stanford. At Helena it snowed over the pass.

It took her two days to drive from central Montana to Spokane, Washington, in her 1939 Ford sedan, at her own expense. Many highways were still graveled, and the weather, as always in Montana, was erratic. But Imogene was an intrepid traveler all her life. Still—

April 12: My disappointment was bitter. My letter did not arrive till today. The principal called once—Wed. The agency hadn't even taken his address.

Had they filled the position before she even left Montana? In any event, her anxiety and the expense of her trip—the new hat and dress, the cost of gasoline, even at $1.08 for eight gallons—all were for nothing.

April 14: I got my first check for writing—$2.

April 26: Got the job back.

The teaching job at the Warm Spring Creek school. After her disappointment over the Spokane interview, it's better than nothing. But she stiffens up—no use crying over what can't be helped, point out the ghosts, and what can't be cured must be endured.

May 23: The Mothers came early & I could hardly get my reports done. I guess the kids had a lovely time. Lots to eat. They went swimming after.

Traditionally, the last day of school was celebrated by a picnic, attended by all the parents and preschool brothers and sisters. One of the warm springs on the creek had been dammed to make a lovely swimming hole. Even in May in Montana, steam rose off the creek, and the little dryland kids were goose-bumped and blue when they climbed out of the warm water into the cold air.

It doesn't sound as though Imogene attended this picnic. She was still feeling let down after her disappointment in Spokane. After squandering money on the new dress and the new hat for the interview that didn't happen, she had to find a way to make her car payments and pay her bills over the summer.

She noted that Dave was getting married—*June 9: Dave told us he & Florence have decided to get married*—next Sunday if all goes well. I'd been hoping but it was still a shock. Told him he could have the car to use—before she heard of a job in southeastern Montana, working on a dude ranch. On June 26, she writes, "Got to Livingston at 3:00—had a job at 4:00—waitress & dishes at 63 Ranch—not enuf help—wranglers—to suit me."

I'm struck by her use of the article—*the* car, not *my* car—as further evidence of Imogene's relationship with her family.

After her summer at the dude ranch, Imogene returned to central Montana with little enthusiasm to resume teaching at the Warm Spring Creek school. On her birthday that fall she wrote, "No catch um yet." Then she began the tedious fall routine of meetings and lessons.

September 5: We went to the teacher's meeting. It was so boring. Broke into my school house to stay all night. No lights.

September 8: Had 11 pupils by noon. Mr. C stopped at night and told me Gremaux's didn't want me back & said I let the kids swim raw.

September 11: Roosevelt speech was at 7:00. I heard the first half. Static bad. He's sure worried about Hitler. I wish Hitler would meet his end.

September 12: I started down to Mother's tonight & not two miles away my car stopped. The gas line or fuel pump. Lyle & Ervin came along & pushed me to Mother's.

Lyle Knutson and Ervin Mossey are neighboring ranchers—brothers-in-law, in fact, whose daughters I am still in touch with. Imogene's diary constantly reflects the close ties of the second-generation homestead community and the unspoken certainty that neighbors will always help neighbors. Her next entries, however, show her difficulties with her car broken down. She can't run her own and her family's errands, can't get to town to buy groceries, can't even afford groceries on top of the unexpected expense of car repair.

September 13: We [Imogene and her mother] couldn't do so much today—short on grub—no soft water. We went out & picked some buffalo berries.

Imogene's lament about no soft water gives a glimpse of nearly-forgotten daily life on those dryland homesteads. Because so much of the well water in northern Fergus County was alkaline—my mother said the water stained my baby clothes yellow, and that sometimes, just to show that they could do it, they would touch a match to the gases from the water and cook an egg over the flame—the women collected rain water or melted snow to wash their hair or to do fine laundry. Imogene is complaining that she can't wash her hair this weekend.

Short on grub. Another reminder that the depression isn't over, not here in Montana, and Imogene's pay warrant and her mother's haven't stretched far enough this month.

September 17: The big boys work on the spring some more. It still has lots of sediment in it.

September 18: Mr. Vanek stopped tonight to see about my exempt card. I would like to buy some more groceries but have only $2.50 left this month & two weeks.

September 22: Polly brot me a loaf of bread & some milk. Her Dad got me a box of groceries at Brooks. With nothing to sew or write I sure kill time.

September 24: A cold rainy day & the weather gray. The kids beastly—just as mean as devils. One broke a window worse & one tore a light fixture down.

October 6: No new pupils [which she apparently has been told to expect.] Outlined my story so I think I can go ahead with it. Finished the 1st quarter. If I can do 5 pages a night it will be done this week.

October 7: Finished the 1st half. Sometimes I think it will sell the first time out & then I don't. Could sure use the extra money.

October 8: Nuts, I should have written but just fooled around & read & wished for more to eat. My warrant has not been signed and I'm out of sorts.

October 13: Mon. Got our 4 new pupils & I believe they will fit in fine with the grades here. Sure have lots of cleaning up to do. Darn old dog came tonight & chased my kitten.

October 14: I can play the song flute—something I could never do on a harmonica. But I can't interest any of the boys. Looks like I will have to depend on the girls.

It sounds as though the Warm Spring Creek school board has invested in Tonettes, those brightly colored plastic approximations of clarinets, for the pupils. Music was a part of the curriculum that most of the rural teachers struggled with. Usually the school had a piano, but few teachers had had more music instruction than they could get in a single class at normal school. My mother was determined that my sister and I would learn to play the piano (after all, we were going to be teachers, and what an advantage we would have, being able to play the piano!). Of course, she couldn't play, but she had learned to read music in her normal school class, and when my sister or I practiced, she could scream, "F sharp!" from the kitchen whenever we missed one.

My grandmother couldn't play, either, but lacking all other resources at one of her schools, she organized a band by having every child bring a pocket comb to wrap in waxed paper and hum Christmas carols through. *Make do* was the motto of all the rural teachers.

October 22: Polly & Paul got in a fight today in baseball. Polly was still mad enuf to slam doors when she went home. I washed clothes tonight.

November 4: Made a batch of cookies. Began to read Darrow for the Defence. Very good book. Am beginning to think about hot lunches.

November 11: Took the radio to school & let the kids listen to the presidents speech. Got my curtains up again. Burnt my breakfast rolls. That irritated me.

November 14: A hellish wind last night. Lights off this morning. I got some water & went to Mother's.

November 18: Bean soup—did the kids ever clean it up. Washed with snow water. Scrubbed my floor & baked muffins & dream bars.

November 26: Believe it or not, the school board did get my warrant signed. I was sure surprised. Asked for a broom, coal hod & water pail.

December 1: Got up a half hour late. The kids liked my new dress. I started the Christmas program. How wild the kids get. I hate the next 3 weeks.

December 7: Took a roll of pictures of Mary. Then I went to Danvers to see about my tires. Then to Ma's for dinner. Finished my crocheted edge.

In 1941, news arrives slowly in central Montana. For us, the date rings with significance, seems to quiver on the page, but for Imogene, December 7, 1941, has been just another uneventful Sunday. Because she has left her radio at school, she will not learn until the next day that, on the other side of the world, the Japanese have attacked Pearl Harbor and the United States is at war.

December 8: Radio reports Japan attacked the H.I. We listened to the president's speech at recess. So we are in World War II. So some people are happy.

Morning recess. Probably about ten o'clock. The radio on the teacher's desk, the dozen or so pupils clustered around to hear, through static, the clipped, enraged syllables of a man whose face they have seen, if at all, in newsreels at the movie theater in Lewistown. What do Roosevelt's words mean to these ranch children with their serious faces? Their books left open on their desks, their breath condensing in thick frost on the schoolroom windows, as always in December. What can possibly be happening beyond the snowbound rim of the South Moccasin mountains that can affect them?

A lifelong Republican in isolationist Montana, Imogene disliked Roosevelt on principle, but her remark, *so some people are happy,* probably has less to do with FDR than with her worry about her brother and other young men she has known all her life who have registered for the draft and now are going to be called to fight. Back on June 10, she had noted that *[Dave] has not been called yet.*

Meanwhile the school routine continues.

> *December 17: This afternoon we got the stage up, the tree, and lots of roping. We also got 90 sacks of treats boxed. Two days to go.*

Finally, at home for the brief vacation:

> *December 25: We always open our gifts Christmas Eve—I got a rollaway box & lots besides. Mary got piles of things. We had a goose dinner. Weather bad. Dave & Florence at Frenches.*

Imogene's family has gathered for Christmas, all but her sister Sylva, who is with her husband in Bremerton, and her brother, Dave, who has recently been married and is spending Christmas with his wife's family. They don't know it, but it will be a last untroubled Christmas, as war and work and accident wait in the coming year. Their tradition is to open their gifts on Christmas Eve, while the house is warm, rather than to let the children get up early on Christmas morning in a cold house before the fires have been lit. By Christmas of 1941, I am still the only grandchild, and I seem to have done rather well with presents.

December 30: My cold went into my vocal cords. Gloria wasn't here, luckily for me. I just live over my stove—can't get the room warm at all. Nurse my cold—don't write.

As I read these lines, I remember how the redheaded woman threatened to resign because the school was so cold. By the winter of 1949, teachers were scarce, and she could risk making the threat. But in 1941, Imogene would have expected to be replaced if she gave a school board such an ultimatum. The cold continued:

December 31: Only 6 kids in school—an easy day. Can talk again. Weather cold—Have a notion to stay here tomorrow and write. Could sure use more money. May not be able to start my car.

Another year done. The cold is bitter. Snow has drifted into the coulees and filled the draws. Range cattle huddle for shelter in the dark, their breaths white, their shaggy coats encrusted. In the distance the shrouded outline of the South Moccasin mountains promises safety, a barricade between these miles of snowy stubble fields and the rest of the world. How much war news has filtered across those miles? Do the ranch families know, does the teacher know, that Japan has invaded the Philippines? That Japan has captured the island of Guam? That on Christmas day the British surrendered Hong Kong to the Japanese?

Hardly a light shines over all these miles of snowbound Montana, except perhaps a few stars winking through the overcast, and of course the light from the schoolhouse windows that falls across the snow. So late at night and so cold, there is no passerby, but if there were, he might hear the tapping of the teacher's typewriter, tapping into 1942.

6

January 1, 1942: Got up late—had had to get up, build a fire & go to bed with a hot water bottle. The car was stiff & cold so I staid at the school house & did odd jobs.

January 2: Only James & Buddy came today. James helped me take my battery out. I let them go about 1:30. Got a letter from Aunt Mary & a mag. Snow is so deep in the gate I'm afraid I can't get thru it [with her car].

January 4: Sun. It finally cleared up but is still cold. The snow plow went by at last. I huddled over the stove all day long.

January 7: Some said it was 18 below but it felt warm to me this morning when I did the chores. Gloria & my seventh grade sure poke about their work.

January 12: Got a swell idea for a story—mean to write it immediately & try it on the American [magazine]. Vaneks brot the school commodities. We got good apples.

January 22: Still an argument over daylight saving. I'm going to find out. Finally wrote to a literary agent. If I could only earn my living by writing.

January 30: Left about 5—got picked up by Mrs. Fritz. She had asked Miss Patton about school time next week. And we do not have to change. Ha! Ha!

I was puzzled by the entry for January 22—what was Imogene going to find out—until I read ahead and realized that there had been an argument in the community about whether or not the school clocks should be set an hour ahead for Daylight Savings.

The United States adopted Daylight Savings Time on February 9, 1942, to boost war production, but a lot of ranchfolk in Montana disliked the idea. If you wanted to get up an hour earlier, they reasoned, why not just roust your bones out of bed and be done with it? Did government fools in Washington really think you could get more daylight out of twenty-four hours by changing the clocks? However, one of the families whose children were attending the Warm Spring Creek school was campaigning for the school to start on Daylight Time, much to Imogene's annoyance.

This entry also reflects Imogene's habit, when the weather is so cold that she can't get her car started, of heading for the homestead on foot (twenty miles!) and hoping someone will give her a ride. Mrs. Fritz is another rural teacher, who has heard the word straight from Miss Patton, the county superintendent, that there will be no setting the clocks ahead this year in Fergus County schools, and Imogene rejoices.

February 3: All I do is read—be glad when I finish the book, only halfway thru. The kids are spring ornery. Hope I get a job before school is out.

February 18: Cold as sin this morning. Fires pokey about burning. Everyone in school. Paul picked off a tick so I guess spring is here.

March 4: Finished my reports for this week except 3 cards not returned. The yard is a sea of mud & slush. My days are full of dull routine.

What she hasn't written about: That on February 15, 1942, the Japanese captured Singapore. That hundreds of women in the Pacific Northwest are enrolling in six-week training programs to become Red Cross Volunteer Nurses' Aides. That people in Seattle are ploughing up their lawns to plant victory gardens. That the draft age, originally 21 to 35, has been expanded to 20 to 44 years of age.

March 5: Got my first vacancy notice of the year from Geyser. That's a town I can drive to but I'd rather locate near Absarokee for a special reason.

Imogene has hinted in her diary entries of her feelings for a man in southeastern Montana. *And there's a cowboy,* she wrote in September of 1940, *but he loves another gal.* I've never been able to identify this man, although I can put a name to most of the men in Fergus County who courted Imogene. Apparently they interested her the most when they were unavailable.

March 20: Birds are chirping at 7:30. And the sun shines on the hills across the Judith. This was a lovely day.

What she hasn't written: That on March 9, 1942, the Japanese had taken Java and captured 100,000 Allied troops. That on March 11, General MacArthur had escaped from the Philippines as the Japanese closed in. That on March 19, Japanese planes attacked Darwin, Australia. That March 1942 saw the beginning of the relocation of Japanese-Americans from coastal regions to sites east of the Rocky Mountains.

April 8: Letter from Dave. He hopes for a job in Alaska. Florence will come home for a visit while he gets a place to stay if he can. What a relief.

Imogene's relief is at her brother's draft reclassification as an essential war worker. However, he will take the construction job in Alaska just in time to experience the war in the Aleutians, and his family will start worrying all over again.

Then, a week later, an explanation of what she is not writing:

April 15: The mornings are lovely. Then a wind comes & it is not so nice. I baked muffins & cake tonight. I say little about the war. It shadows every day.

April 16: Imagine my surprise to see Dave & Florence drive in. We were invited to Jack's for supper. They [Dave and Florence] have a baby coming up in Aug. Such pretty clothes she has made.

April 18: I've had a nice visit even if Ma has not felt well & Dave is going away for so long. I walked up on the hill & down by the dam.

April 27: Got my sugar rationing instructions. What a headache. I guess it only takes 4 evenings tho. I measured out 4 lbs & have lots left. Guess I'll make jelly next week.

Sugar rationing will be a headache for Imogene, not only because she'll have to cut back on her cookie-baking and jelly-making, but because she will be in charge of registering everyone in the school district for their sugar rations. Like the Christmas programs and the school picnics, the sugar-ration registration shows how the rural schools served as a focal point for those sparse and yet close-knit communities in the days before paved highways and television seemed to make communication easier, but, ironically, tended to isolate individuals and break down the communities.

April 29: How I hate to diet & severe dieting is the only thing to take down my weight. By Sept. I'd like to be down to 125 lbs dressed.

Well, at least there's one bright side to sugar rationing. Maybe she can lose weight. But no, Imogene will fight her extra pounds all her life. Her diary constantly reflects her ups and downs, her worry that her friends will find out about her dieting, her anguish at not fitting into her clothes.

April 30: Got a vacancy notice from Alaska. Pay $1800. Would like to get it. Last day of the month. Tomorrow is Sylva's birthday. Gee, we're all getting old.

Such advanced ages—Sylva was thirty-four in May of 1942, and Imogene will be thirty-two in September.

May 5: I registered more than 20 tonight. I bet Thursday is a nightmare. Got asked a question I could not answer.

May 7: Finished registering—only did 4. Sent Roy home sick.

May 8: Got to Ma's & she was fagged. She got supper & I helped her finish her report. Then I packed & we left—loaded to the hilt.

Imogene and her mother are making one of several trips around Montana to talk to school boards and try to line up schools to teach in the fall of 1942. Because it would be her third—and tenure—year, Imogene already knows that the Warm Spring Creek school won't hire her back. She is thankful to have her car. It has kept her in debt and frustrated her with its breakdowns, but at least she and her mother don't have to depend on my father or my increasingly unreliable grandfather to drive them where they need to go.

May 9: Got up too early of course & we had an hour & a half to wait in Stanford. I stopped in Moccasin. Then home to round up the horses. We got them down fairly easy.

May 10: Had quite a branding. A cold day. Got so stiff going up I thot I'd not be able to ride back but I did. We rode thru Martin's pasture & got the cow & calf that ran away.

Cattle brandings were spring festivals during my childhood. On consecutive Sundays there would be a branding at our ranch, then at Uncle Theo's, then at Uncle Martin's. The uncles from town showed up and pretended to be cowboys again, and the aunts brought homemade rolls and frosted cakes and pies and potato salads, and we cousins got reacquainted after another winter apart. Imogene's diary entry revives a host of nostalgic images for me—branding irons heating in a pitch-pine fire, vaccine guns laid in a row on a log, the smell of wet white hawthorn blossoms along the rutted road to the corral, the bawling of cows for their calves.

Imogene is writing here that she rode with my father to bring the cows and calves down from the mountain pasture to be branded. It was her first long horseback ride of the spring, and it left her sore, but she had a good time. Many of her entries during the spring of 1942, especially as she grows more and more disenchanted with teaching, tell of the pleasure she takes in helping my father with ranch work.

May 11: Sam took me to a show. I was dead tired but if he goes to the army it was the least I could do.

Sam. I'm pretty sure I know who he was and what he did for a living, but I'm not absolutely certain, and the memories that could verify mine are vacant or dead. Sorry, ghosts.

May 12: Nerts—still no mail. The school board had a meeting. I guess they are thinking about a teacher for next year. Heh! The Addison school decided on Sun. for their picnic.

May 14: Went to the show again. It rained some more. Got another vacancy notice. I wish I'd get a contract. It hailed tonight.

May 15: There was snow about 7:15. It melted but it was snow. After school I packed the car & left. Jack was at the road on Pardner. But I got down without help.

The ranch where my parents were living, on the Judith River, was a mile or two off the graveled highway. In bad weather the dirt road through the sagebrush from the highway to the ranch buildings was a treacherous journey through gumbo mud. Imogene is saying here that my father had ridden to meet her at the highway and would have let her ride Pardner, his saddle horse, to the ranch house while he drove her car over the worst parts of the road. But she was proud that she negotiated the road by herself.

May 16: Snowed again today. Melts before it touches the ground. Helped Jack & Bill brand 6 calves. Then we went to Uncle Theo's but they didn't brand.

May 18: Sam said he was quitting [quitting courting her? Or quitting his job? He's expecting to be drafted]. I'm glad. We took in a good show. Note from Mrs. Fritz about the picnic. Well, the rest of this week I must work like a dog.

May 19: Baked brownies—used up my nuts & my sugar ration for a week. Washed clothes—cleaned my floor—scheduled the rest of the week.

May 20: The Board of Health were out. What a day for them to come. I have done some packing & the place looks like the Wreck of the Hesperus.

May 21: After school I went in—ordered the ice cream to go to Brooks— got weenies—& such. Took the chicken feed to Doris. Sewed a little on Mary's coat.

May 22: Had a nice crowd—lovely day—went swimming. Was amazed at the backbiting that goes on. Came back and finished my reports.

And so another school year ends with another picnic. Without other employment, Imogene will move in with my parents for the summer. With most of the young men gone to war, she will help out with ranch work in any way she can and pray that she gets a teaching contract for the fall.

What will happen to her within a few weeks is disaster.

May 23: Sam was up to bid me goodbye—could string him along all summer. But what's the use. Got to Jack's & found out he wanted me to take a team up the hill so did not go to Pa's. Made myself a nightie.

May 24: Last night we had a hail storm & rain. The river was high as Jack had ever seen it. Doris lost 35 chickens. I started on skim milk & hope to stay on it till I lose 3 in. Worked on Mary's red dress. Cut out Doris' nightie.

May 27: Went to town with the men—broke a tug. They sold 4 pigs— bought a new mower. I got 2 teeth fixed & did my register & Mother's. Got 4 kittens on the way home. Mary was entranced.

May 28: Jack sent me home for a team. They were not hard to catch but it rained & I had to walk down the canyon. They had quite a time in the wet coulee.

June 2: Jack & I moved the bulls up on the hill. Then we caught two horses & brot them back. They gave a bit of trouble till we got to the main road. Then chores.

June 4: Rain last night so we got up late. Doris washed after Jack worked over the machine. I tried to carry water on Pardner but could not.

June 6: It was 11:00 before I got thru riding around. Wish I had a job. Expect Florence is worried about Dave. Mail does not go thru so fast from Alaska.

In 1999, I asked Aunt Florence about this entry, and she wrote back,

You wrote that the Welches were worrying about Dave during the war. Well, so was I. I was five months pregnant when Dave left for the Aleutians [as a civilian construction worker.] He left Montana in April, was out in Washington, waiting to sail to Alaska for over a month [until he finally got to Dutch Harbor, Alaska.] I think the attack [came on] June 3 and he said they had no place to go, no protection at all, and they ran to the outside of town. I don't think he ever knew how many were killed. He said the Japs flew up and down the streets shooting.

Then I didn't know whether he was dead or alive. The army would-
n't let him write. Kristie was born the 17th of August and he knew I
had to have money to pay the doctor, so finally I got a letter. Big white
envelope. The return address was WAR DEPARTMENT. I looked at that,
and I cried, 'Oh, he's dead,' and Mom said, 'Well, open it.' Here was a
card—*I am well—Dave*—and a check. That's all there was, but what a
great relief that I knew he was okay.

Aunt Florence is right about her date; the Japanese attacked Dutch Harbor, Alaska, on June 3, 1942, then returned on June 4 in a second and more
deadly raid with 10 fighter planes, 11 dive bombers, and 8 low-level bombers.
The civilian construction workers had nowhere to run but to the weeds. American casualties were 43 dead; the Japanese probably lost a handful of men.

*June 13: Florence's first wedding anniversary. I got her the dishes. Had $5
more work done on my teeth. Home too late to get the cows. My school kids
passed, all but Roy.*

*June 14: This was a nice day. We went for a walk. Florence looks well &
seems in good spirits. My tooth keeps on aching. We have had a nice visit. She
likes the quilt.*

*June 15: I sewed on Jack's saddle blanket. Grammy washed & it rained.
Just before we milked Frenches [Florence's parents] came. They thot the road
was awful.*

June 16: This is a day I'll never forget.

In fact, June 16, 1942, was a day that no one in our family ever forgot. It
was my father's twenty-ninth birthday, and my mother, pregnant with my sister
Betty, was at the ranch house baking him his favorite cherry pie for a birthday
supper, while Imogene helped him in the hayfields. After all the rain of the

past several days, my father would have been glad for a hot sun and a chance to get his hay mowed. He sent Imogene with his sorrel colts to mow one field while he mowed another, a quarter of a mile away.

The sorrel colts were beautiful and fast, but they were half-broken, and that day they spooked, perhaps at their own shadows, and ran away with Imogene and the mowing machine. Somehow she was thrown off the high seat of the mower and into the razor-sharp sickle bar. It was one of those moments in a life when all that has seemed placid and dull is suddenly altered beyond imagination. In an instant the sickle bar had slashed through Imogene's right ankle, cutting flesh and tendons to the bone.

As my father told the story years later, he looked across the flats from his own mowing and saw that Imogene had not finished her round. He unhitched one of his own horses and rode her bareback through wild hay and sagebrush to find Imogene sitting up against a fence post. Somehow she had managed to catch the sorrel colts and tie them up, and she had pulled a lace out of her shoe and fashioned a tourniquet for her ankle. "And a good thing she was so level-headed," my father always said, "because I wouldn't have known what to do."

He galloped on horseback to the ranch house and drove back to the field in Imogene's own car, got her in the back seat with her foot wrapped in towels and elevated. In the few minutes before he and my mother started with her for the hospital in Lewistown, I climbed into the front seat of the car to see what had happened to Auntie. It is one of my earliest memories, and I can still see her, propped in the back seat, and smell the blood and dust.

At the sight of my face, she laughed her familiar, wonderful laugh. I knew that nothing terrible could happen when Auntie could laugh. "Look what they did to me, Mary," she said.

My parents drove Imogene the thirty miles over gravel road to Lewistown, trying not to speed over potholes on bald wartime tires. None of them believed that Imogene's foot could be saved. She would be a cripple, she would be unable to work—and certainly not teach, not with schoolhouses to sweep and wood stoves to stoke and hot lunches to cook and springs to clean and baseball to play with her pupils—no, she would be dependent on others for the rest of her life. She was not quite thirty-two years old.

But at tiny St. Joseph's hospital in Lewistown, the nuns rushed Imogene into the emergency room, and the doctor who had delivered me went to work with sutures on the nearly severed foot. The following are Imogene's diary entries, which she reconstructed a month later.

June 16, 1942: This is a day I'll never forget. Jack's birthday. We planned cherry pie & rice pudding for supper. I got thrown into the wheel of the mower & badly cut. We handled the situation calmly.

June 17: Last night the Dr. said my foot was warm when he came so I went to sleep. Naturally it would be several days before we could be sure it was safe. Doris, Jack & Mary were in this evening.

June 19: Due to rain the folks came in this afternoon. Doris visited me all afternoon. Mary said "That's where Auntie is!" I was glad to see them. The Dr. is encouraging.

June 23: I am going to type an account of this summer also. There isn't room here for all the junk I want to rehash & remember when I am old & grey.

If she did type an account of that summer, I've never been able to find it. How I wish I knew the details she wanted to remember when she was old and gray. But all I know is what she wrote in her diary and what has solidified into family legend.

June 29: Today I got to sit up twice & know I can sit up long enuf to get home. What a relief. Had a sore throat & temperature. Darnit. Means more days.

July 4: I ate lunch in the hall listening to the parade go by. I guess the celebration was not much. Lud was in a race & got his name in the paper.

Lud, the man she never forgave and never forgot, obviously out of prison by the Fourth of July, 1942.

Get over him, Imogene, I want to tell her. Get on with your life. He isn't worth it. If he had your backbone, he'd pull himself together. You think he doesn't have options? He could hop a freight, like your brother did, and go where the construction jobs are, couldn't he? He could go to Alaska and run for his life with the other workers when the Japanese attack Dutch Harbor.

But he doesn't.

July 7: I had two different hemorrages this summer—neither very bad— only they worried me. The Dr. took off the cast & did not put any thing more on—only bandage. He hopes my foot will not be too stiff, but it just drains & drains & it seems like I'll be here forever.

July 9: Every week he keeps saying one more week & then I get so blue.

July 20: Gee, today Dr. S told me he'd let me go home Wed. So I got a card right out to Doris & can only hope she gets it in time to come.

July 22: Doris, Ma, & Mary came for me. All the excitement. An Alaska job. Tore around bidding people good-bye. The trip home not bad. Haying when I left. Harvest now.

July 27: Harvest is coming on & all have to work so hard & there is so little I can do but play with Mary & sew. I embroider blocks for Doris' baby quilt. It has x-stitch animals on it. Mary always wants to help. She likes to go out doors with me. If the gobbler comes he is all I can manage on crutches. I have been offered a school in Idaho at $140 for nine months. Wrote to hold them off till I can hear from Alaska. Ma of course does not want me to go to Alaska. But $1800 is a lot of money.

Imogene always told me that everyone in Fergus County knew that she had nearly lost her foot, and that no school district wanted to hire a woman on crutches. How, after all, would a cripple carry spring water, cook hot lunches, stoke a wood stove, and play baseball with her pupils? And so, Imogene said, she began sending applications out of state, where no one knew her story. In truth, as her diary shows, she had been looking for a better-paying job out of Montana for several years. What she has not yet realized in July of 1942 is that the war has brought about a teacher shortage, and her applications are going to meet with better luck.

Oh, yes, the turkey gobbler! The great peril of my childhood. As a toddler, I liked to chase the turkey hens, but I lived in fear of the gobbler, who would knock me down with his wings. I would scream for Imogene to save me, and she would come hobbling on her crutches to beat him off.

July 31: Today I tried to get on my shoes and could not. That one foot was badly swelled. I measured it & it was an inch larger than the left foot.

August 1: Was able to get my black oxford on. What a relief. No doubt in 6 weeks I can wear my other shoes. Dr. S will never know how glad I am he saved my foot.

Then begin the hints. She's made a decision for reasons that she undoubtedly has hashed over with her sister and brother-in-law; she's about to embark on a journey with a destination she doesn't bother to note in her diary. And it's not just that she's not telling herself what she already knows, but that she's fighting her fears. If she doesn't put into words what she's about to do, if she doesn't use future tense, she won't have to face the future until, thankfully, it becomes the past.

August 10: My foot is not quite healed. The Dr. told me I could drive a car. He had me take a step without my crutches. I guess I'm more scared than hurt.

August 13: Packed my stuff in the attic & the garage. Told Mary I was going to visit Grandma. "Don't stay" she told me.

August 17: Getting odds & ends tended to. Tomorrow I must go to town & see the Dr & find out about my bill. My budget is driving me crazy.

August 20: What a day. The tie rod got loose. I had a headache. Couldn't get all my car work done. Saw the baby [Dave's and Florence's daughter, Kristol]. Florence had 30 hr. [labor]. Frenches took me home.

August 22: I got all my packing done here. If I ever marry, wonder what I'll do with my junk.

Imogene never explains whether she was offered the job in Alaska, or why she decided against the job in Idaho even at the salary of $140 a month, which sounds so good in comparison to the $80 a month she had been making at the Warm Spring Creek school. She does continue to note the ranch activities, the gradual healing of her foot, and the birth of Dave's and Florence's daughter, Kristol Lee, on August 17. But somewhere between the lines, she has negotiated the next big change in her life, and now she is loading her car and preparing to leave Fergus County. On August 26, she writes, *Got 30 miles W. of Missoula. My ankle is badly swollen tonight. I quit about 7:30. Spent about 12 hrs. on the road. Ate at McDonald's Pass.* She's on her way to a new teaching job in the tiny community of Napavine, south of Tenino, Washington, and, whether she realizes it or not, a transformation.

The Washington Years

August 1942–
January 1945

7

/ / /

August 26, 1942: Got 30 miles W. of Missoula. My ankle is badly swollen tonight. I quit about 7:30. Spent about 12 hours on the road. Ate at McDonald's Pass.

August 27: Went to Ellensburg. Staid in a camp. Guess I'll get in in fair time tomorrow. Have about 225 miles to go. Will be glad to get over Snowqualmie tomorrow.

Again I begin with my own map of the mind, superimposing it over the highways that Imogene traveled that August, driving her black Ford with its stick shift through heat that rippled through the sagebrush and must have made an agony of her swollen and bandaged foot every time it had to touch the gas pedal. I've driven that highway more times than I like to think about, and not always in an easy frame of mind, but least I never had to cross the Rockies and head westward with one foot half-severed. Imogene would have

79

left the homestead near Denton as early as she could get away—7:30 in the morning, if she's right about the twelve hours on the road—and driven just about 300 miles, averaging 25 miles an hour over gravel roads and only a little single lane pavement. From Missoula to Ellensburg, where she stayed her second night, would be about another 300 miles, another twelve hours of driving.

Most of that route is Interstate 90 today, but past the Rockies it still shimmers with mirages in August heat as it rolls through the sagebrush and broken hills of eastern Washington. Desolate, interrupted by the swoosh of cars at eighty miles an hour over the asphalt ribbon. The curious thing about distance, though—genuine geographical distance—is the detachment that comes with it. Regrets seem to dissolve with the mirages. Another start seems possible. Consider Imogene's new start, consider the distance of her journey, chuffing along at her average 25 miles an hour, twelve hours a day for three days. All is reduced to the heat and the pain in her foot and the need to get across Snoqualmie Pass and then another hundred miles south to Napavine.

August 28, 1942: Got here after 4. Traffic thick. Went past Ft. Louis. Saw slugs of soldiers. Mrs. Curtis helped me carry my things upstairs. Seems nice.

August 29: Got more unpacking done. Got groceries. Called on the supt. & met the janitors. Bernita [probably Bernita Lark, a talented musician and teacher she had known back home in Denton, Montana] came home or rather to see me. She does not like her place.

August 30: Wrote letters. Went to Bernita's for a chicken dinner. Spent the afternoon in gossip about people we knew & schools. She has met more teachers than I have.

August 31: Nothing panned out. Only 16 in the 4th & 40 were expected. I have 23 in the 3rd—a total of 39. I guess my room will be largest. The Grade school has a fair faculty.

After three days' driving, crippled, in late summer heat, she arrives in Napavine late on August 28, unpacks and visits the school on August 29, and by August 31 is teaching a combined third- and fourth-grade classroom of thirty-nine students. I ponder the sentence I just wrote and wonder whether there really is anything more to be said about Imogene's character.

The Napavine elementary school is expecting a swell in enrollment, perhaps because of the families of service personnel at nearby Fort Lewis, which was a major induction center in Washington State during World War II. Imogene has more students in her combined third and fourth grades that she ever taught at one time in a rural school. But the Napavine school not only has electricity and running water, but it has janitors! What a concept!

She has not let anyone in Napavine know that she nearly lost a foot in a mowing machine accident over the summer, or that she's still on crutches and in pain. And now I amuse myself by writing an imaginary sketch of that first day in Napavine, where the superintendent of schools sits behind his desk, intent on details in the August heat. Although the faintest breeze brings the scent of ripe grass through the open window behind his desk, he wears the decent wool suit and starched white collar and necktie of his profession; he doesn't dream of air-conditioning or the casual comfort of a golf shirt and slacks. He hears the slow thump of rubber-tipped crutches in the corridor before he looks up and sees the girl with the huge brown eyes and the brown hair pinned up in braids: the awaited young woman from Montana, who will take the place of a teacher lost to the Bremerton or Seattle shipyards. From the sheen of sweat on her face and the tendrils of curls that have escaped from her decent braids he can see that it has cost her something just to walk from the high school parking lot, through the doors, and down the hall to his office, and it's on the tip of his tongue to say, What the hell! What happened to you? What makes you think you can get through the first week of teaching, let alone the school year?

But school starts tomorrow, and he's got to have a third-grade teacher. He won't be any worse off to give her a chance, and maybe by the time she collapses, he'll have found a substitute. And so he rises from behind his desk, holds out a hand—"Miss Imogene Welch?" and then, as she fumbles free of a crutch to shake his hand, he notes the serious, tucked-in corners of her mouth, the set of her head, the straight line of her back. At least the girl's got guts. She just might make it.

September 1: A long hard day. I tested the 3rd grade myself. They behaved better. One 4th grader stole a pencil. We worked late on books & supplies.

September 2: Woe is me—this book system. My Eng. turned out to be High School. 4 of the 8th grade girls asked me to take them swimming in the river. It wasn't bad either.

September 3: Tonight I was not nearly so tired as before. Had the kids ironed out so did not need to stand all the time. Found out I had to go to town in the AM to get a Dr.

Years later she told me that the real killer that fall was playground duty, which kept her on her feet. She was so tired that she went to bed every night for her first month in Napavine, wondering if she would be able to get up in the morning. Finally came a night when she knew she'd be all right, that she'd make it through the fall. My fictional school superintendent was right about that spine of hers.

September 4: No catch um yet. The years slip by. The war raises the odds agin me. Too tired Friday night to go to town to celebrate.

For years it had been her regular birthday entry: *no catch um yet.* On September 4, 1942, Imogene is thirty-two years old. This September 4 is the last *no catch um* entry.

September 5: Went to Chehalis & blew my self for a Gruen watch. Marvelous looking. Also an umbrella, & a new pen. Bummed all day with Bernita— took in a fair show.

September 6: Sunday. Up late. My foot looks good in the morning. I honestly can kill more time on Sunday & get less done than any one I know.

September 7: Bernita came & we sure killed time. I have all but one pillow fixed. We visited Mrs. Zimmerman. We ate salad here & supper at Mrs. Buroker's [an older, married teacher].

September 8: Joyce [a friend in Montana] does her last day of nurse's training. I bet she enjoys a rest. Mother starts at Deerfield [a rural school in Fergus County, Montana]. Had the faculty reception tonight. I had to laugh.

As Imogene completes her first week of teaching in Napavine and faces the next week, I read and reread her entries and think about what she is not writing. It's not just the absence of war news, but the absence of context that gives me pause. For example, Imogene apparently has rented an upstairs apartment from a Mrs. Curtis, and although she must have signed the rental agreement sight unseen, she's reasonably pleased with her digs (compared with poor Bernita's, at least.) But where are the details that would bring back to life a street, a house, a landlady's blessedly friendly face after the ordeal of three twelve-hour days of driving? What door at the top of what flight of stairs opens on what space?

Elizabeth Hampsten, in her groundbreaking study of midwestern women's private writing, *Read This Only to Yourself*, gives me a clue to understanding Imogene's diaries. Hampsten notes that women's letters tend to be filled with news about other people—illnesses, letters received, visits and gossip—but while the women often record the weather, they tend to say very little about the landscape or other details of their surroundings. As I look back over these pages, I realize that it's I who have described the schoolhouse on the knoll, I who deepened the frost on winter windows in Montana and watched the light from those windows fall on snow and listened to the tap-tap of typewriter keys into the night. I'm the one who has driven through the sagebrush of eastern Washington in August and watched the mirages shimmer and disappear.

"But the more estranged from place a woman feels (an estrangement among these writers that is parallel with social aspiration) the more she is apt graphically to inform others of her whereabouts. As for the professional woman writer, she is almost always an outsider," writes Hampsten, and I feel as though she's talking about me. I'm the one, after all, who stands apart, observing, detailing, writing, and revising.

My immediate problem, however, is that I want to describe a residential street in Napavine, Washington, in 1942, and I can't. The school in Montana? I've walked through that door, I've hung my coat on a hook and sat at one of those desks and run my fingers over the embedded initials of pupils before my time. The highway? I've driven it. But the street in Napavine?

I have clues, of course. I've visited Napavine, I know that its present population is 745, and that, even with wartime activity at Fort Lewis, it couldn't have been much more than that in 1942. I've seen photographs of its main street taken in the late 1940s, and I know enough about its climate and its trees and undergrowth that (already having imagined a school superintendent, after all) I can imagine a quiet graveled street a couple blocks south of the school, shaded by big-leaf maples that in August are just starting to rustle overhead with a premonition of fall. Compared with dry Montana, the lawns look lush and green to the exhausted woman at the wheel of the black Ford, although in truth the grass and leaves are drooping with the stress of late summer. To her it all looks too lush, perhaps, too much like Technicolor, not quite real. Right now she can't remember why she has wanted to live in Washington, how long she has waited to drive down this street and pull over at, what number shall we say it is, 217, a bungalow painted white, of course, with a screened porch. She parks by the fence and drags herself out of her car, barely able to put her weight on her swelling, agonizing foot and ankle. Thinks how she's going to walk as far as that gate, past the sweet peas clustering through the woven wire, up the porch steps to knock. But thankfully, the screen door opens and here's white-haired Mrs. Curtis in her housedress and apron to greet her—"Miss Welch?"

September 9: Did my first stint in the O.P. Nothing happened. I was tired all day. Put my last pillow together & sorted out a lot of art junk.

Imogene has immediately plunged into war work, indicated by the mysterious initials "O.P." At first I thought that O.P., to which she refers again and again throughout her two years in Napavine, had to do with entertaining servicemen, an activity that was just getting underway in Washington State in the fall of 1942. But it isn't until September 26, several weeks later, that Imogene remarks that servicemen have had "duty" at O.P. and she has gotten to see two soldiers "up close."

O.P. seems to be required work; in a much later entry, Imogene will refer to a Mr. Pierce, who forgot his shift and expects to get in trouble for it. And it is intensive work. Imogene writes of shifts that begin at 6 A.M., shifts that run from 5 to 9 P.M. O.P. is a constant in her life while she's in Napavine, but after she resigns to take another teaching position in Tenino, just up the road, she never mentions it again. It's an irritating example of the way she never explains to herself what she already knows, an example that underscores the private nature of the diaries, written without expectation of a reader. Also it's a conundrum; nobody knows what O.P. stands for, everybody I ask makes a guess. The likeliest hazard is from James R. Warren, whose book *The War Years: A Chronicle of World War II in Washington State* has been particularly useful to me. He responded to my inquiry in a letter:

I figured [O.P.] might stand for "Observation Post" . . . Yesterday the Seattle Chapter of American Ex-Prisoners of War met and I posed the question to them. After some discussion, they agreed that the common meaning of the initials was "Observation Post."

1942 was the first full year of World War II and the possibility of Japanese air attacks was a major concern. Cities were blacked out and civilian lookouts were posted in observation posts throughout west-coast states. Many of them were women. They were posted in high places, atop hills, in high buildings, and sometimes in shelters built in high trees to watch for enemy planes. Thousands were involved as look-outs and service personel in the area sometimes helped the cause.

September 10: Decided on our art skedule. Are program is nuts but there is lit-tle we can do to help it. I had a kid would not salute the flag. Found a solution.

September 11: Went to bed at 8:30. So darn tired. Bernita & I got down town so late the P.O. was closed. Then we got nailed for O.P. Sat. 5–9 P.M.

How I wish I knew what Imogene's O.P. station looked like. I suppose it's too much to hope that she got to sit in a tree. Surely she would have men-tioned the tree!

September 12: Bernita & I wanted to roast weenies but we ended up in Evens back yard. Went to the O.P. & I got my button holes done. Miss Lincoln came & visited.

Daisy Lincoln (I've changed her name) is another teacher at the Napavine elementary school and a new friend. Unlike Imogene and Bernita, she grew up in southwestern Washington, so she can show the sights to the young women from Montana. Soon the three young women will be inseparable.

September 13: We, Bernita, Daisy Lincoln, & I went to two churches in Chehalis [Methodist and Catholic] & to Burokers for dinner. Then I came home & slept.

At the end of her second full week of school, Imogene is creating a context for herself, of "letters . . .visits, gossip, and news," to cite Elizabeth Hampsten. On the one hand, Imogene is cherishing news from home (her friend's nursing training, her mother's starting at the Deerfield school), but on the other hand she is driving twenty miles to the larger town of Chehalis to shop, finding her way to church, accepting dinner invitations, and making new friends with young women teachers. These women's friendships are crucial for Imogene; references to Bernita and Daisy will recur again and again in her entries over the next several years as they move together from school to school. Already they're so close that they attend two church services, Methodist and Catholic, to be with each other.

In more ways than the physical pain of setting that injured foot on playground gravel, Imogene is rapidly finding her footing in this strange town. Still, as she notes the news in letters from home, her thoughts are very much back in Montana:

September 14: Ma's school started today. That surprised me. I get awfully tired. We are getting our schedules made over new. Due to gas rationing Bernita & I want to go see the Pacific soon.

September 16: Got my ironing done after a fashion. I always feel so tired after school I need to rest so much I can't get anything done. 3 months today I got hurt.

September 17: I collected art things tonight. Margaret had me down for a waffle. Afterward Miss Long & I went to Bernita's & talked out our trip.

September 18: After school we all went home and packed then Daisy came & we took my stuff to Burakers. I will stay with Bernita.

September 19: What a day. We stopped to call on a friend of Daisy's, looked at Longview. Got a keen cabin, fireplace & everything. The Ocean was all we had hoped.

> *September 20: We spent the morning at the ocean & ate enormous meals.*
> *Gathered driftwood, got souvenirs, watched logs being salvaged. The fog came*
> *after 2.*

These entries about that first visit to the ocean are quite descriptive, compared to most of Imogene's daily jottings. She may have noted the details—
the driftwood, the logs, the fog—in part because she was sightseeing and
thought it was the thing to do. And yet her omissions call for my attention.

The Ocean was all we had hoped—what had these young landbound women
hoped for? What Imogene seems most to have enjoyed is the outing with her
friends. The excitement of planning, packing, spending the night before the
trip with Bernita so as to get an early start, stopping to visit Daisy's friend,
and then the "keen cabin, fireplace & everything."

I'm intrigued, however, by Elizabeth Hampsten's observation that, among
the ordinary midwestern women whose letters and diaries she studied,
estrangement from place paralleled social aspirations. Compared with the
women whom Hampsten studied, Imogene and her friends are relatively
well-educated, even affluent, for all their agonizing over their small expendi-
tures. Imogene, indeed, had aspirations of becoming a writer. And yet her
brief entries reflect those of Hampsten's women and also the diaries of the
emigrant women on the Bozeman Trail (1863–1866) studied by Susan Doyle,
who quotes an entry written by a Nellie Fletcher in 1864 that could have been
written by Imogene: "Kate Caldwell was over to see us at noon. I was writing
home. Chell & I went home with her & they showed us their Photograph
Albums. Kitty gave me a beautiful bouquet of flowers."

I wonder if, for Elizabeth Hampsten's term, estrangement, I can read self-
consciousness, as in that flashing moment of realization: *I'm the one they're*
laughing at! I'm the one who made that boy cry!

Except for a few passages like the description of the mowing machine accident, Imogene's diary entries seem almost wholly devoid of self-consciousness,

perhaps because of that habit she acquired, almost a rote exercise, of the scribbled line or two at night. Writing in her diary, she's quick and careless with spelling and grammar, doesn't bother with corrections or care what her page looks like. When she thinks of herself as a writer, as she does in the sonnet "Scent of Wild Roses," she's not only capable of exploiting the emotional quality of sensory detail within a conventional rhyme scheme, octave and sestet, but she also proofreads her work and arranges it attractively on a sheet of letter-paper.

But not in her diaries. There's never a sense in the diaries that she expects anyone else to read what she's written; these entries are for herself, alone.

So why is she writing her daily entries?

One reason, as other women of her age who have kept diaries have suggested to me, is that scrawling her few lines at bedtime is a way of bringing closure to her day, a way of telling herself that she's made it through another day and she stands a chance of making it through the next. She may or may not have finished all her tasks, but at least she's got them corralled on her page. Writing down her chores, she at least achieves some control over what might otherwise seem as endless and insurmountable as the ocean waves.

Another reason, I think, is that she's telling herself who she is. In new territory, she's beginning to spin a new narrative about herself; she's no longer the girl who fell in love with a cowboy, and she's beginning to realize that her story isn't necessarily the story her Montana relations might tell, of the good-natured teacher-sister whose (unmarried) life is on hold but who can be counted upon to lend her car and lend money to her family. I think she's reinventing a harder, more self-assured persona, who uses a breezy, self-conscious slang—"no catchum yet," "the odds agin me"—and who brings a cold professional eye to her new teaching duties. It's a persona I'm beginning to recognize, one that she will keep separate from her Montana identity, but which will strengthen with the years.

Imogene loved the ocean all her life. After she moved up to Port Angeles, she saved her money until she could build a house on a bluff, overlooking the

Strait of Juan de Fuca, and she kept binoculars by the window and watched the shipping, and the way the fog rolled in and out, and how, on clear nights in the distance, she could make out the lights of Victoria, Canada. Meanwhile, living landlocked in Napavine, she will visit the ocean every chance she gets.

September 21: We saw two deer on New Waukum Hill last night [coming home from their trip to the ocean]. Today was a pip. Two of my kids sick, 3 in a fight. No art. The Co. Supt. Came out.

September 22, 1942: The PTA Reception was tonight. After school a bunch of us went to town to see about our certificates. I got nailed for O.P. at 6:00 AM.

September 23: A small bunch of soldiers hit town yesterday & had duty in the O.P. So I got to see two close up. Was I ever tired tonight. My reports are staring me in the face.

September 24: Finished my reports & then went out to chit chat with Bernita. I rested after school & felt good all evening.

September 25: The teachers had a little confab. Nothing was decided. Gave my kids art. Rather dull, I thot. Hope to spend this weekend catching up.

September 26: Went to bed at 9 & got up at 9. Feel grand. Called on Daisy—spent 2 hrs. in the O.P. After supper we called on Bernita. Our trip [to the ocean] was under $3 each.

September 27: We went to Catholic & Methodist services. Then I came home & worked at odds & ends. Sure will be short in my accounts. Am getting the writing bug again.

Imogene's "writing bug" seems to surface whenever she feels particularly hard up. Right now, at the end of the month, after the indulgence of the weekend at the ocean (less than $3 each!), she's thinking again how it would ease her circumstances, how it would ease her guilt at spending money on small pleasures for herself if she could just sell a story. I remember feeling the same way when I was a pregnant undergraduate student, taking creative writing courses and thinking, if I could just sell a story. If I could just earn those few extra dollars. Crass? Maybe, but it's part of the incentive that kept nineteenth-century western women like Mary Hallock Foote turning out their novels and paying the family's bills with the proceeds. *At least I'm doing it for money! At least I'm not indulging myself and wasting time better spent on others!*

A few days later, on October 2, Imogene will report, *Aha! Got my warrant today,* and that she immediately went shopping and bought herself some goldfish.

8

September 28: So much stronger than I was a month ago. Three of us went to the school house to do ditto & such. I met Miss Wilson's sister.

September 29: Teacher's meeting with the county nurse. We have to have morning inspection every day as a health preventive. I baked me a supper tonight including meat loaf.

Typically, Imogene notes the differences she's encountering in the Napavine school. There were no regular health inspections in the rural schools in Montana, or ditto machines, either. When I attended the Warm Spring Creek school, the teacher had a recipe for a kind of gelatinous substance that she poured into a jelly roll pan and let set overnight. Then she mirror-wrote on it with a pungent blue ink and pressed down paper to make reproductions. In this way she actually produced several issues of a school newspaper.

October 4: Daisy could not start her car so we went to her church in mine. We were going to Winlock [a nearby town] to a show but Bobby [Wilson, another young woman teacher] got sick so we went for a stroll. My fish died.

October 5: Lovely & sunny again this afternoon. My bank book [checkbook, her first] did not come yet. Darn it. My grocery bill runs higher. I repotted a plant tonight. I can't get down to write.

There! You see! her conscience, honed in depression-era Montana, would have been lecturing her. You went out and wasted money on goldfish, and what happened? Served you right when they died. Now, if you could just earn a little money through your writing!

October 6: Got my checkbook at last. Went to the P.T.A. Mrs. Pierce sang & Bernita played the violin. I got a promise of being able to buy 2 or 4 pairs of nylon hose.

October 7: Wed. Anyway I get two [days from school] off. Armistice & Institute. I & Dorothy went to the school house & dittoed for 2 hrs. We got lots done but I let all else go.

October 8: After school we went to town house hunting for Daisy's folks. Soldiers, sailors, all over town. Friday comes & a good thing it is, too.

October 10: On regular shift from 1-5 Sat. at the O.P. After 7:00 PM we went out to Emery's to ask about church & Red Cross yarn. They are very nice.

Daisy is going to teach Imogene to knit for the Red Cross. After some struggles at the beginning, Imogene's knitting goes so well that she hardly puts it down. Within a couple of months, she's on her second sweater.

October 11: Went to church in Centralia & I got the giggles. Letter from Ma bragging how Kristie is so handsome—looks like Dave.

October 12: Talk of an adult education class in typing at Winlock. Bob Wilson taped a kid's mouth shut. I had to laugh.

October 13: Tonight we went to Winlock & took in a class in typing. We decided on 2 nights a week, 15 hrs. for 6-8 weeks.

True as ever to the work ethic pounded into her, Imogene has loaded herself down. She may not have to carry spring water or cook hot lunches on a wood stove for her pupils, but she's teaching full-time, working long shifts at O.P., and now adding the typing class. The typing class apparently is an effort at self-improvement; a few days later Imogene remarks that she hopes to be able to pass a test as a typist at the end of the class. She doesn't seem to aspire to a career as a secretary, but rather to polish her stories professionally and enhance her work when she goes back to college to renew her teaching certificate.

Still, she does think of getting out of teaching, which continues to have its drawbacks, as her next entry shows.

October 14: Shook one of the brats today for hitting a girl. They were pushing in line.

And finally, after living for six weeks in a town full of soldiers, she works up enough courage to try something riskier than an outing with the other young women teachers:

October 16: Went out to Bernita's & got my nails done in Revlon——Chilli bean color. Hot stuff. We plan to tomcat Sat. nite. Stopped to see Daisy on the way home.

October 17: Tried to learn to knit again this P.M. Got it all ripped out & knit on the first row. Daisy's sister came out then. I went for Bernita [to go tomcatting].

October 18: We decided it [tomcatting] was not to be repeated. I got a pro-position & a proposal. Today we went to church & the kids ate breakfast at my place. Then we fixed lunch & went to the park.

Imogene's "proposition & proposal" line is humor, I think, meant to mini-mize a situation that made her feel uncomfortable. Years later she remarked to me that never a year had gone by, between her eighteenth and fortieth birthdays, when she had not received either a proposal or a proposition and sometimes both. So why is a woman so anxious about being single also so resistant to social situations involving men? One answer is that she's telling herself what she thinks she wants (marriage), while steadily moving toward what she really wants (independence.) Is this the true answer? Or have I imposed it upon Imogene's text? I can never be sure.

October 19: Mon. I got a new pupil. Two of my pupils are behind in arith. I've got to start new art projects too. Nuts. Tomorrow is typing.

"Until I went to Napavine," Imogene once told me, "I thought Gloria Walton was hard to teach. But Gloria started to look pretty good to me, compared to some of the kids I taught at Napavine."

It's likely that Imogene was seeing the effects of the war on her third- and fourth-grade pupils. Some of these children will be coming from families sep-arated because of military service, some will have been uprooted because their families are following war work. Again and again Imogene will note her classroom difficulties caused by such flux.

October 21: Had an educational movie & were my kids mean the rest of the day Only half an hour for 7-8 art but at last I got all my art grades checked.

October 22: We took in the Institute. Heard good singing. My car would not start. And my sink plugged up. Was I on the prod. Heck—Darn—plenty of curses!

October 26: My battery was dead as a nail. With the aid of Daisy, Mr. Pierce,
& all the neighborhood boys I got it rolling. Went to school & worked on reports.

Her car is a mixed blessing, as it has been since she has owned it. Like so
much technology, it frees her in some ways while it hampers her in others.
Here in Napavine, far from her dependable brother-in-law, Imogene turns to
friends and especially to the school community for practical as well as emotional support. The breaking of old bonds and forming new ones is a gradual
process; it's a shift in expectations and point of view and feelings. The social
process frees Imogene in some ways while it baffles her in others, and her
frustration and exhaustion creep between the lines of her diary entries.
Heck—Darn—plenty of curses!

October 28: Daisy went into town to see about her radiator. This was the
coldest day so far. I got so tired made up my mind to tumble into bed. Dim out
so shades must be pulled.

Napavine is far enough inland that a full blackout isn't thought necessary,
but Imogene has to go around and pull the shades in her upstairs apartment,
grumbling to herself, before she can collapse in bed. Back in Montana she
slept in the attic of her parents' two-room shack. Sweltering in summer, frigid
in winter, no shade at all on the single small window that looked out on rip-
pling grass and the two converging tracks of a wagon road. After dark, no one
within miles would watch that window suddenly materialize as a square yellow glow, then vanish when the lamp was blown out.

But here in town, well, maybe eventually she'll get used to drawn shades
and the loss of country privacy.

October 29: My car wouldn't start. What a worry. Bernita drove us to
Winlock. We were late needless to say. I get so nervous. Daisy came down to
see about moving in.

Daisy is moving into Imogene's apartment with her, probably so both women can save money. It will be a mistake. Within a few weeks, Daisy is getting on Imogene's nerves, and probably Imogene on Daisy's.

October 31: What a pouring day. Daisy had to tow me to Chehalis. Back to O.P. She moved while I watched. I ironed & worked while she watched. Had Bernita for dinner.

November 2: Went to town after school My car was fixed at the tune of $4.90. Nothing much wrong. Got my R. cards done all but attendance.

November 3: Had to go to PTA. Was rather bored. Gas rationing soon. My cold worse. Got my report cards done. My knitting is started right at last. Hot dog.

November 4: Report cards out. Knit an hour and it shows. Gosh—no cooking next week [because she and Daisy are taking turns]. Whoopee. My voice is going. Am reading a new book The Day Must Dawn.

November 6: Voice better in the morning—worse at night. The nurse called. Also Rodger's mother. I put him in remedial room. I got a head acke also.

November 7: Daisy shopped today [her turn]. I smirked. We put towel bars on the screen. Letter from Doris. Bet she has a boy.

Back in Montana her sister Doris is expecting a baby any day. Imogene is excited about the new baby, but wrong about its sex, as her entry for November 14 will show.

November 9: Daisy did not go to school today. We decided she must have flue. Her week to cook much to her sorrow. I called Shafer & got him to stop the Winlock kids.

November 10: Decided to start the milk diet again so I can wear my black dress. Daisy still not recovered but back in school. Vacation tomorrow.

November 11: Got my dirty hair fixed, some knitting down & my wash. In the evening we went to Chehalis & took in a show. I invested in B. pills fer my grey hair.

November 14: Such rain. Card from Doris saying Elizabeth Anne arrived Nov. 9. A bounce of a girl. My knitting is going apace now. Bernita & I decided agin goin to town.

Except that Bernita must have changed her mind and gone out, anyway:

November 15: Out to Buroker's for dinner & Bernita told us of her adventures last night. Met a soldier & had a keen time—& I, I was curled in bed.

It's one of those moments in Imogene's diary when, as Elizabeth Hampsten puts it, "the sound of a voice seems recoverable." The repetition of the pronoun I, the quality of the participle, "curled," break through the exhausted litany of who went where for dinner and whose cold has developed into the flu. And yet the language is not self-conscious compared with the deliberate folksy-humorous attempts with which Imogene hides embarrassment or shame—I invested in B. pills "fer" my gray hair; we decided "agin goin" to town.

She's present between these scribbled lines; I can hear her when I listen hard enough.

November 16: Teacher's meeting tonight. Gas rationing on the end of the week. Have to work hard at my knitting to get past the hard part before Daisy [who is teaching her to knit] goes to S.

November 18: Wed. Took in Fantasia. Very good. Had Bernita down to stay all night. I came home from school with a mean headache but took an asperin & it left.

November 19: Shafer told me to keep Ralph & Roy in. They've been throwing apples at the girls. I sure had a time getting my tire no. for gas rationing. Nuts.

November 20: Letter from Sylva & she's gone to work! Daisy & I went to do our bit at gas rationing & it was not bad at all. Then I went down stairs & knit on my sweater.

November 21: Letter from Doris. They are threshing at last. She calls the new baby Betty. I got the blues & really bawled. Knit a lot in the O.P. All Red Cross work is wanted in Dec!

November 22: Had to do a lot of knitting over to mend mistakes. The girls got home with wild tales to tell of life in the big city. Bernita's heart throb called today.

Got the blues & really bawled—as November wears on, Imogene is stricken with homesickness and envy of her sister Doris, with her husband and her ranch and her new baby. Perhaps she's depressed; she's used to Montana's clear skies, and now she notes the November rains again and again. Also, she may be withdrawing from her friends and their social life; she'd rather stay home and knit while Daisy and Bernita explore the excitement of Seattle. And apparently Bernita has found a boyfriend, perhaps the soldier she met the evening that Imogene stayed home to knit and get a good night's rest.

November 24: To Winlock for the last typing lesson. Mrs. Buroker & Mrs. Holt went along. They had Daisy & me out for dinner amid much misunderstanding. B's heart throb came.

But rain or no rain, another ocean visit is planned for the Thanksgiving holiday:

November 25: We got out an hour early much to my great delight. Then I packed the grub & washed clothes & did other odd jobs & we are set to tumble into bed.

November 26: We got off in a winter rain about 9:00 A.M. Pulled in about 12:30 & looked at the breakers rolling. Sure got wet down at the beach.

November 27: It was quite bright out today. We went up to the end of the spit, talked to soldiers, looked at a wreck—rode on the beach, got stuck. Had quite a day.

November 28: We tried to get down to the light house but couldn't on account of the army. It was my turn to begin to cook today. We knit & played checkers & gloated.

November 29: I got breakfast in the morning—hot cakes—coffee, eggs— sausage. Then we packed & left. We got home early—around 3. I made out my wool order. Can knit in a car.

December 1: PTA this afternoon so school was out early. Due to a wind-storm the lines were down so no electricity & no water. We had Bernita & Mrs. Holt for dinner.

December 2: After school we came home and did our dishes. I did a lot of embroidery on my Christmas bibs. At 8:00 we went to dress rehearsal [of the senior play]. I am getting a cold.

December 3: Teacher's meeting that lasted till 5:00. I don't think much of Xmas plans here.

Is she thinking of the elaborate Christmas entertainments at the Warm Spring Creek school, all directed by herself? The play she wrote, the stage constructed out of wires and safety pins and borrowed sheets, the rehearsed songs, the memorization, the wildly excited children? The hours of sewing

candy into net bags? The tree with its construction-paper chains? The head of
the school board in his Santa Claus suit? *I hate this time of year*, she wrote at
the time, but now, in rainy Napavine, she sounds wistful, with her thoughts on
her family back in Montana. For the time being, she's laid aside her knitting
to embroider bibs for her two new nieces, Kristol and Betty, born less than
three months apart.

> *December 4: Found paper today for Xmas cards. Went to the senior play*
> *& it was much better than dress rehearsal. Came home & built up the fire &*
> *drank hemo.*

> *December 7: Was it cold at school today—the temperature never got over*
> *60 & mostly it was 50. Sure good to get home & warm up. Gift from Doris*
> *[came in the mail].*

It's the anniversary of the attack on Pearl Harbor, but Imogene doesn't
mention it, nor has she mentioned the landing of Allied forces in North
Africa, nor the battle of Guadalcanal. War news may be so overwhelming that,
by this time, she deliberately blocks it out. Not allowing herself to think about
the newspaper headlines is how she manages to live from one day to the next,
making her Christmas preparations, missing her family in Montana, wishing
she could see the new babies.

> *December 9: I got several packages off tonight. Got in an hour of sewing on*
> *my quilt I want to wash. Only got about 1/4 done. The kids broke a gym window.*

> *December 11: We went to Burokers for dinner & ate clam chowder. Soon the*
> *O.P. shifts change. I didn't get a notice yet. Hope I needn't sub. Got my book order.*

> *December 12: We went to town early. I got my coffee ration book. Also some*
> *cheap crystal candle sticks to decorate at Christmas. Got Daisy's gift done*
> *& B's started.*

December 16: Got all my presents made & wrapped but Bernita's. My cards are all written & sealed too. Now I can clean house & get settled once more.

December 17: We started to decorate in my room. Will finish tomorrow.

December 18: Tried to have the kids make wreaths. They didn't make any fronts or backs. They tore some up to make over.

December 20: Daisy had a lovely dinner, chicken, dumplings, mincemeat pie. Our house looks quite like Christmas. The tree is cute—holly & red candles.

December 21: Got our tree up at school & decorated at last. I can't get a lick of work out of the kids. Mrs. S on hall duty. Brats skipped out early. $5 [her Christmas present] from Ma.

December 23: Went to town after my lisence & didn't have my title & couldn't get a drivers license on account of my eye. And even have to get glasses.

December 24: Got the film from Aunt Mable & it was very nice. We made two batches of candy & it turned out fine. Mrs. Emery brot me wool & I got my 2nd sweater started.

December 25: We ate dinner with Daisy's folks. We each got a little casserole & a few other small gifts. Had a wonderful dinner. Played Chinker Checks. A nice time.

A nice time, a lovely time, a wonderful time. The table that Dorothy has set in the apartment she and Imogene share, the tree with its red candles and holly. Later, Christmas day itself with Daisy's family, kind people who have invited the two young women from Montana so they won't feel all alone. Of course Imogene feels lonely. Of course she thinks of the tree her brother-in-law will have cut and carried home on horseback to set up in the log ranch house, she thinks of her carefully wrapped gifts, whether her sister likes the embroidered baby bibs—of course she's homesick.

The cure: another trip to the ocean.

December 26: After breakfast & the mail, we pulled out. Had a time to start Daisy's car. How mad she gets. We picked up a sailor. Got to West Port at 12:30.

December 27: We gathered ourselves a bunch of shells and rode around & looked at the ocean. After lunch we started home. Took in a show in Chehalis. I got my hair fixed.

Then, the grueling trip by public transportation to Bremerton to spend what is left of her Christmas vacation with her sister Sylva:

December 28: Finally got off for Bremerton. The bus was so crowded. I could make better time by Tacoma so I went that way. Some sailors showed me up the hill.

December 29: Ervin showed me how he tuned up a car & I got all greased. Sylva lectured me as usual but I told her off too. Played cards at night. Roberta [one of Ervin's younger sisters] is getting married soon.

Imogene's brother-in-law Ervin grew up on a dirt-poor Montana homestead with little education and no future. When the call went out for workers at the construction of the Fort Peck dam in 1937, he hitched a ride north and was lucky enough to sign on. He learned how to weld from an older worker at the dam, who took the time after hours to teach him, and from there he went on to work at the Grand Coulee dam and then into shipyard work in Bremerton. Ever after, he took pains to teach others what he knew. In late December of 1942, he's trying to free Imogene of her dependency on male relatives or mechanics to keep her car running, and she's eager to learn.

In 1992 Ervin taught me basic carpentry and gave me his handsaw, which I still use. If *make do* was the motto of those depression-era women, *learn how to do* was Ervin's.

December 30: Got back to Chehalis—Had my eyes worked on. Drops did not blind me. He asked me about head injuries & I thot of two after I left. Daisy's dress progresses.

December 31: I made pudding & worked on my accounts. Guess I'll finish them when I get my next bank balance. I bought a new stamp book. Did my nails but no knitting.

And that's it for 1942. She's home alone for New Year's Eve, doing her nails, worrying perhaps about her damaged eyesight. Is she remembering New Year's Eve a year ago, how she sat up late typing in the Warm Spring Creek school? What of her hopes and dreams?

Well, she's finally got her job in Washington State. Got herself moved down here to Napavine, learned the ropes, made friends. We know that her foot has healed, because she hasn't complained about it in months, hasn't complained about being overly tired except in a routine way. Like generations of women before her, women displaced by the Civil War, women on the Oregon Trail, women on the Bozeman Trail, she's learned to treasure letters from home, to keep alive the vital connections in any way she can. Meanwhile she's depending upon her new women friends for the emotional support, the social outlets, that her mother and sisters once provided for her.

"[The frightened woman's] evasions are true to the life of survival," remarks Elizabeth Hampsten, "though not adequate to history or fiction," and she's certainly right about the inadequacy of the hints and the incompletions.

And the evasions? Imogene may not be frightened, but she's living with constant stress. What she has accomplished seems pretty remarkable to me, but is she happy with the progress she's made, the new job she wanted, with the better pay? Does she regret the close-knit community life she left behind? She doesn't quite dare to think about it directly, to count up what she's got and what she paid to get it.

Imogene's not writing, she barely mentions "getting the writing bug," but does she regret those long snowbound evenings at her typewriter, last winter? She doesn't tell us.

9

/ / /

"The . . . single quality that marks the diary as absolutely distinct from nondiurnal forms of writing [is] dailiness," writes Jennifer Sinor in *The Extraordinary Work of Ordinary Writing: Annie Ray's Diary*. "Dailiness prevents the diary from being reflective and forces the writer and reader into the immediate present. . . . Dailiness means that the diary does not cohere around an organizing event or principle. . . . Writing in the days refuses occasion, climax, and closure."

> *January 1, 1943: Resolution time again. I aim to write——get thin, not laugh at Daisy, & try to go the "U" & make $300 besides. Dinner at Shafers [the elementary school principal and his wife]. It was lovely. Bernita got home & I lost the bet but he's sending her a ring.*

I wonder whether Sinor's observation about daily writing is more descriptive of the nineteenth-century diary she examines than it is of Imogene's diary. Certainly Imogene writes in the immediate present. Certainly she uses language to smooth out occasions. Particularly in the early Washington years, she will consistently describe a dinner party as "lovely," although as time passes and she's more certain of herself, she'll allow herself to be more tart. And certainly, as her January 1, 1943, entry illustrates, Imogene uses what Sinor calls "decentering;" that is, her resolutions, her New Year's dinner, and her noting of Bernita's return all receive equal weight, if only because the events are given brief and equal space and because they are arranged (I think) more or less in the order they happened. But can we really say that she's unaware of occasion or closure, or that she's not more interested in Bernita's engagement than she is in the Shafers' "lovely" party, surely one of those stilted dinners where the school principal and his wife scoop up the unattached teachers and make sure they aren't alone on a holiday? The entry seems to me to vibrate with the tensions between the three best friends: Daisy and Imogene have laid a bet whether Bernita will come home with a ring on her finger. Imogene has lost the bet, but Bernita's engaged, all right. Is it to the "heart throb"? His name will turn out to be Jake, and he'll come to dinner a time or two with Bernita and Daisy and Imogene, but Imogene won't be impressed by him. *Bet she doesn't marry him after all,* she'll write in a year or two.

In a school photograph taken of Imogene at about this time, she stands at the back of her class of third-graders. She's wearing her glasses and a raincoat and the same small, fixed smile that appears in the studio pose taken when she was sixteen. Now, at thirty-three, she's smiling a having-her-picture-taken smile, perhaps, because I don't recognize it. The smile I remember was wide and generous, and her laughter overflowed from it. Was she a happier woman with her nieces than she was with these thirty-two scrubbed children who squint into the sun? She looks plump in the school photograph, her face round and unlined. Which is the woman she believes herself to be?

Young. So young.

She plans to attend the University of Washington in Seattle this summer. She will earn a level three teaching certificate, and she will earn at least three hundred dollars from a part-time job, enough to live on. And write.

And get thin.

January 2: Got substituting on the OP from 9–12 so did not go to town for my lisence. Took Bernita home in the evening. This month I just haven't money enuf. Feel blue.

January 4: Back to school & it didn't go so badly. Sure traded stamps with the kids. By the time school was out it was raining again.

Imogene knows the ropes now, so she isn't as anxious about her teaching as she was in the fall. Her foot feels okay. But she's not going out with the girls as often, she's finding other ways to ward off the blues, and she's started a stamp collection to keep herself busy when she isn't making lesson plans or knitting sweaters or embroidering pillow cases. Her stamp collection probably started as a response to the foreign and military stamps that she and her pupils' families were receiving. Eventually it will swell into several albums.

January 5: Rainy again. Stamp trading. Went to PTA & saw 3 airplane films & got a kick out of the officers. Got my 9–12 OP shift on Thur. PM that I've wanted.

January 6: Went to town tonight but my glasses had not come. Managed to get my car lisence but that was all I got done. Had B. for dinner & took her home in a thick fog.

We'll hope the fog was from the weather, not from the lack of glasses.

January 7: Mrs. Moore sent us a can of salmon and a receipt [for salmon loaf, probably]. I made it tonight & it was very good. My glasses came but I could not put them on. I guess Daisy gets disgusted.

January 9: Got my drivers lisence by paying $2. This cop said I didn't need glasses to drive. Damn, man; I was mad! Bernita staid for lunch. Daisy made scones for supper.

January 10: Out to Buroker's for dinner. This morning I cleaned the apt. good. Letter from Ma saying Dave was home. We went to see Daisy's baby niece christened.

January 11: Finished B. Blake. Counted my stamps—have over 350. Daisy is fighting a cold. Occasionally we talk about going to Montana in the spring.

January 14: B. got her ring. I think it a little loud. We plan the party for Tuesday. I was on OP duty & knit. I have my blue sweater started. That is hard. Easy now till the pattern.

Oh, come on, Imogene! Bernita's ring is a little loud? Aren't you being just a little snippy about it?

January 15: Friday—a pretty snow. Glenn got in a fight & got a black eye. Good for him. Letter from [illegible]. Makes me think more than ever of going to the U.

January 18: Our water pipes are frozen on the side. Wish there'd be no school. How my bunch fussed. Thot of the Montana bunch who take this in their stride.

January 20: More snow. Lots of schools & factories are shutting down. Both Napavine & Chehalis shut till Monday. Curses. There goes our spring vacation.

January 21: It snowed all day. Knit 3 1/2 inches on my Red X sweater in OP. No mail. Anyway it is a nice vacation.

January 23: Daisy & Bernita went to town. I stayed home, ironed, got my accounts & budget done. Daisy was tired & crabby. Who wants to go to town on these roads.

January 25: Hot damn. More snow. And my sweater is two inches too big. So I learned the pattern, I hope, & started over. Acquired a dozen good stamps.

January 26: Made bread & rolls today. What a vacation. Told the girls it did me more good than Christmas when I chased around so much. Sure hanker to go home this summer.

The fiction writer takes a deep breath of the unexpectedly chill air, so cold for southern Washington, even in January. Wades through knee-high drifts to the middle of the street, where somebody in a pickup truck with chains broke a trail earlier today. Follows the tracks for a block or two, stops outside the gate of the 1912-era bungalow behind its woven wire fence, where last summer's sweet pea bed is buried in snow. Every tread on the stairs leading up to the apartment entrance wears its mound of pristine snow, so the young teachers who live upstairs haven't been out today, although it's a school day, a Tuesday. School must still be cancelled.

The fiction writer ascends the stairs without disturbing the snow. Doesn't bother opening the door on the landing or trying to see through the foggy glass pane, but materializes inside the apartment as though she herself is the ghost, yes, the ghost writer come to watch this living woman finish kneading her bread dough, rounding it into a buttered bowl, covering it with a clean dish towel, and setting it next to the heat register in the floor where she can be sure it will keep warm enough to rise. It's not really necessary to bake bread in town. Even if her car won't start, she can always put on her coat and scarf and overshoes and walk over to the City Market on Main. But bread-baking is a hold-over habit from years of ranch life in Montana, and on such a snowy day she likes the feel of the dough growing smooth and elastic in her hands, and the yeast smell as it rises, and the heat of the oven on her face as she lifts out the hot brown loaves. She's been thinking about Montana, especially when the other teachers complain about the snow, and the smell of baking bread brings back the best memories. Her mother's kitchen in the homestead shack, her sister's kitchen in the log house at the ranch. Wood stoves and good company. Yes, she'll go home this summer if she possibly can afford it.

But she's also been reading the vacancy notices that start to come in the mail at this time of year, from school superintendents anticipating the holes in their teaching staff as the women flock into the shipyards for the better-paying war work. How much more she could earn if she goes back to college and upgrades her certificate. Yes, she definitely should take some classes at the University of Washington this summer, she definitely should try to better herself, otherwise she'll end up sharing this upstairs apartment year after year with the likes of Daisy Lincoln.

January 28: Letters from both Ma & Florence. Sure glad to hear from them. How Dave must enjoy being with Florence & Kristie Lee. They'd moved & it took him longer to find them.

Or—instead of summer school and back to teaching, why not a real adventure?

January 30: We went to town—saw a Waac. B. & I went in the Navy Recruiting office. He said, "Think of telling it to your grand children." A bad argument. I got a dish—the girls got fish floats.

January 31: Sunday. I baked dark rolls. Bernita came for dinner & then fixed our hair. Daisy did her nails green. B & I talk about the Waves & Waacs.

February 2: PTA where we looked at war pictures & some lovely local ones of the Mts. More I think of the taxes, the more I like the Navy. Teachers are growing more scarce.

February 3: Daisy's brother came out for supper. Enjoy hearing him tell army experience. I ironed a cloth for the table & got dinner.

February 5: On the spur of the moment we went to Winlock to a basketball game. Napavine lost. Rain, rain, rain, a wet night indeed. Yep, if I can, I'm gonna join the Navy.

February 7: Out to Burokers for dinner. I started a sleeve & got the ribbing done. Letter from Ruthie, made me think of the Montana bunch. Got my box of stamps at last.

February 8: Ha, got on pretty well with my pattern. Meant to do 4 more rows but got at my stamps & ran out of time. It snowed again—huge flakes.

The fiction writer wonders, why all this energy directed into knitting? Embroidering of pillow cases? Stamp collecting? What kind of an unattached thirty-three-year-old woman would rather curl up with her knitting than go out on the town with Daisy and Bernita. Bernita met a soldier, and now she's wearing an engagement ring. Why won't Imogene make an effort, especially when she's so wounded at the recruiting sergeant's remark about the grandchildren she believes she'll never have?

The fiction writer's task is to answer such questions, and her first impulse is to develop a character so wounded by the betrayal of Lud that she never again trusts her emotions. And yet, after so many years have passed, will readers really believe in a fictional woman who still nurses her hurt, still doesn't trust herself, still withdraws with her knitting at the first sign that a man is interested in her? Isn't some stronger motivation called for here?

No, it's more as though she's closed off a part of herself. Not that she has intended to, not that she even knows she's knitting and embroidering and pasting stamps in a kind of self-hypnosis, a lulling of herself into emotional limbo.

The fiction writer, of course, knows something about emotional limbo.

February 9: Tore into Chehalis & got valentines. Got a valentine from Sam. He's a corporal now. Everyone is having trouble with their antifreeze. I'm going to have mine out.

Sam, who took her to the movies in Montana until she decided there was no point in stringing him along. Now he's about as interesting to her as antifreeze.

February 10: Yesterday I got the rest of the wool I ordered the 1st of Dec. Letter from Sylva today. Poor gal—had to work 12 hr. shifts with overtime. I've worked 14 hrs. for a buck.

February 12: Daisy & Bernita decided to hit for Seattle tonight. I told Daisy I'd take her OP. Mr. Pierce forgot his & I guess some will hold it "agin him."

February 13: Went to bed with a tickling throat & got up feeling worse. After OP & shopping I went back to bed. A letter from Pa did not help. I spent the evening in bed—but couldn't sleep.

February 14: Didn't get so much done today. The girls got home about six with stories of their weekend. I got my hair done. Didn't knit at all.

February 15: Tonight I went to bed early & lit the cresolene lamp. My cold has stuffed up my head & I feel horrid. 7–8 art in the morning.

February 16: Asked B to supper—she was low—went out to Burokers to sample her valentine candy. Daisy got feeling hard toward me over what I thot was a harmless remark.

February 18: Letter from Ma. Guess she is ok instead of what Pa wrote. Daisy took my OP so I counted my stamps—533 mounted. Teachers meeting tonight not bad.

The dementia that soon will swallow Imogene's father in a fog of anger and confusion is showing its signs, although none of his family yet recognizes the symptoms for what they are. Something is wrong, his daughters agree, but they think he's being lazy, or inept, or just plain cussed on purpose to make their own lives more difficult.

Although there's no knowing what he had written in the letter that distressed Imogene on February 13—that her mother was sick?—in one of his surviving letters to Imogene, in August of 1943 , A. P. daydreams on paper:

My dear daughter . . .

I am planning, when Ma goes to her school, to go to Minneapolis and visit brother Dover, & sister Belle. I expect to go with some one from Lewistown and share expenses. After I get through visiting in Minneapolis I want to run down to my old home town Manitou [Saskatchewan, Canada]. I want to walk around old Manitou and see who of my old friends who are left would remember me.

Well, Mussolini got it in the neck and I feel the war will end by Sept 1st. I hope I am write. Won't it be grand to see the boy [Dave] come home . . .

Love from daddy

To my ears his delusions sound harmless enough, even the wishful thinking about an early end to the war, but the voices of ghosts echo in my head: Where does he think he's going? To *Canada?* How does he think he's going to pay his way? I hope he doesn't try to borrow it from me. No, nor from me. What's the matter with him, anyway? Doesn't he have any consideration for Ma? For the rest of us?

February 19: B & I got our Waves application blanks. After supper we went for a ride in my car—ended up at a movie in Centralia. Coming home Daisy kept at my [car] window till it went clean down.

February 20: Today we went for a ride & got the gr[ocerie]s. I went out to work on my car window & Daisy & Mrs. C came out & we did it. Did I feel victorious.

*February 22: I got my register done while the girls went to school &
sewed. B & I have it counted up—8 weeks & we should know—9 more &
I'll be ready to raise my rt. Hand [and be sworn into the Waves].*

*February 23: Got rung in tonight on rationing but I got it all ironed out
anyway. Mr. Pierce would come in & talk when I wanted to study Washington
Manual.*

The new rationing system that will come into effect on March 1 is so
complicated that it's a wonder anyone understands it. Food will be rationed
according to a complicated point system based partly on amount and partly
on scarcity. Special classes are being organized to teach housewives the point
system, and Imogene may be involved in one of those classes.

*February 25: I got a lot of embroidery & knitting done. Served rationing also
& told Mrs. Harper off. Who is she to tell me off. We have a baseball game planned.*

*February 27: Got my first medical. Wouldn't it be a joke if I do pass the
physical! Got some fancy pillow cases tho I knew I shouldn't. If we get a raise
I am going to get a silver key ring.*

*February 28: Finished my sleeve. Made out a stack of bills. Next month
I'll be easy financially if they only pass that bill [to raise teachers' salaries].
Sorted stamps this P.M. while the girls sewed.*

*March 2: PTA tonight. Urged Bobbie [Wilson] to come home with us for
coffee. Had a high bid chinfab about jobs & teachers & such. Teachers are scarce.*

*March 3: My cold makes me feel below par. Finished the 4 inches of rib-
bing on my sweater front. I'll just get it done in time to enter the Navy.*

Details of illness permeate Imogene's diary entries during this late winter
and early spring. Her colds. Her headaches. Other people's colds and headaches.

In many nineteenth-century diaries, "headache" is a euphemism for menstruation, but it's not a euphemism for Imogene, who calls her periods "the curse." She really is suffering from severe headaches. In the back of her five-year diary for this period, she kept track of the dates of her headaches and whether or not the pills she had been prescribed were giving her relief (usually not.) Possibly her headaches are connected to her vision problems. Maybe the doctor who asked her about head injuries was on the right track. Maybe she hit her head during the mowing machine accident in June of 1942.

It's also possible that her headaches and frequent colds have to do with emotional stress. The fiction writer could spin quite a web from that theory.

March 6: Took my exam. It could have been worse. B. got a letter from a Calif. hospital & Schafer told her if she did get it they would release her.

March 8: Heard the $30 raise was passed. If I get it I promise myself a silver key ring, & two playing card sets. Mr. Jean is leaving for the armed services.

March 9: Got my picture proofs. The full face is crummy. The profile not bad but I cheated. Got my accounts under control once more. Hope I get in the Navy.

March 12: Moved Bernita tonight. I got a row of the pattern done right. Now to finish it this weekend. Letter from Pa. Didn't read it yet. Might like to teach in Winlock.

Bernita, thinking that she may give up her teaching job and go to work in a San Francisco hospital, has given up her apartment and moved in with Daisy and Imogene. It's not a good idea, the three women in that cramped space, and Imogene's diary entries show her irritation.

March 15: Got all my reports done & my sweater, all but two rows. B. might finish the term here. She's a changeable kid. And bad to throw things around.

March 16: The kids wanted another chocolate cake so I baked one after supper. I did my nails green "agin." And this month is nearly gone—more than half.

March 17: Got my report cards out. We went to Winlock & got gas. This may be a good plan [getting teaching jobs in Winlock] if it works. I wish Bob W[ilson]. would go with us. Dorothy got touchy, I was so late at the store.

Then a weekend at the ocean:

March 18: We lay our plans for the beach tonight & got our lists all made. B. took my OP shift so I washed & cleaned house & next week she gets to cook.

March 19: Quite a dither getting off. B. likes to take her time & then Daisy just froths at the mouth. O—dear. Not too good a cabin.

March 20: We stopped at Copalis Beach—not bad—not like Long Beach. Walked up the shore—very invigerating. We did not like the cabin at Pacific Beach.

March 21: Had clams fried for dinner. Very good. Watched dogs trained for beach patrol. Bernita takes her shift of cooking hard.

Then home again for same old, same old:

March 22: Curses—my last check was overdrawn. A cold day—and windy. Looks like Daisy got a bunch of new pupils.

March 23: Didn't pass the St. Manuel [test in the manual arts] so if I go to summer school I'll have to take that course. Daisy & Mr. Pierce almost locked horns over the remedial room.

March 24: Last night we tore in to see Casablanca. Very good. We were going to dress rehersal but had colds. I'm so hoarse. Asked Mr. S[chafer, the elementary

school principal, whom she likes] for a letter for the Waves. If I can't get in
I'll come back [to teach in Napavine].

March 26: I moseyed over to see the play. It was pretty sexy—to much to
suit me for a H.S. play. B was sick & staid home all day——she wants to be
pampered & doesn't do her share—milk bottle & things.

I try to reconcile this entry with the aunt I knew. Surely Imogene never
was prudish! Of course not. She was the one adult I could talk openly with,
always my confidante—and yet this thread of sexual opprobrium runs through
her diaries. Too much sex in the high school play. Too much flirtation among
the young unmarried teachers. Too much making up to the men. The fiction
writer wants to develop this thread, spin it into her web about a repressed
woman whose one real attempt to find intimacy with a man frightened her so
badly that, without realizing it, she has withdrawn into herself.

So far, though, I've managed to keep the fiction writer quiet. Or, if not
absolutely quiet, at least I've drawn some definite lines in the sand around
her. I've let her imagine some of these faceless characters, let her describe a
street she's never seen, let her construct a house on that street with its
upstairs closed off as an apartment with its own entrance, meant to provide a
little extra income for kindly, widowed Mrs. Curtis—why widowed? well,
there's never a mention of a Mr. Curtis, and it was Mrs. Curtis herself who
helped the crippled new teacher from Montana lug her belongings up those
stairs. Yes, let the fiction writer provide the smell of baking bread and also the
sharp stink from the bottle of green nail polish, the smell of cosmetics everywhere in this cramped space where three young women have crammed their
belongings. The oldest of the three women getting fed up with the clutter and
the perfume, and the talk of the other women's boyfriends and their catty
jibes about the size of her hips. It's her apartment, after all!

But she's been brought up to get along, to laugh off her hurt, to pretend
she doesn't mind the younger women's messiness and their easy assumption

that they're the ones who matter. She's the one who's headed for sexual nullity, after all. Without a man, she's the one who doesn't count.

It's when the fiction writer begins to speculate that she gets into trouble. Where, after all, is she getting this thread she's spinning, if not from her own guts? What does it have to do with Imogene's diaries? Why doesn't she speak for herself?

March 27: Went to Chehalis. It rained horrid. Forgot Daisy's checkbook. Got my Wave application mailed. Have 900 stamps in my book & a few more not in.

March 28: Got my sweater done & guess I can actually wear it. I guess I never really believed I would. Think I'll like the coat one better. We all have to nurse colds. I got dinner.

March 29: Took up stamp buying for the school. My room also has to sell Blue Birds for the children's home. Then we want to start a stamp club.

March 30: Collected $8.50 out of $14. Not too bad. A rainy day. New McCalls [magazine] with several good eating ideas. My new sweater going nicely.

March 31: Had a head ache—not bad—just nursed it along. Sure get to know people living with them. B. sure can't take responsibility.

April 1: Went to the Adna play & got out early today. Didn't get my letter [of recommendation for the Waves] from Mr. S[chafer]. He's so darn busy. He had it for me when I went on OP.

April 2: Gee, he [Mr. Schafer] was really swell. I got all the app off to Portland tonight. My kids are hog wild over stamps. It sure makes good motivation in Language.

April 4: A lovely day. We had Jake [Bernita's "heart throb"] come for dinner. He obviously thinks he has something, poor guy. I am getting on fine with my cardigan.

Imogene, I can't tell whether you're sniping at Jake himself, or at Bernita as the "something" he thinks he has.

April 5: No mail. No stamps. Daisy & Bernita went to bed at 7:15 while I was taking a bath. I read & knitted. A quiet evening.

April 7: After school I took off with Mrs. Harper & her husband. Made Seattle in time to catch the 8:00 P.M. ferry [on her way to Bremerton to visit Sylva]. Got there at 9:30. Folks [Sylva and her husband, Ervin] at a show.

April 8: Doris Noel's birthday. Sylva had 8 for supper—a rabbit dinner. We played a game later. On my 18th birthday taught school.

Sylva has been raising rabbits to make her meat coupons stretch. Doris Noel is one of Ervin's younger sisters. The birthday must have been Doris's eighteenth, which has set Imogene thinking about her own eighteenth birthday, teaching in the Baulley Dome school, and what that first year was like. One of her pupils had been Florence, her future sister-in-law.

"She had no control over those kids, boys as old as Imogene almost," writes Florence. "When we had noon hr. we'd go on hound & hare chases. The hare kids always left school a few minutes before the hound kids took out after them . . . in the Judith River breaks. Imogene was always with us & then when 4:00 came we all got back to school got on our horses & rode home."

April 9: Went shopping was lucky & found a box of aplet candy for Mother's Day. Do a lot on my knitting. Sylva wants me to make her a sweater.

April 10: Sat. Rode around a little. Think Sylva lives in the nicest part of town. The view of the Mt. is lovely. It [Sylva's house] is quite unfinished of course.

Her observation about Sylva's house seems so casual, seems to carry no more importance than the rabbit dinner or the box of candy for her mother that she was so lucky to find in wartime. But she's got the house in Bremerton on her mind. If only—well, she can dream, can't she?

April 11: Got back about 7:00 to find Bernita on her way this week. Told Daisy I was glad. But the navy wrote me it looked like I could not qualify. Such a disappointment. I'll write them a sales letter.

April 12: We were told it was a $300 raise to stay here. It [teaching in Napavine] would sure be a good job if Schafer stays. Bobby Wilson got a Vancouver contract. I went to Chehalis to see the recruiting officer. We went to a show. No washing done.

April 14: Ha! Bernita left & what a relief. It was a bad mistake to let her move in. Glenn Rooney is fighting again. He is the most defiant youngster I ever met.

April 17: Well, I made it down to the Wave office & they told me my eyes did not meet the qualifications & my wt. was agin me too! Damn!

The Navy's rejection must seem like another dead end to her, another chance for adventure and romance at an end. What now, but to contemplate a lifetime of teaching and sharing an apartment with Daisy Lincoln?

But no, she's got more backbone than that. She's got another idea.

10

/ / /

April 18: Back home again where we could chew the fat well in privacy.
Had another brain storm. This time I want a job in Bremerton & to buy a house.

It must be Daisy Lincoln with whom Imogene is chewing the fat. How much
is she telling Daisy about her disappointment at being rejected by the Navy?
How much is she sharing of this new revelation she's had, that she doesn't have
to be married to buy a house of her own? What is Daisy thinking? That she's
glad she isn't Imogene, that she's glad she hasn't given up and declared herself
sexually neuter by gaining a lot of weight and sitting around at night, knitting?

Wet fir trees behind Mrs. Curtis's house point at the overcast sky and filter
the last of the light through the open windows upstairs. At least the air feels
softer, begins to smell of mud thaw and budding lilacs. The evenings are growing longer, the evergreen shrubs beginning to stir with the sense of another
summer just ahead.

"Shouldn't you turn on a light?"—"Oh, I can still see well enough to knit."—"But you'll ruin your eyes!"

The knitter jabs at her wool, irritated. If only the other girl wouldn't pick at her, but always she has to pick, pick, interrupting the faint clack of her knitting needles, the gentle drag of yarn through her fingers, just when she wants to give in to the mindless rhythm and be lulled, not to sleep, but back into her easy wool-gathering, yes, wool-gathering is the right name for it, the gathering of strands that lead her where she wants to go.

"A house like my sister's. Two bedrooms."

"A house?" says Daisy, in her sharp, high pitch, like a yelp. "I wouldn't mind having a house, when I'm married. I'd buy those white criss-cross curtains, with ruffles, what do they call them—"

"Priscillas are what those curtains are called," says Imogene, less annoyed. She allows herself to be drawn into the daydream they have in common, permits herself the shared pleasure of *what they'll do when they're married,* when their real life begins. "I'd get some iris and transplant them along my back fence—"

Thinking of her flowerbeds, letting them materialize in thin evening air, she has let her knitting drop into her lap.

"Maybe," says Daisy, wisely, "you'll meet someone at the U this summer."

To meet somebody. The suggestion stirs Imogene, embarrasses her. She hasn't said or done anything, has she, to give Daisy even the slightest hint of how she longs, yearns to meet a somebody whose face she never quite dares to give features to. What if he, what if anybody were to guess how she feels! To guard against discovery, she remarks, "I can have a house without having a heart throb," and in saying it, realizes that it's true.

A useful analogy: the fiction writer as ghost. An unseen intelligence who details the flattened backyard grass where winter has slept, the yard sodden from rain dripping from fir needles, who then finds the upstairs window, locates the two young women, possesses the consciousness of the one with the knitting needles, and then vanishes. Only the very critical reader will sense her presence in the way she understands characters and knows what their secrets are. A less suspicious reader, lulled by the rhythm of the thread she spins, will merge with her character and experience her fictional world directly, unaware of an intermediary, unless the fiction writer makes a mistake, slips, and snaps her thread.

The writer of creative nonfiction (that curious, defined-by-what-it-is-not genre) may, on the other hand, draw attention to herself. Whether she insists that every word she writes is literal truth, or whether she denies the possibility of absolute truth, she will claim that first-person pronoun for herself. I am I! Mary! The very one who scrutinizes the lines that her aunt scribbled in her diary sixty years ago, who parses those cryptic sentences and speculates on what they reveal or conceal.

Unlike the ghost of fiction, she—*I!*—may press herself on her reader, ask her reader to believe that she and the persona who narrates her aunt's story are one and the same. If she can't avail herself of the fiction writer's power of invention, what she can do is assert her authenticity. I am I! I am Mary! And, reader, I assure you that I can guess how Imogene hid her feelings because I grew up as she did, learning to stand outside myself, watching and hiding my feelings. If I can't slide through closed doors like the ghost and inhabit other people's heads, at least I can tramp around in my own pages and warn Imogene that she'll never get over the old strictures on behavior, never get over the fear of ridicule. What? My grandmother's granddaughter allowing the world to see her running after a man? Making a fool of herself over him? Won't happen.

I can also assure you, reader, that Imogene's revelation—*I can have a house without having a heart throb*—is a remarkable one, at a time when it was dinned into every girl: of course there's a war on right now, which means you may be going out and doing the men's jobs until the men come home, but still! Your life doesn't begin until you marry, until you marry, until you marry.

April 19: Monday. After school I did my reports—went downtown, bought defense stamps, gro. & got the mail. Home late. Wrote 5 letters—getting set for summer school.

April 20: Oh, it rained & rained last night & today. Had a round with Glenn again. I should get busy & write a short story but I just kill time with stamps.

April 21: Wrote my application to Bremerton. Daisy says I should spend $40 on a new outfit & put in a personal. She went to a Dr. tonight & said she learned nothing for $2.

April 22: Got at writing—but I don't have much punch. It is raining again. How I do miss sunny weather. On OP I got in some good licks on my sweater.

April 23: No lights—so no heat or water at school which gave us a vacation. I tried to get gas for the trip [to Montana for a week or two, as soon as school is out]. No go I guess. Applied for the Waac—now I've decided its Bremerton & a house I want.

April 24: Daisy went to Longview to see a Dr. I finished 2 stories. Wrote a big stack of letters. Got a good letter from Mother. Hope she does get a house in Lewistown.

So she really is writing, and not just letters home.

Imogene's mother is thinking of retiring from teaching at long last and living in town with its conveniences and ease. Electric lights, plumbing. Shopping within walking distance. She'll have her little pension, which will just cover her and A. P.'s expenses. Imogene's concern is for her mother; in the long war between A. P. and Mary, Mary has claimed the loyalties of both her older daughters. Unburdened herself to them, shared her worries about A. P. and also, alas, her contempt for him. His spinelessness, his ineptitude, and now his wandering mind. Theirs hasn't been a marriage to inspire Imogene, certainly, for all its querulous years of grief and privation. Still, everyone gets married, and for women, marriage is an end in itself. No need for higher ambitions for a woman, no need for a better job, no need to write stories—and oh, yes, it's only because she needs the money so badly that Imogene writes stories, she's careful to explain to the diaries that no one reads but herself. Meanwhile the tension between her expectations and her fear of (or hope for) independence is perhaps the cause of her headaches, her tears, her blue spells.

April 26: Got our contracts today. Have to sign them by May 3. $1620 does not look so bad—but I wish it was a big town so I could plan to buy a home.

Sixteen hundred and twenty dollars is almost double the $80 a month she was making at the Warm Spring school in Montana, but of course her expenses are higher, particularly the rent for her apartment, even when it's shared with Daisy. Forty dollars a month is what she'll consider for an apartment during the coming year, which works out to a third of her salary.

April 28: Put in some good licks on my stamp album. Daisy badgered me about my weight & I retaliated by going on a diet till school is out to lose 20 lbs.

Daisy does seem to be taking Imogene on as a project, advising her about her clothes and her figure. After all, maybe it's still not too late for the fat girl to take herself in hand and make herself desirable. Maybe the fat girl can still catch herself a husband. Daisy can but try.

The problem is, who wants to live with the giver of good advice? Not Imogene.

And what, by the way, ails Daisy? Why her frequent visits to doctors? What is Daisy's life like?

May 1: Lost one belly inch at the waist. Went to town—bought a hat, purse & gloves & then decided not to go to Bremerton because they wouldn't let me know soon enuf [because she has to turn in her Napavine contract by May 3].

May 3: I turned my contract in signed & got back to find the teachers in a huddle over a rumor the high school was abolished. If it is I'm going to ask to be released.

May 6: We went to town tonight to see Random Harvest. I'm on my last 4 gal. Of gas. Curses, I wish this war was over. I want a home & furniture.

May 7: Friday again. Oh, if Mr. S[chafer] only stays. Finished my sweater sleeve. Also a book "Peace in Our Time." Our house is filthy. Daisy seldom does a good job of cleaning.

Rumor has it that Mr. Schafer, the school principal whom Imogene likes so much, is applying for other jobs. There's a Mrs. Schafer, of course. Interesting how often the men Imogene really, really likes are the married men. The unavailable ones.

May 8: We got the summer school bulletins. What a headache. I'll never get a degree—but if I can get my certificate this summer that will help.

May 9: Felt low—the curse & just blue generally. Got my mail under control. Am on the second sleeve—the last lap of the journey.

Imogene constantly is writing letters or mentioning that she's received letters from home. In an era where no one has heard of e-mail, and where nobody would place a long-distance telephone call except in dire emergency, letter-writing is an obligation and receiving letters a welcome breath of air from elsewhere, much looked-forward to.

"No letter from Imogene," my mother will complain, rolling down the car window on the hot scent of sweet clover along the county road, opening the mailbox, and rifling through the mail. "It's been a week. What's the matter with her?"

Meanwhile in quiet inland Napavine, where the county roads are bordered by tall grass and Shasta daisies and the hills are enclosed by firs, Imogene will note in her diary, *Wish I'd hear from Doris. It's been a week.*

May 10: Looked up rail connections home—can leave Fri night & get to G. Falls before midnight Sat. Then I can catch a bus or train to Hobson or Danvers.

Another sign of the times. On the one hand, she can't drive back to Montana in her car, because gasoline is being rationed and she doesn't have enough gasoline coupons. On the other hand, the public transportation available to her in the 1940s is enviable. She can get everywhere in the Pacific northwest by train or bus, even to places like Danvers, Montana, which has only a general store, a saloon, and a couple of grain elevators in addition to its train station.

May 14: Gee, I'm blue tonight. Always get this way dieting—but I've lost 10 lbs. Now to get to 150 lbs. At 145 I think I can wear my black dress which should be good for the summer.

May 19: Teacher's meeting tonight. Nothing to stop us from doing all our reports before this week that I can see. I decided not to go to Seattle this weekend. Got my hair done.

May 21: Daisy went to Seattle. I finished my sweater & a number of small jobs. Broke my diet but I think I'm started on my 3rd 5 lbs. Wish it would be gone by Fri.

May 23: Worked on my reports & started to pack. Daisy home—full of adventures—& a new job. Next year I'm going to stay all summer in Mont. So can pack after school.

May 28: A lovely day & things went nicely. In the evening I got a head-ache. We went to tell Mr. Schafer goodbye & he had a job in Tenino & asked us to come along & both of us with contracts signed.

May 29: Meant to go to Seattle but stayed over to see if I could get a release [from her contract in Napavine, so she can accept Mr. Schafer's offer of a job in Tenino]. Have spent the day packing. Then the school board has to meet Monday instead.

Surely it's a compliment to both Imogene and Daisy to be asked to move along with their principal. Now, if they can just get out of their Napavine contracts—and in fact, it will happen; Napavine will release them, and they'll soon be apartment-hunting in the slightly bigger town on Tenino, about twenty miles up the road. An undated newspaper clipping that Imogene kept and that I found among her papers notes that Marvin Schafer will be the school superintendent for the coming year (1943–44), and that among the new faculty are Miss Imogene Welch, primary, and Miss Daisy Lincoln, remedial work. Annoyed with each other, trying to pretend that they're still friends, they'll move together. It's a promotion and a pay raise for both of them.

May 30: Left Seattle at 9:30. Barely made the train.

May 31: Spent the day on the train between Spokane & Gt. Falls. Got in about 11:30. Beat it to the Falls Hotel & was lucky to get a room. Tomorrow I'll shop.

June 1: Really spent money in the Falls. Got lockets for the kids & a dress for myself & a slip for Ma & a shirt for Dad. They were a few minutes late to the train.

Another artifact. I hold in my hand the heart-shaped gold locket that Imogene bought for me in Great Falls, Montana, on June 1, 1943. Its chain is broken, and it is dented with the tiny marks where some child teethed on it—probably my sister Betty, who was seven months old in June. Or is this Betty's locket? Does she have mine? They were, as far as I can remember, identical.

June 2: Horrors! I never saw such a cold, horrid rainy day. It was so horrid I didn't ride up to the ranch. I helped move a hog & milked one cow. A bitter, cold evening.

June 3: Rain again—cold—horrid. Mary is broken hearted because I came upstairs to write. She can't let me out of her sight. "She never sang me any new songs" she mourned to herself, on the stairs.

Imogene is spending most of her two weeks at the ranch with my parents, and I am enchanted to have her. Unlike my mother and father, she has time to pay attention to me, and she's a fresh breeze, a burst of laughter and a new source for songs and stories. "I'm an old cowhand, from the Rio Grande," she sings, "my legs ain't bowed, and my cheeks ain't tanned, but I know all the songs that the cowboys know, I learned them all on the radio," and " 'Tis to little Joe, the wrangler, he'll wrangle never more, his days with the remuda they are o'er."

"What is a remuda? Why are his days with the remuda o'er?" I asked, even at that age wanting to know more of the story.

"Because he died."

"Why?"

"Because his horse fell with him."

"Then what happened?"

"I don't know what happened next! It's just a song!"

When I was old enough to wind the crank of her Victrola and set the steel needle on a .78 record, I listened by the hour to the strange cracked voices and twanging guitars that emanated from the spinning black disc, as though transmitted from another universe:

—and there in the horse corral, a-standin' alone, was a little caballo, a
  strawberry roan—
Lay that pistol down, Babe!
—but remember that Red River Valley—
You are my sunshine, my only sunshine.

*June 4: We just sit & visit. My time is so short I hate to do much. I rode
up to Ma's last evening. Everything [probably meaning her father's peculiar
behavior] is just the same. My Mother is a wonderful woman.*

My grandmother is a wonderful woman for putting up with A. P., is what
I think Imogene means. Imogene admires her mother for her backbone. For
her endurance, for making the best of a hard lot, for all the qualities Imogene thinks she herself lacks. Really, she tells herself! If her mother can bear
up under so much adversity, surely Imogene can bear up under hers. After
all, what does Imogene have to complain about? That she's single? And fat?
That's all.

Does she ever ask herself whether a backbone can become too rigid?
Does she wonder if her own sense of pleasure has been stifled by her
mother's stoicism?

*June 5: Sat. Ma & I went walking—the feed is good. Rainy & wet—I
won't get to see my horses or get them bred. Went thru my boxes.*

*June 7: Went to Denton—got Mary paper dolls. Saw lots of people I
knew. It was quite muddy. Want to go to Lewistown & visit the hospital but
likely won't get to do so.*

*June 9: Went to see Florence—got well wind burned. Kristie Lee is a sweet
doll. Yesterday I had to get the folks to walk to Jack's [about a mile down
through the Judith river bluffs]. Wished for my car—it's a hard trip for Ma.
Let Pa go & worried how he & Doris would get on—but all went well.*

June 10: Pa headed for home but it was so muddy Ma waited. I know how lonely Mary feels & try to show her my love. I love Betty too. She is cunning beyond words, but Mary is lonely for she must learn to share now.

June 11: Rode home today & washed & got set to pack & go back. I'm glad Ma can take her pleasure in her plans of the future. Her life has been hard & disappointing & yet she gets much from life. God, I'm afraid my greatest pleasure will have to be work.

June 12: Got to Jack's late. Doris helped milk while I cared for the kids [and then she, Jack, and Doris went to a community dance]. Jack mostly visited so we did not dance much & I would have liked to. Oh, I envy Doris her husband & girls. We got home about 4:00. Just like the days when I was in circulation.

June 13: We girls slept. Jack took Mary so we could. Then they took me to town [to catch her train back to Seattle]. A pig was ailing. They had to get the vet. It was fearfully slippery on the way between Danvers & Hanover.

June 14: Slept in the basement of the Falls Hotel last night. Was startled to find my suitcase was left behind in Lewistown. It will have to follow later. Got train sick & urped.

June 15: Got to Seattle at 8:00. Daisy came down—we went to Grukams, got my car—& unpacked. Then we went down town to look for a job & got one in a box factory at 65c.

June 16: To college again. Classes at 8-10- & 11. The 2nd hr I looked over the campus. Wish I were not so shy & retiring. Oh for money & time to get acquainted. I learned to rivet.

The University of Washington was a somber campus during the summer of 1943. The university had curtailed all nonessential functions, including social events like the varsity ball and junior prom, and transformed much of its curriculum into war-related studies or adult education programs for workers in the war industries. The summer program had been curtailed, although public school teachers like Imogene, returning to renew or upgrade their teaching certificates, apparently had little difficulty enrolling in the classes they needed. Still, the campus itself was beautiful then, as now, and Imogene was impressed and rather intimidated by it.

Although Imogene doesn't mention it, June 16 is my father's birthday and the anniversary of her mowing machine accident.

June 17: My wrist is sore & swollen but like my job. The bosses are keen. Next to me is another school marm—older—dignified. Oh—I'm lonely—lonely.

June 18: Went to work at 5:00. I guess I can manage on $3 a day. But I'd like to make more. Oh, I want so many clothes. I'm the most inwardly unhappy person. Outside it doesn't show at all.

No, her unhappiness doesn't show on the outside. Her hiding of her feelings is complete. None of her family ever guessed that she suffered from depression, although she fought it all her life. "I never saw Imogene cry," my mother told me, years later. "Never." But her diary entries during her summer at the University of Washington show her preoccupation with self at war with her outward demeanor:

June 20: Ate out—not to rave about—75c. I'm bawling blue. Daisy is out calling. I have 11 letters to write. I wonder why the girls want so to improve me but not themselves. They feel & act so superior. My heart & feelings bleed internally.

June 21: Mon. Full tilt into another week. At any rate the summer will pass fast tho I won't have very much fun. Am getting things straight so the afternoon can be spent in the library.

June 23: Little nagging today. Monday she lost some junk & blew up at me—yesterday a sneer at my blouse. Some things a lady doesn't do.

What are some of the things a lady doesn't do? "My girls would never appear in public like that," my grandmother once told Aunt Florence, who was dressed in slacks.

June 29: Test in Eng. My coat came from the Bon [Seattle department store] & I like mine better than Daisy's. I got the pictures I took of the babies too. We went to work but found out no work till next Tues.

June 30: I shopped. Meat is so high—most of our stamps just waste. Am glad Ma used so many of mine. I checked out a book & have to turn it back. If they'd keep them all on reserve!

July 1: Wish I'd gotten butter. We are nearly out of spread. Am getting time to do a little mag. reading—a nice vacation till next Tues but a pay check is a handy thing.

July 4: Went out to Long Lake for a picnic dinner. Some went swimming, boating, fishing. Ate a wonderful, plentiful picnic lunch.

July 6: Lots of letters. Pa yips as usual till I hate to read his letters.

One of the letters she may have received was from her spinster aunt Mable in Sioux City, Iowa. A lifelong teacher herself, Mable writes to encourage her niece and to catalogue her own preoccupations with salary:

Dear Imogene,

I was sure pleased to get your letter from Seattle and to hear what you are doing this summer. You seem to be hitting it hard as usual. Glad to hear about your new job for next year. You must plan to go on and get your degree. If I had mine I would be pulling 480 more dollars this next year, and blame it all some of the girls who are getting it haven't more than a semester more credits than I have; but to get my degree now expect I'd have to go a year or more and so think it is not worth the effort. We had a $50 bonus for last year and this year my contract calls for $1920. But by the time they take out for pentions, victory tax and now federal tax don't know what I'll really be getting.

July 7: The night crew got laid off tonight. We only worked 4 hrs. The Coast Guard has a priority over the Army. But the Day Crew likes to jump the night crew.

July 10: Sat. Shopped & washed. Daisy studied at the lib. So I had the apt. to myself. How I like to be alone.

July 18: Sun. We went berry picking, each to his own. I got raspberries, cherries. Had a chicken dinner——a nice day——but I got tired. Also the curse.

July 20: Tue. Test in Manual. A farce. Don't know how I did. Worked at the cannery [where she's found work after being laid off at the box factory]. Don't like it but hope to stick there for the summer. So noisy my head rings.

July 23: Worked 11 hrs, from 7–7 last night. Came home just groggy.

July 26: 2 cards from Pa——in a sweat about the money. Crimeny. Still have not recovered from the grave yard shift.

July 31: Went to work alone. Daisy went to a concert. I sure do not like this cannery job. The damn clacking, backbiting women.

August 1: Sunday. Slept till noon. Ate out. Daisy was visiting. She went to work & I put in the evening on my English paper.

August 2: Bummed around on the "U Way" thinking about clothes——didn't buy any.

August 5: Were going to work tonight but were notified the peas were late. We went to "Ladies in Retirement." Daisy heard from an apartment $40 [in Tenino]. Told her to count me out.

August 6: Went to work tonight. Daisy quit at lunch because she wants to go to tennis. Letter from Dave. He likes Alaska in the southern part.

And here I have the very letter Dave wrote, postmarked July 30, 1943, and addressed to Miss Imogene Welch at 4719 21 Ave NE, Seattle. "Well how do you like Seattle by now. Personaly I don't like it with the boom on as it is to crowded. I much prefere Alaska with its wide open spaces."

After the excitement of the Japanese attack a year ago, the construction crews are probably whiling away their free time, speculating about Alaskan hunting and fishing, wondering what life might be like as commercial fishermen. "The fishing season is open now," Dave reports in the same letter. "From what I hear they expect a poor season. There was a 400 lb halibut caught in a fish trap not far from here."

August 7: Got home at 6:00 AM. Slept—shopped. Daisy home from tennis in good spirits. Has decided to take the apartment. Now if I can only get a place I will like.

August 10: Heard from Mrs. Furness [who has an apartment for rent in Tenino]. No oven—but I'll try to get Mrs. C's stove—if she'll sell it. My Geog. [assignment] got stepped up to this Friday.

August 11: Made almost $20 in my pay checks. Hope I can work thu August 28. Cracky. I got tired tonight. Sure glad we were working only half a shift.

August 12: Put in a good lick on Geog. Hope it goes well. I've enjoyed my reading. Test in Hist. tomorrow too, so I'm not going to work tonight.

August 16: Went to dinner at Miss Blair's. Very nice. Got to read the Tenino paper—it had the list of teachers. I drew the 2nd grade—hope I got a good room.

August 19: Hope to get in 3 full nights and 3 5-hr. shifts this week. Kay Uhle is kind of playing up to the men. I still like her.

August 20: Only one more week. I can hardly wait to establish my own domicile. Lovely——lovely——lovely.

August 24: I cut Geog today having gotten my report done on Mon. Decided tomorrow I just have to study. I can't possibly work.

August 26: Tests in history and English. Went shopping. Got a few duds— some towels for Mrs. Graham. Things are sure winding up fast.

August 27: Got to bed about six. The alarm did not go off and Daisy was late for her 9 o'clock exam. She burns me up. It was not my fault.

August 30: How wonderful to relax and sleep [in Bremerton for a brief visit]. Sylva had rabbit for dinner. I like them as much as chicken. Sylva is a good meat cook.

September 2: Got my hair fixed for the entry into Tenino. Ervin said I should stay over longer but I want to get strung out for school and unpacked.

Is Imogene aware of the subtle shifts of diction in her diary? That the emphatic *we, we, we* of the days when she went everywhere and did everything with Bernita and Daisy has shifted to the first person pronoun? *I've enjoyed my reading—I'm not going to work tonight—I hope I got a good room—I can hardly wait to establish my own domicile. Lovely, lovely, lovely.*

And now it's the beginning of another school year, the true beginning of any teacher's year. Imogene will leave her sister's house in Bremerton and travel in the heat of early September down to Tenino, hoping that her beauty salon shampoo and set won't have wilted and straggled by the time she arrives. A beauty salon set: she's spent money and had her braids cut, so the weight of her hair doesn't drag down the natural curl, but allows it to wave around her face, full and dark and soft. Maybe, maybe the hair-do is another break with tradition, as she jounces in the slow, crowded bus to a new apartment and a new school.

Imogene as a toddler on the Montana homestead

At the homestead, circa 1917. Back row: Sylva, Mary Welch, Imogene; front row: Doris, David

Imogene Welch, age thirteen, on the Montana homestead

Imogene, age fifteen, Coffee Creek, Montana

Imogene's high
school graduation
portrait

Imogene riding Paulie on the Montana homestead, circa 1930

Imogene, age twenty, in front of the house on the Montana homestead

Imogene with her colt, early 1930s, Montana

Imogene with Kristie Lee, 1943

Imogene at about the time she began teaching in Tenino

Christmas program at the Warm Spring Creek school, 1950. Mary (Clearman Blew) is at far left, back row; her sister, Betty, is second from left, front row.

Imogene, age
seventy-eight

11

/ / /

September 3: Left Bremerton at 7:30, got to Tenino early. Saw Mrs.
Shafer—ate at Daisy's—I'm not crazy about her apartment. Got to Napavine
& back [a forty-mile round-trip for her belongings, packed in the back seat
and trunk of her car].

Tenino. For years it was known to me only as a way my aunt had of beginning a sentence: "When I was in Tenino—" But always, the rest of the sentence is lost to my memory. What was she telling me that I should have paid
attention to?

Today the population of Tenino is about 1300. Its population before the
war was around a thousand, but perhaps it was a more of a market center than
it is now when Imogene moved there in 1943. A picture postcard of its main
street, taken in the late 1930s, shows unshaded pavement and sidewalks, with
power lines and a single streetlight. Single-story buildings in the business
block, for the most part, some of them built from undressed stone with brick

facades. A Model A truck is parked beside the Tenino Feed Store, a few more cars beside Puget Sound Power & Light and the barber shop and the drug store, and Campbell & Campbell, which offers dry goods, shoes, and hardware. There's a fire hydrant on the corner, and a fellow in a dark suit, white shirt and tie (no hat, so he's probably just stepped out of his office for a breath of air, or perhaps to watch the photographer), leaning on the pillar outside the real estate office. The far end of Main Street is faintly shadowed by firs, because this is the Pacific northwest, but Tenino is still a quiet little farm town, not so different from the dusty towns of Montana that Imogene won't feel at home. *I like not too big a town,* she'll note in her diary.

No sign of a motion picture theater in this photograph. The teachers probably pool their rations of gasoline and drive to Chehalis if they want to see a show.

> *September 4: Another year has rolled around. [Imogene is thirty-four today.] We went to town & I got a lot of things I wanted. Bought a bookcase. How Daisy loves to tell me what to do.*

> *September 6: Teacher's meeting today. I liked Mr. Fox [the elementary school principal] but his kid is a pain. Dang, I offered to take the 3rd & got in the little school. I have the best room tho. Notice the teachers pair off.*

Another picture postcard, taken by the same photographer who captured Main Street: the Tenino public school. Unremarkable, recognizable as any public school anywhere, with its brickwork and flagpole and many-paned windows. Behind it, a heavy phalanx of firs, and more firs faint in the distance. In front of it, a muddy, track-marred space of sparse grass and rock. Could the school be newly built in this photograph? Has a playground not yet been constructed?

How glamorous the idea of my aunt's school seemed to me! A real school, like the ones pictured in the outdated science readers and language arts readers she brought back to me.

But how surprised my aunt's third-graders would have been at my idea of glamor, for they would have believed, as all children do, that their world was mundane. Boring. Imogene's third-graders knew that true glamor lay on the dangerous edge, perhaps in a world their teacher told them about, where children no older than themselves climbed a stile and braved range cattle to fetch drinking water from a spring.

September 7: First day was not so bad. I had 32 pupils—24 desks— all of which were changed. So we had lots of recess. Card from Aunt Mary [in Iowa].

September 8: Mary Cramer [the English teacher at the high school] stopped last night and we had a gab fest. Like me—she wouldn't live with Daisy. When I live alone I always talk too much.

September 12: Went to church. Daisy just strains herself to give the impression we are pals. I tried out a new pork chop dish. Not bad. Wrote letters.

September 13: Have to apply for sugar & [ration] Book #3 again. Guess what. Mice. I got 2 traps—one no good. Next week I'm going to get going on both my diet & ex.

September 17: Was sure stiff on the 4th grade. I never saw such spellers [an ironic note, considering her spelling.] 14 of the 3rd can not read in a 1st Reader & 15 can only read in 2nd readers. I bet they think I'm a Grind.

September 21: Faculty reception & I had a good time. But Daisy came over & spoke & made a cutting remark because I didn't introduce her to Mrs. Buck.

September 24: Daisy & I went swimming in the old quarry 90 ft. deep. So hot this afternoon. Letter from Mother. Says Pa is failing. He's seemed too forgetful for a long time to me.

Details fall together. There's a quarry near Tenino, and that's where the stone came from for the buildings on Main Street. I'm amazed at myself, at how much I can learn from such scant entries.

Imogene was unlike a lot of prairie-raised girls in that she knew how to swim. She'd taught herself in an irrigation ditch near the homestead, floating in the shallow, muddy water and squinting up through the weeds at bursts of sunlight until, plop! A frog thrown by her younger brother or sister, my mother or Uncle Dave, hit her in the stomach and sank her. But—perseverance—she spat and recovered herself, yelled threats and tried again, until, eventually, she did learn to swim and later qualified as a lifeguard.

Pa is failing. Yes, his dementia is progressing, Imogene.

September 25: Got my hair done. Letter from Sylva. Only one week left in this month. Hope my certificate comes so I can get paid. I need money so darn bad.

However badly she needs money, she's continuing what will become a lifetime habit of having her hair done in the beauty shop. A small luxury, and maybe a small defiance at the old strictures.

Beauty is only skin deep!

Maybe so, but I'm going to have my hair done, all the same.

September 27: Hot dog—got my 3 yr. Certificate. Teacher's meeting. We have ration book 4 to do soon. I hear they will cut down still farther on gas soon. Spelling [trying to teach it to her third-graders] is about to get me down.

Her three-year teaching certificate means that she won't have to go back to summer school for another three years. She's thankful for the breathing space, for not having to return soon for the grueling combination of studies and working at a box factory or a cannery until she's ready to drop. She can treat herself to a summer in Montana, she can take her time.

I know I'll never get a [bachelor's] degree, she writes at one point, although in fact she does, one day.

> *September 29: Damn! Daisy is moving into a house—not that I care about that but she wants to sleep here the 10 days between. I won't like it but I can't say no.*

> *September 30: One of the Jr. H.S. boys got killed at school today. We had the 1st PTA tonight. A nice crowd. I was asked to be secretary.*

Oh, Imogene! What is the story here? Why do you dismiss the death of the boy in the same line as the PTA meeting?

Because I have the place and the date, I could almost certainly learn the boy's name and cause of death. A social historian researching life in small-town Washington State during the 1940s probably could find a newspaper account of the fall from the tree where he shouldn't have been climbing. Or the dash he shouldn't have made into traffic. Or the rough tackle on the playground, head hitting one of those rocks that never got moved after the construction of the school, the other boys scared and defensive, we didn't mean, we didn't mean. But I'm not a social historian, and why does the boy's death matter, finally, in Imogene's story?

(She's new in town, remember. This is her first year teaching here, so she can't join in the conversation among the older teachers: Oh, yes, he was in my fifth grade in such-and-such a year, I remember when, and so on.)

The writer of creative nonfiction is constantly questioned about the ethics of her craft. What can she decently write about other people? Which secrets should she allow herself to expose? Ought she be writing at all? Because isn't she, in a sense, selling herself? Selling herself and her family and friends, selling her very landscape, her very culture, to prurient readers who at the very least think that they're getting the real thing and, at the worst, that they're getting the low-down, the dirt, the ugly underside.

Oh, of course she asks herself these questions constantly, not that her answers will please everybody, but she does ask.

Meanwhile the fiction writer, of course, is busy making other, more cold-blooded choices. Can she spin some significance out of the death of an unknown boy in 1943? Hang a plot around him, turn him into a sacrificial victim for her art? Never should it be said that the fiction writer, safe behind her mask, is a pure vendor of virtue, she who also spins her web out of other people's misery, but does it invisibly.

> *October 2: Today there were pint jars in town. I got 2 doz. Also some tomatoes. I guess I'll can some pears too. I got my canning sugar. We looked in 3 furniture shops.*

The careful wartime restrictions, the scarcity of jars, and the careful use of ration points, which allow for canning and preserving.

Imogene first would have learned to can fruit and make jelly at her mother's elbow, helping at the wood stove in the white heat of the homestead shack. Later she would have taken home economics in high school, just as the Tenino girls in 1943 take Vocational Home Economics from a Miss Phyllis Loutzenheiser, just as I will take the required home economics courses in Montana junior high and high schools in the 1950s. (The Tenino boys, of course, are busy with Vocational Agriculture, taught by Mr. Robert Kerstetter, just as the boys I went to school with took the obligatory class in shop.) In home economics class I will learn to sew by hand and also on a foot-treadle sewing machine, although the home economics room possesses a couple of electric sewing machines (as does my mother, who sold a calf right after the war and bought herself an electric Singer.) I will learn to make baking powder biscuits and pie crust from flour and lard, and I will be lectured on the frugality of hot oatmeal over more expensive, more convenient cold cereal for breakfast. After all, when you're married, you'll have to make ends meet on your husband's pay check. It's important to know how!

Every woman of Imogene's generation, and mine, too, knew how to cook and sew and preserve. How often her diary notes the pork roast she managed to get with her meat ration points, the meatloaf she baked, the cake she baked. Despite their heavy teaching loads and their war work, she and Daisy and Bernita sat down to real meals. Every night.

October 3: I got sore at Daisy again. Darn her. I'll be glad when she gets moved. I canned my tomatoes. Hot dog. She got quite a bit of elderberry jelly.

October 4: Gee, we whipped thru our reports in no time. Mr. Fox [the elementary school principal] sure has a system. I washed, broke up crates for kindling. I moved some coal. O, for my warrant.

October 6: Hot dog. Daisy pulled her freight tonight. How wonderful to have my own vine & fig tree alone. Such luxuory & joy.

October 8: We took the kids to Bambi. I liked it & had seen it before. Now at last I can send for my sewing machine. Nuts, my money never goes far enuf.

October 10: A rainy, grey Sunday. I mailed a handful of letters & picked a bunch of Calif. poppies. Sure like my house this way with Daisy out of it.

She's either cooking on a coal stove or, more likely, heating her apartment with coal, which doesn't seem to have been the case in her Napavine apartment. But she's used to starting fires and testing an oven by stretching her hand inside to gauge the temperature, even if she does have to lug her fuel up those stairs. And it's an upstairs apartment, that much can be deduced from her references to "going down" or "going up."

Let's imagine one of those old frame bungalows, two stories, that probably was built in 1910 or so. Retired couple lives there, rents out the second floor to stretch the pension. Upstairs is slanted ceilings and dormer windows that look out on maple trees and a sparse little lawn that the landlady's husband tends. One bedroom, a bathroom behind the kitchen, and a little living

area with papered walls and splintering fir floors. By one of the dormer windows the teacher has set her comfortable chair and her lamp and the bookcase
she bought a few weeks ago, but already her shelves are full and her books sit
in stacks on the splintering fir flooring. But never mind, it's her own clutter,
her knitting and her unfinished embroidery and her novel with her place
marked with a fingernail file. And never mind the apple boxes full of stamp
albums, photograph albums, more books, she'll get around to unpacking if
she can think where to put things. Under the bed, maybe. Stacked on the shelf
in the closet. She doesn't care, and she doesn't care about the graying wallpaper, the landlady's dusty curtains that sag at the hems, the total absence of
what could be called *decor*.

What she does care about: at the end of the school day, afternoon already
darkening into twilight, staggering up the stairs with her arms full of coal or
groceries or schoolwork to be corrected, opening her door and dropping her
load with relief on the floor. Starts a fire, breathes deeply. Peace and quiet at
last. Familiar shadows. She sighs, turns on a lamp, kicks off her shoes and flops
in her chair. Lets herself absorb the familiar odor, the mixture of tracked-in
leaves and coal dust and her own shoes. Her own bed waiting, after she's had
her supper. But first, while she decides what to cook for herself, she'll just sit
and be quiet. Maybe she'll reheat what coffee is left in the pot, read for awhile.
She's got some new library books, bright covers, historical romances. Dust
curls collecting on those fir floors. Let them. Let her sit in peace, no yelping
Daisy to criticize her or hurry her or carp about the cleaning. What luxury!

*October 12: Tonight I went to the Arabian nights & found it lovely photo-
graphy but the action very like Wild West. Crimeny, it's been cold for a couple
of days.*

*October 13: Went to Red X tonight. Put in two hours. Not bad. Letter
from Florence. She is worried about Dave. He has moved. I will be glad when
she hears.*

October 14: PTA. A small crowd—perhaps 50—I am secretary. Nuts.
Mrs. Sullivan talked about Russia. Mary C dropped in for a few minutes. C&C
[the Campbell & Campbell department store in Tenino] has sheets at $2.50.

October 15: Friday at last. Show in the A.M. I got a new magazine. My
groceries came late. Decided Monday to diet 6 weeks in a deffinent attempt
to lose 30 lbs.

October 17: Worked on my reports. Decided to reduce & promised myself
a garment for every pound I lost. Want to lose 45 before school is out.

October 18: Finished my reports tonight all but my notes. Mrs. [Helen] Corn-
well [fourth grade teacher and music instructor for the elementary school] asked
Daisy & me to her house tomorrow for dinner. Wed. teacher's meeting in Chehalis.

October 20: Went to Chehalis to W.E.A. [Washington Education Association].
Looked through the shops. So little choice. Guess I'll send for sharkskin to make
blouses [when she gets her sewing machine]. I'm going to have a play suit too.

October 21: PTA executive board meeting & I got home at 11:00 & so
to bed. Am reading Quentin Durwood & find it very interesting. Got a new
Goodhousekeeping.

Good Housekeeping, that ur-manual of conventional womanhood! Then as
now, it's filled with housekeeping tips, recipes, advice on rearing children for
the reader it assumes is a married woman. For Imogene, *Good Housekeeping* is
a reminder how out of step she is with the rest of the world. Single. Childless.
Uninterested in elaborate decorating schemes that, in any case, she can't
afford. But what *Good Housekeeping* does contain in the 1940s that it doesn't
contain today is plenty of fiction. Short stories, novels in serial form. That's
what Imogene likes to read. What with *Quentin Durward* and the new *Good
Housekeeping,* she's set for this evening. Let the light darken, let Daisy Lincoln
fuss with her interminable place mats and tea towels. Imogene will tell herself

she should be doing chores, should be writing, but then she'll turn another page. Far away there's perhaps a little late traffic on Main Street, a truck changing gears, but in her space is lamplight and blessed quiet. If she still dreams of romantic passion, perhaps she's coming to believe that the likes of Quentin Durward are best contained within the covers of a book.

October 22: Took in the H.S. dance for an hour. It seemed to have been a success. Came home, did divers things—to bed at 1 o'clock.

October 24: Sunday—a dull gray, rainy day. I got lots done—canned applesauce, but didn't get to church. I ought to get in the habit. Like to write home on Sunday.

Her church-going has sadly slipped since the days when she, Bernita, and Daisy went to Catholic and Methodist services every week. As she gets used to the routines of town schools, makes more acquaintances, and feels more sure of herself, she's less inclined to try to impress others and more likely to settle back into her own comfortable, solitary pleasures. Doing what she feels like doing. Reading, knitting, embroidering. Still, she's drawn into the life of the community:

October 25: Teachers meeting to prepare for rationing. I hope we don't have to ration clothes. I want to make some new ones. Oh, when can I get down & wear my black!

October 28: Mr. Boling brot our bear meat today. Say, I fixed mine, & it was darn good. I've eaten better meat, but for wartime or any time, bear meat is o.k.

October 31: Dinner at Daisy's. How odd she is, and such a poor cook, and how she likes the niceties—a tablecloth. Got my reports done & precious little else.

As twilight gathers, Daisy spreads her freshly ironed tablecloth and lights her candles. She had hoped to find orange or black candles, for Halloween, but plain white were the best C&C had to offer (it's wartime, after all.) However, she's assembled a centerpiece of maple leaves and the last few button chrysanthemums from her backyard, and she's set a carved pumpkin on her front steps. She's proud of her little house, proud of what she's accomplished in the three weeks she's lived here with her little domestic touches of cushions and curtains and family photographs in silver frames, and proud of its shining cleanliness after days of putting up with Imogene Welch's sloppy ways. No dust curls in Daisy's corners, no hopeless clutter of books and sewing materials, no water spots in her sink, no baked-on grease on the fireproof casserole dish she lifts from the oven and sets in its prewar metal holder. She's serving macaroni tonight, with baked squash on the side, and she's unsure about the squash, it looks stringy, but anything fresh is so hard to find. And it's just Imogene Welch coming to dinner, after all. Happy-go-lucky Imogene, she won't hold the squash against Daisy.

Daisy's home, with its candles and cushions and odor of Dutch cleanser, is her stage. Here she shines. Waits for the evening when it won't be just Imogene Welch coming to dinner, but, well, she can't visualize his face, but rather sees the back of his shoulders, in uniform. He's the true audience for whom she practices. Hopes he arrives before her slenderness becomes stringy, her sharp face beaky.

Daisy loves Imogene, but oh, she wouldn't be Imogene for anything!

12

/ / /

November 2: Sent Betty her birthday check [for her first birthday, on November 9]. Doris wanted to get shoes for her. Letter from Florence & pictures of Kristie Lee. She is sweet as can be.

November 3: Red Cross tonight. I have a cold developing. It rained & rained & rained. I must get my car in a garage. Have so many projects I can't finish any.

November 4: PTA. Not to large a crowd. I had a nice enough time. Lots to eat—nobody likes to eat but me and a man or two.

November 7: Daisy came to dinner. We get on fine if we see each other once a week. I am nursing a cold along. Weekends go so fast.

November 9: Hot dog—Armistice Day this week and no school. So that is when I'll do my dratted accounts done. Then to write. I should do a story this month.

November 10: Long confab with the nurse over June. Mr. Fox said not to let her tell me how to do my job. With 33 pupils, a teacher can't give one too much time.

November 12: Bought a tongue & boiled it tonight. Took 14 pts. & cost 1.00 [a serious dent in both budget and ration points]. But I'm always going to diet. Made me a wish chart—115 lbs.

November 13: Went to Chehalis. Took Mrs. Cornwell, her kids & boyfriend. How her kids act! I got the rest of my knitting needles & patterns.

November 15: Milk program under way. I got 2 new pupils—my room is full again. I reseated a lot of people and I guess tomorrow I'll reseat a lot more.

November 19: Hot dog. Only three days of school next week. I have a big washing to do so I'll have clothes to wear at Sylva's [for Thanksgiving].

November 23: Teacher's meeting tonight. Lasted till after 5. I told Helen C. I bet half of it was because [Daisy] Lincoln wouldn't oversee the 5th grade kids that day.

November 24: Wed. Thru early. I pulled out about 5 [apparently she managed to get enough gasoline to take her car]—got into Bremerton at 8:00. Not a bad trip. Took much fancy work & hope to get in some good licks.

November 25: Ervin had to work so Sylva had a big turkey dinner and all the fixings. Just some of Ervin's family. Sylva is the one who always has the crowd in.

November 26: Friday. Sylva & I caught up on visiting. She feels hard toward Pa. I agree Pa is only honest as long as it suits his purpose.

Anger will possess Imogene and her sisters and brother when, in a few years, they'll be called upon to do something about their father. Blame will be passed around: surely it's somebody's fault! Pa's fault for being inadequate all his life! Ma's fault for being overbearing! Blame: a way of insisting that events are not out of control. That A. P. could, if he only would, straighten up and behave himself.

Sylva will take her mother's side, Dave will take his father's side, Doris will refuse to allow her father to live at the ranch, in her care, and Imogene will try to help her mother and avoid conflict. It's beginning to dawn on her that she's well off having a life of her own in distant Tenino, her own den at the top of those stairs where she can dump her load of coal and groceries and fling herself in her familiar chair with a cup of reheated coffee. Blessed peace and quiet!

Yes, as the stillness settles around her, the dim walls, the books in stacks where she left them, she closes her eyes in the knowledge that no one will walk through that door without knocking, no one will disturb her evening. Her coffee is a little weak, but that's how she likes it. She'll hoist herself out of her chair in a while and cook something for her supper, but not just yet. Not just yet.

Her hands, looking for something to fill them, grope by the side of her chair and come up with her half-finished pillow case. Needle threaded with rose floss and stuck through the fabric, embroidery hoop snapped in place. The familiar motion of her fingers and the soft sibilants of the floss as it slides through the linen. Comfort in repetition, over and over. Her mind is free to float. Family tensions dim, school reports seem less ominous. She'll have it all to worry about, but not right now. Not right now. No.

November 28: Picked a bunch of mums. Sylva gave me a plant, some catchup too. I left at 2 & got home at 4:30. My reports were tough.

November 30: Tore in to get my report cards done. Going to bed early & try to catch up on sleep. Criminy, I wish my weight would go down.

December 2: PTA tonight. The best pie for supper. I had chocolate. I suppose that is why I do not lose. Mrs. Buck died very suddenly last night.

December 3: Mother wrote Dave got home the day before Thanksgiving and they were expecting him for a short visit. The [Buck] funeral is tomorrow. I don't see how I can go.

December 8: Went to dress rehersal. It was not so hot. Mary [Cramer, the English teacher who apparently is directing the high school play] is kind of perturbed. Had her over for coffee. Hope to see more of her after the play.

December 10: Another letter from Pa. Curses, I wish he wouldn't write like that. I staid home & read. Should have gone to the class play.

December 13: Knit tonight. Only 2 rows in half an hour. Letters from Mother & Doris. Betty broke her arm. Darn, I can't get there [to Montana] till Christmas Day.

December 19: Went to church twice. Enjoyed good local singing. Have my nighties done but buttonholes & embroidery. Made my Christmas candy.

December 20: Went to a shower. Had a nice time. Dress rehersal [probably a rehearsal for the elementary school Christmas program] was rotten. Wed. is going to be a queer day. Will get my hair done tomorrow.

December 21: Program over. Went well. A nice crowd. My clowns acted up till Mr. Fox worked them over. I got my hair done. She did a lovely job.

December 23: Had a nice party and got off on the 4 o'clock bus [to catch a train, probably in Seattle, to travel to Montana]. Had a two hr. wait in Tacoma. My connections promise to be good.

December 24: Caught a cold & headache all day. Neither read nor knitted. Ate dinner with a sailor.

December 25: Jack met me [at the train station, probably in Danvers or Hobson.] I sure feel rotten. Jack went for the folks [Imogene's mother and father] before breakfast. Dave & Florence & K.L. came in the evening.

/ / /

In the depot at Danvers the stationmaster has set up a little fir tree and strung it with foil and a few celluloid ornaments. He leans back in his swivel chair, visiting with my young father while he waits for the train from the west. The potbellied coal stove kicks out heat that steams the windows, otherwise the stationmaster and my young father, Jack, could watch the snow blowing across the three or four streets of this tiny prairie town, drifting in front of the post office and the pool hall and between the grain elevators. Danvers has not yet shrunk to nothing. Although Old Man Longin has closed for Christmas, his dugout store is still a viable business where ranchers can buy canned goods and hot dogs and sliced bologna from his case, and where, even in wartime, a few Hershey bars are tucked away for the very smallest children.

Farther away, on the other side of the county road, are the white-painted schoolhouse and the community hall and the Catholic church, so faint through the blowing snow that my father barely made them out in his headlights when he drove in from the ranch this afternoon. In every other direction are stubble fields and snowbound prairie and no signs of life. The cattle are weathering it out in the coulees and the rabbits and coyotes have holed up while the wind whines and the twilight gradually encloses the town and the railroad tracks and the little depot.

Jack has loosened his mackinaw and the tattered black silk scarf he wears for winter warmth around his neck. Props his bootheels on the hod. No hurry today, nothing to do but wait, although back at the ranch, in the log house by the river, his wife and mother will be flying around, getting a late Christmas dinner, while four-year-old Mary gets underfoot and Betty with her cast on her arm naps in her crib.

"Looks pretty damn fierce out there," the stationmaster agrees, "but the almanac says there's a chinook on the way, probably tonight. Your sister-in-law coming in from Tacoma?"

"Yeah, she tried, but she couldn't get a seat until today."

"Always liked her. Always ready with a laugh. She must have finally got over that accident she had, with your team and the mowing machine a few years back?"

"She's done real well. Always going to have that scar, of course."

"Helluva thing. How's she like it out there in Washington?"

Jack shrugs, uneasily. He's the son and grandson of settlers, himself, he can't imagine living anywhere but in the midst of this high prairie where he was born. Can't imagine why anybody would want to live anywhere else. The changes brought by the war must be endured; he's seen his younger cousins in uniforms, heading for far parts of the world. He'd be in uniform himself if he didn't have so many dependents, if he weren't in a crucial occupation. The upheaval will go on, he knows, until General MacArthur whips the Japs and the Allies whip the Germans, as is just and as it must be. But he hates the turmoil, the constant shifting, everybody on the move.

"Don't think she'd ever have left, but they pay their teachers so much better out there," he says, finally.

The stationmaster shakes his head, commiserating. "Always hard to have to leave."

Together they gaze at the flames leaping against the glass in the little pot-bellied stove, while the wind howls around the eaves of the depot and shakes the rafters and drives snow across the vast plain of Montana, the frozen sage-brush and jackpine of the river breaks, the cutbanks and eroded hills of home.

In the early dark, the sagebrush flat above the Judith is still tortured by the wind, which has changed direction. Out of the west now, it attacks the snow-drifts, drives them back, whips the tips of grasses and sets the brush along the coulees to thrashing from the roots. A chinook wind, just as the stationmaster predicted, warming the prairie from thirty degrees below zero to forty degrees above zero in less than an hour. The frozen ruts between the two lines of fence will be mud by morning, but for now the old tires bounce along, following the headlights past the gleam in the window of old Pete Husted's cabin, through a wire gate and across the sagebrush, heading for another distant yellow square of light. Imogene bounces with the tires, into the ruts and out again as Jack drives. What she can see in the headlights has the distortion of the well-known after long absence. The last fence corner, the bare shadow of the box elder tree. She can hardly wait.

Jack pulls up at the fence around the log house, turns off the headlights and kills his motor. Gets out and lifts Imogene's suitcase out of the back of the pickup while she struggles the long step down to find her footing in the dark. Lamplight beckons from the kitchen window as she gropes her way, and then the door is opening, a flood of warmth, and Doris cheering at her arrival.

Mary crowds past her mother—"Auntie! Auntie!"

"Brought your big fat auntie for Christmas!" agrees Jack, following with her suitcase.

Imogene giggles at his remark—she always giggles, even when it stings—and scoops up Mary. Holds the little girl's warm, squirming body close.

"So did you have a good trip?"

"Pretty good. Lots of sailors on the train. I caught an awful cold, though. No, don't kiss me, honeybunch, you don't want to catch it. Oh! Everybody's here! Ma—Pa—"

Her mother looks tired as she stands to greet Imogene, her father rumpled and a little unfocused. Nobody hugs, except for the children, it's not that kind of family. Somebody like Daisy, Imogene thinks with a touch of contempt, might think they were a little chilly. But it's not chilly at all, it's a kind of dignity, and she's relieved to be back inside its familiar boundaries. Home at last. Or at least as close to a home as she's got, now, her mother's home or her younger sister's home. *I'm a homeless rat,* she'll write in her diary.

Her old envy of her sister stirs. What Doris has. Her log house here on the

Judith river, her kitchen with its splintered floor and coal stove and a sink with a pump. Her cowboy husband, her two little girls.

Betty, wakened from her nap, toddles like a mouse from the shadow of the table and Imogene reaches for her, but Betty will have none of her. Betty is her mommy's girl. She wraps her arms around Doris and hides her face.

Doris stoops and picks up her baby, arm cast and all. Lets her nestle. What a heart-stopping moment it had been, the high chair rocking, crashing over, the baby spilled on this awful old floor—Doris had been more concerned at the time with the bump on Betty's head, only noticed the swelling on the little forearm after she had calmed her and calmed herself. Greenstick fracture, the doctor had said. Remembering, Doris pats her baby. Feels her breath on her neck, the tickle of straight wispy hair. Doris knows that her sister loves the little girls—and just look at Mary, making over her—but her sister can't possibly know the moment when breathing stops and time seems to make up its mind; will the high chair fall, will the baby hang suspended for all eternity, will the baby hit the floor, will the baby live?

Imogene may be their own mother's favorite, thinks Doris, but she's the one who has given her these grandchildren.

Fifty years later, Betty will read Imogene's diaries and exclaim, "I had no idea she was so sensitive about her weight! Do you remember how our dad used to call her our big fat auntie? How dreadful that must have made her feel!"

Yes, a late Christmas dinner in 1943, but a happy one, whatever the family tensions. Nearly everybody gathers around Doris's table for the turkey and the trimmings and the suet pudding that follows; only the oldest sister, Sylva, and her husband couldn't make it home for this holiday. Nobody here seems particularly concerned about the war, except for its inconveniences. They can afford to be detached, after all, here in sheltered Montana. Dave has been deferred from the draft as a civilian construction worker, and, as a rancher in a crucial food-producing occupation, my father's draft number will never be very high, although most of his cousins serve in the Pacific, including the invasion of New Guinea, just a few days before this Christmas dinner. But for Christmas of 1943, life in Montana seems in stasis. It's Imogene who is changing, Imogene who is drawing away into another life in faraway Tenino.

> *December 26: Sun. We went down & looked at the cattle. A nice outing—lovely sunny weather. I can't believe it is so nice. Betty does not make up quickly.*

> *December 28: Sewed on Betty's dress & knitted & visited Ma. Pa is more forgetful every day. Ma was provoked because Doris didn't curl Betty's hair.*

> *December 29: Wed. This P.M. we went up & visited Mrs. Holt. I told Ma I never did think Bernita was in love & I bet she never marries Jake.*

> *December 31: Fri. Went to town—got nothing done. Betty surely fought having her cast off. The Dr. [Solterro, who operated on her foot after her accident with the mowing machine] was glad to show my foot to his son.*

It's the first mention of her foot in a long, long time, because in spite of all expectations it has healed completely. All her life she will laugh at Dr. Solterro's pride in showing off his reconstructive surgery to his son, just as she will wear the deep scar, like a bracelet, around her ankle for the rest of her life. But for now, it's her last evening at home, and she'll spend it with her family, from whom she continues to draw emotional support.

13

/ / /

January 1, 1944: Left the Falls at 7:15. Train a little late—more crowded after Shelby. What a way to spend New Year.

January 3: First day of school in 1944. Gee, I just slogged thru. Think Fox is going to try to get me to send kids to the remedial room. Nuts.

Back at school again, Imogene settles into her routine. She sounds like a more contented woman—she's had her Christmas vacation in Montana, which has given her a lift, she's got her schoolroom organized by now, and she's making a wide circle of new friends. She isn't worried about her foot giving way under her, and she's pretty sure her job is secure. Also, she's beginning to like teaching. Knows the ropes, knows what she's doing, doesn't let the kids get under her skin. Enjoys them, even. Her diary entries for the coming months will note dinners, wedding showers (another sign of wartime, lots of wedding showers), parties, meetings, gossip—and far fewer complaints.

There's a life to be created here in Tenino, if she can just figure out what it is.

January 6: PTA executive meeting. Kind of fun. I'm six rows behind on my knitting. Ma sent my overshoes [probably forgotten during her Christmas trip home]. June brot me some real good U.S. stamps.

January 8: Got my hair done. Ran up to Schafer's & got Jamaca Inn to read. Emersons were there. Nice to see them. Letter from Mother. She said nice weather yet.

January 9: Went to church. Thot I'd catch up with my odd jobs but got so interested in Jamaica Inn I didn't even get letters written except to Ma.

January 12: Worked a long time after school. Got 4th grades done & 3 sheets of arith & my new skedule figured out. Are the kids ever wild and wooly.

January 17: Got a book, Chuckling Fingers from the library and read all evening. So tomorrow I must do my reports & such. My sewing machine should soon be here.

January 18: Did my report cards—and semester grades. Read a mag. story & finished Chuckling Fingers. A good mystery. Got no knitting done.

January 22: Such a lovely Sat. I got my house clean, my washing done— went to the library. Got Whispering Cup & Kings Row. Didn't do all my knitting.

January 23: Schafers had me up to dinner. Had a nice time. Got lots of knitting done. But little else. Started Kings Row. It's a long book—2 weeks on it.

Knitting, knitting, knitting. This constant tallying of the trivial creates what Jennifer Sinor calls "a site of safety," the ordinary sphere in which "nothing is produced. Nothing is made to rest in the public. Nothing is erected. Nothing gets created. The note left on the counter is thrown away, the answering machine messages are erased, gas is used to drive to the grocery store, and dinner is eaten in the space of fifteen minutes. Unlike extraordinary works— say, for example, art or philosophy—which testify to being in the world, which transcend the ordinary and the mundane, the ordinary is marked by consumption. We eat, we wear, we toss, we clean, and we use the mundane that surrounds us. We save, we frame, we preserve, and we honor the nonordinary in our lives. . . . Progress is measured by acts and action. . . . Things [in the ordinary sphere] can only be consumed."

And yet for Imogene, knitting marks progress. She may be "just slogging through" the fourth-grade curriculum, the kids may be "wild and wooly" after the Christmas holidays, but at least she can measure her knitting and see that she's got somewhere.

Got somewhere. Where? Imogene has been imbued with the self-discipline that requires a schedule, an implicit timeline, the taking for granted that life requires a narrative. One moment follows another and one stitch follows another in an assurance that she's not wasting time. As to the narrative she's creating, her language provides a clue. *Gee. Nuts. Nerts. Crimeny. Hotcha. Hot Dog.* In the secret life of her diary, Imogene's just a little jazzy. Free to be dismissive. Congratulatory of herself in her small triumphs. A young woman (she's still only thirty-four) who doesn't have to be told what she should like or dislike, who can sort out the fools from the faithful for herself.

You can do it, she's telling herself. You *are* doing it. You're going to be okay. You are okay.

January 25: Home late—cold better—had quite a round over some gym shoes. Did lots of correcting and dittoing. Gee, some are lazy.

January 26: Went to the Dr. tonight & had my throat worked over. We joined a Med. before Christmas. Three of my 3rd graders are so lazy. I swear I'll work their pants off.

Medical insurance! What a concept! This will be the first time in her life that she has not had to pay for every cent of her medical care. It took her years to pay the doctor's bill and the hospital's bill for her wounded foot.

January 28: Had a movie for the kids. I felt awful. Just droop around with my cold. Am going to get a new pupil Monday. He is an attractive looking child—but a problem.

January 30: We went to work on a Girls Choir. Hope we can put it thru.

January 31: Went to Mrs. Mosers & I guess we got the ball rolling for the choir. I sure put in a day at school. New boy was nice. Mr. Knight was down to borrow my typewriter.

February 2: Cecelia seems to have told her mother I hit her. Told the nurse I have never touched her. Seems we may have a new nurse. Most of us won't be sorry.

February 4: Hot dog, my [sewing] machine came at last [shipped by my father, from Montana].

February 5: Got my machine uncrated. Cut out a dress but can't sew by lamplight without marking the pieces. Got to one shoulder on my sweater.

February 6: Got to tired at school again today. Couldn't work this evening. Hope the shower for Miss Morgan is after school Wed. so I'll have my evening.

February 7: Got my hair done & little else. Besides PTA there are 2 showers coming up. Got quite a bit done in school today. Had kids help correct papers.

February 8: Sure did a lot of gossiping. The party seemed to be a success. But, gee the teachers are catty. Perhaps they don't mean it.

February 10: PTA. Small crowd—interesting meeting. Many of the teachers were not there. Gave my boys quite a lecture & licked two before I got thru.

According to her former students, in later years Imogene kept a size 13 tennis shoe in her desk drawer to threaten unruly pupils. A joke developed: She used to throw the shoe at us!

No, I didn't! I never threw shoes!

Oh, she did, she did!

February 11: Fri—at last. Finally got our Valentine box done. This evening I just lay around & exulted because it was Friday. How fast time goes. They are having bad dust storms at home.

February 15: Saw Mrs. Mathews about Bluebirds. Hope she takes the leadership. Went to a teachers meeting. Mr. Fox seemed a little out of sorts.

February 16: Called on Mrs. Hull to see if I can interest her in Bluebirds. I'll be glad when I can relax over that.

February 17: Still looking for a Bluebird leader. Mrs. Hobart will be one. Mr. Schafer helped me start my car.

February 22, 1944: Cut out my seersucker and got the skirt basted and the sleeves made. What a life. No girls leaders at all.

February 23: Had our organization meeting. 12 girls signed for Campfire & 10 for Bluebirds. But no leaders. So I took the Bluebirds.

February 24: Went to Mrs. Kykans about the Bluebirds. She had a BB book for me. I can start now. She told me of some old PTA funds.

February 25: Good letter from Mother. Got Mrs. Russel to be Camp Fire leader. Talked to Bob Austin about Cubs. He wants them on the PTA program.

February 29: Heh, seems like I ought to ketch me a man this year. Hope the Bluebird get off to a flying start tomorrow. Got some art patterns tonight.

Instead of grousing for having the Bluebirds foisted on her, Imogene quite seems to look forward to her troop of ten little girls. In the coming months, her diary entries will note the activities she plans for them, the hikes, the little treats. It's evidence of her gradual acceptance of her professional life, her pleasure in her community activity and her friends. But what about the "ketch me a man" remark? Has she met someone? Later she will hint, in the subtlest way, that she's interested in a man. But by now she's so chary that she won't even confide in her diary.

Elizabeth Hampsten observes that the midwestern women whose private writing she studied depended upon other women for emotional sustenance. It was men, however, Hampsten notes, who made the critical decisions in these women's lives. "Women's history," she says, "in this traditional and admittedly oversimplified view, is a history of following directions from men." Is this also true of Imogene?

She certainly draws upon other women for emotional support, especially after moving to Washington State and away from her family. She's constantly being invited to dinner, or inviting to dinner, or going to talk with one of the other women teachers. Even Daisy Lincoln, for all that she annoys Imogene, is an important constant. But what does Imogene say about men, who are apt, as Hampsten points out, to be "fathers, brothers, husbands, sons . . . employers . . . clergymen, doctors, and commercial entrepreneurs"?

Hampsten's point is well illustrated in those earlier diary entries, written while Imogene was teaching at the Warm Spring Creek school in Montana, in which she expresses her concern about school board members. The board had hired her, and could fire her, and could make large differences in her life, depending on their willingness to support her if parents complained about her teaching or her discipline, or even, God knows, her cooking hot lunches or taking the children swimming. From her point of view, the board members were given to unpredictable behavior and were only too likely to make their decisions on the basis of rumor or whim.

Once she gets to Napavine, and later to Tenino, she's less directly affected by a (male) school board, but reports instead to a (male) principal and school superintendent. She admires Marvin Shafer, who gave her the chance to move to Tenino when he himself changed jobs; she looks forward to visiting with him, and socializes with him and his wife. About Mr. Fox, the elementary school principal in Tenino, she's less forthcoming. She keeps a weather eye on him— *Mr. Fox seemed out of sorts tonight*—but she doesn't worry overly much about him or see him as a serious threat to her security.

Who are the other men in her life whose decisions affect her?

She's grateful to Dr. Solterro in Lewistown, Montana, for saving her foot, and she's amused at his pride when he shows her off, or shows off her foot, at least, to his son who is joining his practice. But she shows no sign of hero worship or a crush on Dr. Solterro, and in fact complains about the length of her hospital stay.

Clergymen? She must have gotten acquainted with a few men of the cloth during her church-going, but she hardly mentions them.

Her father? Nobody pays attention to any advice of his, least of all Imogene. And she's seen little of her brother since the war started.

The men who matter the most to her are her sisters' husbands, Ervin and Jack, and it's interesting that she trusts them, feels at ease with them and welcome in their homes, and yet keeps an emotional distance from them. She does not, for example, always turn to Jack or Ervin for advice or follow the advice they volunteer, and she hides her feelings from them letting them tease her about her weight, for instance.

The other spinster in our family was my great-aunt Mable. Like Imogene, Mable was a teacher. But Mable, a generation older than Imogene, led a much more circumscribed life than Imogene ever did. As the last daughter living at home with her widowed father, it fell to Mable to keep house for him and, on occasion, drag him out of saloons. After he died, she boarded with the Short family in Sioux City, Iowa, until she retired from teaching. She became very attached to Mr. Short, who was a socialist clergyman. He gave her radical reading material and changed her political views. In her old age, living with my grandmother (she never lived in a home of her own, never, not even her own apartment), she clung to her socialist views in spite of her Republican family. She was the only one of her brothers and sisters who voted for John F. Kennedy in 1960, and they called him "Mable's president" ever after.

Mable retained her childishness all her life, in the best sense. Visiting our lonely ranch when I was six or seven, she went out to the woodpile and hammered together a pair of stilts out of lumber she found there, then taught me to walk on them. She loped beside me, ready to catch me if I wobbled and fell on the ruts of the dirt road, and I remember feeling charged with my height, with my sudden elevation, and being so amazed at the old lady's sense of fun that I kept glancing over to reaffirm that, yes, she really was white-haired. Years later I was amazed all over again when she dropped down to the floor, limber as a girl, and sat cross-legged to play board games with my children.

Even making allowances for the difference in the times they grew up, when I compare Imogene's life with Mable's, I'm struck by Imogene's adventurousness and her determination to be her own woman. In part, of course, Imogene has been molded by her family's struggle for survival on the Montana homestead frontier, which, if it did nothing else, certainly developed staying power. Also she has the role model of her mother before her; my grandmother, along with her edicts about beauty being only skin deep and praise to the face being open disgrace, also taught her daughters how to turn their hands to whatever work was to be done, how to shoulder whatever loads fell upn them, how to continue. Finally, Imogene has the opportunities created by wartime, as women flock into jobs previously closed to them.

But about this new romantic interest, if indeed she has one, she's secretive even in her diary.

March 1: Well, guess the Bluebirds did O.K. Had 12 out. We are going to make clothes pin dolls. Hope that holds them awhile.

March 7: Got my hair done—home late—worked on my accounts—chinned with Alberta. Maybe I should take the 3rd grade next year.

March 8: Found out how Jack Austin got his black eye. Keith gave it to him. Had Bluebirds.

March 10: Ran up to see Helise [Knight, a friend Imogene has made in Tenino, who has moved with her husband to Fort Lewis]. It was not hard to find at all. This housing project is better than some I've seen. Went to a keen show.

March 11: We [Imogene and Helise] talked of love & sex & our relations & other people. She has lived a full life—& nothing has soured her.

March 14: How the kids adore the paper drive. I'm reading a book "Cow by the Tail." It's a good one of early days. If one does not buy pork, ones meat choice is small.

March 15: Took the Bluebirds on a hike. They talked me into it. Must not be stampeded again. Finished my book. Got nothing else done.

March 17: Friday. June brot me a shamrock to wear. Had to go to a show. Come home early. Didn't do a thing after I got here. Hope to get control this weekend.

March 18: Have 9 gal. of gas I can't get in my car. Have a notion to see if I can drain some in a can. Got a library book. Cleaned house. Next week I want to go to town.

March 21: Nurse was out late tonight—they may close school for 2 weeks—how I hope—what a vacation—I could get caught up with everything.

One of the school children has been diagnosed with scarlet fever, and the nurse fears an epidemic.

March 22: Nerts—a nurse checked the kids & sent 4 home for a week. I sure could use a vacation. It rained horrid. Bluebirds had to play inside.

March 23: Hot dog! School out till April 3. Ten whole days of vacation. Isn't it wonderful.

Apparently the nurse found more cases of scarlet fever and changed her mind. Indeed, a local history of Tenino notes that the schools were closed from March 23 to April 3 to help prevent a scarlet fever epidemic. Imogene doesn't seem particularly concerned with health issues, however. For her, the epidemic means a good rest from her classroom.

March 28: Mr. S [chafer] was around with warrents. We were hired back with a $100 raise. He told me Daisy was leaving so I spread that fast to Bunny & Helen.

March 29: Decided after I got my seams sewed on my green skirt to run up to Sylva's. Have the urge to talk to her.

March 30: Finished the little pinafores. Hope the girls like them. Am making good progress on my knitting too.

March 31: Fri. Finished the hem in my seersucker. Sylva & Ervin take great pleasure in their yard, especially this time of year.

April 1: Already have the urge to go back to my own shanty. Guess Sylva & I will go home in June by train.

Imogene's talk with Sylva likely had to do with their father's worsening mental state. They both continue to get worrisome letters from Montana, and neither of them knows what to do.

April 3: Gosh, the kids were lazy [after their scarlet fever interlude]. Had 7 out. Went to church this evening, I've sure a long list of things to do.

April 5: Enjoyed my 3–4 boys PE class tonight. Had the Bluebirds club. Mailed the kids [Mary and Betty] Easter pinafores. They were cute, if I do say it.

An enlarged snapshot shows me astride a rusted tricycle, with my little sister leaning against my knee, both of us posed against a background of alkali and sagebrush in our new Easter pinafores that Auntie finished for us on March 30, 1944, and found time to put in the mail a week later. The pinafores really were cute, and so were the little girls, with their hair in big loopy curls to please their grandmother, who thought straight hair was ugly, and their aunt, who had sent the pinafores.

April 7: Took the 3–4 grade boys for a hike in the woods for flowers. What a good time they had. Went to Mrs. Cornwell's get together. Her kids behaved.

April 10: Had a keen baseball game. Did Bunny, Helen & I ever chew over Daisy again. I'll always dislike her but she doesn't bother me like she does Bunny.

April 11: After school tonight we really chewed the fat over Daisy. I asked Mr. S. if there was any chance of her being principal. He said no.

April 12: Mrs. S had 32 out to Bluebirds. Guess we must find an extra leader. Mr. Fox wanted me to take the gym tonight but I couldn't on account of the girls. He felt tough.

April 18: Mr. Schafer was up with other contracts. Gave us another $60 raise. Got my hair done—my last sleeve started. Got my first lessons.

April 21: Had a letter from Ma about a stunt Pa pulled making trouble & worry for everyone. He told she was sick & had Turner out to see her.

A. P. seems bound and determined to make trouble for his wife. For years he's allowed himself to be shunted aside, treated at best like a troublesome child—"A.P. was a dear old man . . . [He] was telling me a story," wrote Florence about a visit to Dave's parents. "I was so shocked when Dave's mother said, 'Hush Pom' & he never said another thing while we were there"—and maybe his anger has been festering, or maybe it's just a random symptom of dementia. But in April of 1944 his family still seems to believe that he could pull himself together, if he just would.

April 22: It was a beautiful day so I monkeyed around instead of sewing or writing. Got a new mag. So killed time instead of working.

April 25: Operetta practice horrible. I did a bunch of master copies in arithmetic. Don't see how I can finish. Put in a good evening on my writing.

April 28: The H.S. decorated for the dance and successfully broke up our operetta practice.

May 2: Got a little sewing done—a little writing. Mrs. Thomas said wasn't it too bad Dorothy wasn't coming back. I said we'll get on beautifully without her.

May 3: A hot day. In practice I paddled about 6 kids. Poor things. I feel for them. Teachers meeting. Laid a trap to catch kids stealing money.

May 10: Took the Bluebirds on a hike. We crossed a creek on a log, and a fence on another, got in nettles, chased a snake, caught a frog.

Lucky Bluebirds, to have Imogene to chase snakes and catch frogs with! My sister Betty and I envied her pupils who had her for most of the year, welcomed her during her summer visits with the eagerness of two little girls growing up on an isolated ranch. Auntie could be counted upon to play with us, teach us new songs, and read the stories that our work-exhausted parents had no time for. She would hike with us into the slough and tell us about tadpoles, she would pull on a pair of blue jeans and go horseback riding with us, me on one of the ponies and my timid little sister in front of her in the saddle.

On one of our rides, as we followed a wagon road around the base of a shale bluff, the pony shied and threw me off. Getting thrown happened to me often enough that I should have been used to it. But with Auntie on hand to offer sympathy, I groaned and carried on and pretended I'd hurt my ankle and couldn't walk. She had to climb off her horse and lead Betty and carry me, while the pony ran off somewhere—"There I was," she said later, "with one kid acting half-killed and the other cheering, 'Yay! Yay! Sissy got bucked off!'"

My mother always said, darkly, that it was a good thing Imogene never had children of her own, because she would have spoiled them rotten. She must have been considerably less gullible with her schoolchildren, however, because she regularly notes her disciplinary measures—that she "paddled about 6 kids" or "licked four." It had been a long time since, as a teen-aged teacher, she played hares and hounds all afternoon with her pupils.

May 13: Letters from both Florence & Dave. Always makes me lonesome. Doris & Jack on a ranch deal. I wonder if Mother won't stop teaching & move to town.

My mother has written that she and my father are negotiating to buy the home ranch, which had belonged to my great-grandfather and which, after his death, is being sold through closed bids. It's an exciting time for my parents, with the prospect of leaving their sagebrush and alkali for the better grass and pasture and sweet creek water of the home place, but it must also have roused all Imogene's feelings of envy: if only she had married a rancher, she too might have walked among her own hills and planted her own gardens.

May 16: Gave the tests today. Two of mine were not there. Not bad. They are doing better than last years class. I ate out. Curses—that picnic tomorrow.

May 17: Went on the picnic. Guess the kids had a good time. Finished my reports. Quite satisfied with my test grades.

May 18: Had a lovely pot luck dinner with a group of ladies. Also ex. com [PTA executive committee] meeting tonight. Now exactly 10 days of school left.

May 19: Got my 4th spelling done. Am ready to tie into my final reports. Letters from Pa & Ma. If I don't get my gas tickets it's going to be bad.

May 23: Gee, next year's class is going to be a lulu. How wonderful to have half that know how to read. I'm really looking forward to it.

June 2: At long last. I'm never really happy the last day of school. Got my car serviced & my kitten. Mary Cramer stopped for just a minute—she's blue.

June 3: Went to Chelhalis, paid all my bills. Bought books for the kids [Mary and Betty].

June 4: Went to Sunday School & church because R. was there. Nuts. Where am I going. So lonely. Visited Schafers but the kids were going to a show.

Who is R? Is he the romantic interest she hinted so gently about, back in February? In none of her entries does she remotely suggest that she's had dinner with a man, seen a movie with a man—so either she's censoring her own most private writing, or else the romance is mostly in her imagination.

Could R be a woman?

"Could she have been a lesbian?" one of my daughters once asked me, and the term seemed so distant from Imogene's context, so much a part of our own glib generation, that I could hardly begin to answer. How would Imogene have referred to a woman who loved other women? Would she have spoken, as Radclyffe Hall did in the book the dean of students at Western Montana College told Imogene not to read, of "the love that dared not speak its name?"

Marriage preoccupies Imogene. Although the fiction writer might spin a story in which her cultural background and her naivete are what keep her from admitting that she really wants a woman partner, what Imogene says over and over again is that she wants a husband. Meanwhile I, the nonfiction writer—I! Mary! who has had two husbands—I wonder if she knew what she was wishing for. If living with Daisy Lincoln drove her half-crazy with day-to-day irritations, what did she think living with a husband would be like? Did she get her idea of marriage from the romantic novels she had been reading, like *Jamaica Inn?* Marriage as a blissful happy-ever-after that begins on the last page? If so, she couldn't have been paying much attention to her parents' marriage.

No, I think that if she's a lesbian, it's in Adrienne Rich's definition of any woman who derives her primary emotional satisfaction from other women, and that that has more to do with her rigid upbringing and her insecurity about her looks than about her sexual preference.

I think R is a man. Whoever he is.

Meanwhile, unsuspecting of great events in the making on the other side of the world, the two sisters, Sylva and Imogene, load their luggage and their presents for the family in Montana into Imogene's car and set off. They're preoccupied with family worries. But somewhere, whether at a gas station or a lunch counter, they hear the news over a radio:

June 6: D-Day——invasion——we got in on the middle of a broadcast.

14

/ / /

June 7: Ate supper in Missoula, went thru several splashing showers, got to Helena while it was still light, got a good cabin for $2.

June 8: Curses! A flat tire. Was I mad. Didn't get off till 1:30 but got home before 8:00. In Denton the gas station man looked at me with suspicion.

After all, she's been away for years, and she's driving a car with Washington State plates. In the eyes of the gas station man in Denton, Montana, she's a foreigner.

In her seventies, as part of her creative writing class, Imogene wrote a story about driving through Montana with her little dog, stopping for coffee, and being regaled by jackalope and sidehill-winder stories, which rural westerners like to use to draw the line between themselves and outsiders. "Don't try to feed me that line," Imogene wrote in her story, cherishing her secret insider status, and fed the local gang a line of her own.

Imogene's detailing of geographical space seems to me a departure from the ways that many nineteenth-century women denoted space in their diaries. Jennifer Sinor points out that, at the same time her several-times-great-aunt was "documenting dailiness," in 1881, her itinerant blacksmith husband was tracking his travels throughout the west by noting how many miles he covered in a day and how much he earned. Imogene, in the freedom of her car (for all the headaches of dead batteries, stuck windows, rationed gasoline, flat tires), measures how far she has traveled, how much she has had to pay for accommodations, where she makes connections (if she's traveling by train), what the conditions for driving have been like—and by these references we can measure how far she's traveled in independence from the prairie women of Elizabeth Hampsten's study, who kept their focus close and indoors in order to shut out the unimaginable.

June 10: We went to town [from the homestead], it was quite muddy in Denton. We picked chickens & got ready for the big day tomorrow.

June 11: Florence & all of Doris' came. We had a nice day. The kids were sweet & went for the kitten in a big way. Sylva left with Florence. She'll go home in 2 days.

June 13: Doris & Jack were riding after cattle & stopped for lunch. Ma & I walked out & got some flowers. I did quite an ironing while she baked ham.

June 15: Ma & I hit out to scout around for schools. Went to Geyser [a small community about fifty miles from Denton. Coffee Creek [only a few miles from Denton] sounds good. Wish she'd get that. But Pa is such a problem.

June 17: Rain, rain & cold. I feel like I was caged—to cold to type—I can't really talk to Ma & Pa—just listen to their reminiscences.

That two-room house on the prairie north of Denton, with its attic bedroom, the bedroom her mother still thinks of as Imogene's, is no longer home, but a cage. Its frame is constricting now, its space cold, and Imogene experiences a new kind of loneliness. She has indeed walked a long way from her parents' ways, and she hasn't found a way to speak over that distance. On this day of pouring rain, she'd probably welcome even a conversation with Daisy Lincoln.

June 18: Still cloudy. Butchered a chicken. We ate it for dinner. Ma & I walked a long way. It looked like rain so I told her I would go down to see Doris.

June 20: Played with the kids & sorted out my attic stuff. Books are in fair condition a shame to have left them there. I'm a homeless rat.

June 22: I went to Lewistown & Ma took her exam [to renew her teaching certificate]. I tended to a few little things. Met Jack, Doris on the way home.

June 23: Ma has not been well today. Her trip to town & the exam was pretty tough on her. I can't help but worry & Pa is no help to her at all.

June 24: Ma still isn't so well. After dinner I went down to Jack's—got the cows on the way.

June 26: Doris hoped to wash, so rainy she just couldn't. I helped her clean house. Poor kids can't play outdoors when it is as sloppy as this.

June 29: We went to Denton, found Ma did not get Coffee Creek [school], tried Arrow Creek—unsuccessful. Disappointed. I rode out to see the cattle. Saw a coyote.

July 4: Ma had peas, new potatoes & fried chicken. A very quiet 4th but I don't know when I'll spend it with the folks again.

July 7: Took Ma to Buffalo & Straw & believe she may get a job. Rough roads. Saw Anna Micock & others. Got a headache. Bought a dictionary & more crochet cotton.

Straw is a forgotten community today, nothing more than a name along the railroad tracks, blowing grass and a few deserted buildings, but in 1944 it had a post office and grain elevators besides its teacherage and school. My grandmother did get the Straw school that fall, and she and my grandfather moved the fifty miles south to live in the teacherage. By that time, my grandmother had been teaching continuously since 1922, never more than two years in the same school, and now she was well into her sixties and old enough to retire, if only she weren't so worried about A. P. and how she was going to pay his bills.

The polio epidemic was frightening the countryside during the summer and fall of 1944. All over America, swimming pools were being closed and children kept away from movie theaters and crowds, and still the dreadful illness crept even into remote Montana. My parents were planning a rare Sunday away from the ranch to visit my grandparents in Straw, when a postcard came from my grandmother. Don't bring the kids over here, she wrote. A little girl in Straw has polio.

I cried with disappointment. I loved my grandmother, who would tell me stories and answer my questions with endless patience, unlike my harassed mother—"I don't know! I don't know! Don't cross-examine me!" she would scream, at her wit's end—and I didn't understand the threat of polio at all, until a few years later, at the county fair, I saw a woman in an iron lung who was being carted around the country on public display, and her paralysis and the muted roar of the contraption told me why we had not gone to Straw.

This summer I drove past the turn-off to Straw on my way out of Montana and saw the remains of the community, the tattered grain elevator under the shadows of clouds, and the few silvered shacks surrounded by wheat fields and looking so benign and empty of the emotions that had filled it for a few days during the last months of World War II. Straw was where my grandfather had the breakdown that was the beginning of an end for him and my grandmother, where he ran capering across those wheat fields by moonlight, crying back at her, "You can't catch me!" and she chased him for a while and then walked over to the depot and woke the stationmaster to use his telephone to call my Uncle Theo and ask him to saddle a horse and ride across the river to get a message to my parents, that they must get up and get dressed in the middle of the night and come to Straw, that she needed them.

For me, a name—Straw—a glimpse of emptiness—and then the ghosts waken, warning me to be silent even as they clamor to be heard. There's no pleasing the ghosts, that's one sure truth for the nonfiction writer.

July 9: We ironed. I dressed a chicken. It has been rainy, cloudy, windy, cold. I rode down to Jack's in the evening.

July 10: I rode herd on the kids. They were hoping I'd come. First time this summer I've been up river.

The first time, in other words, that she's been to the new ranch since my parents bought it. For Doris and Jack, this summer must be a frantically busy time, what with trying to keep up with the work on the lower ranch and still get the haying done on the new meadows. All the rain that Imogene reports is delaying the haying—they'll still be stacking the last of it in August—but she pitches in, helping wherever she can. From the following entries it is clear that she and my mother worked almost every day in the hayfields, along with the usual cooking and cleaning, clothes-washing and child care. I wasn't five years old yet, and my sister was a year and a half, and my mother must have been grateful for Imogene's help. *How tired Doris looked tonight,* Imogene will note several times this summer.

July 13: We put in half a day putting up hay.

July 14: Jack went for a stacker. Took all day. Doris & I explored & picked berries & rhubarb.

July 15: They worked all morning on the stacker. We got in a good whack at the hay in the afternoon.

July 17: We finished stacking the field & moved the stacker after dinner. What a trip. Willow brush 10 feet high. Crossed Spring Creek & Little Jud[ith river, which ran through the new ranch and met to flow into the Big Judith river].

July 22: Sat. The rope [on the hay-stacker] snapped some tools into the air. Cut Jack's chin. Doris & I took him to the Dr. Had stitches.

Another early memory of mine: one of those ranch accidents happens out of the blue. No warning. One minute all is going well, the next minute the sudden snap of rope, the flash of metal, and my father's bleeding face. My mother and Imogene probably packed the gash as best they could, loaded him into the old pickup, and headed for Lewistown as fast as they dared on wartime tires, with my father fuming because he wasn't driving, probably swearing he was okay, no need for such a fuss. For Imogene, the episode must have brought back memories of her own haying accident, two summers ago, and how lucky she had been, not to be crippled for life. How lucky my father had been, to have escaped another of the dangers all ranchers lived with, never spoke of, made the best of. Lucky not to have been blinded. Or killed.

July 23: Sun. Doris went for Jack. We hayed in the P.M. Got a nice stack started but cleared such a small patch of ground.

July 25: Doris hayed today. She wanted Jack to lay off & get Ma to come & care for the kids but Jack wouldn't lay off.

Of course not. He wouldn't lay off, he still had hay down, and already it was late July.

July 28: Fri. Jack's chin is healing fine. Tomorrow he hopes to get the bandage off. So glad it was no worse. It could have been really bad.

At last, she can risk thinking about what might have been. Jack blinded, Jack dead. So glad, she allows herself to say, so glad it was no worse.

July 29: Kept the kids. Pete [Husted, a neighbor] went by & said Pa had sent him two letters in one day. Wanted $100 for the use of team & Pete hadn't gotten them.

Another bad omen. Imogene can't read the future, I'm the only one who knows that within the coming year A. P. will caper in the moonlight out at Straw. But she's worried; she's expecting a jolt, like the flash of the mowing machine sickle or the wire singing into my father's face, and the demon of bad luck sneering at them, there, take that! Don't ever think you'll get out of this world unscarred!

Oh, yes, the reason for that old stricture of silence was survival. To speak of danger was to acknowledge it, and just as my mother and Imogene kept their worst fears to themselves when my father's chin was gashed, so also the deterioration of A. P. is discussed in fragments and undertones. They can't ward off the bad-luck demon, but they can word-starve him enough to live with him.

Curious, given this dread of words, that Imogene wants to be a writer. Or maybe not so curious. To fear the power of words, to covet the power of words—are these impulses really so different?

July 30: We went to hay. Ate at Theo Jr. Rebie's were down—Bob home— looking fine. Got soaked in a shower. Harry S[tevens] has a lame back— can't work on horses.

From the sounds of this passage, my parents are still living on the lower ranch, in the sagebrush, but driving upriver to get their hay in. Uncle Theo, of course, has been living upriver all along, and he and Aunt Thelma have invited everyone to a Sunday dinner, including Uncle Joe and Aunt Rebie, who live in Great Falls, and their oldest son Bob, who is home on furlough from the air force.

Harry Stevens was known all over the countryside as the Horse Doctor. In his youth he had apprenticed at a racetrack, and eventually he extended his practical knowledge to doctoring all animals. By 1944 he was in ill health, although he continued some of his quasi-veterinarian practice, and I remember him as an elderly man in shirtsleeves and braces and a fedora, helping my grandmother to caponize chickens. In a few years he would be dead, and real veterinarians with real college degrees would set up their practices, but the real veterinarians would lack Harry's aura. Harry was uncanny. He might be able to probe deep enough into his illogic to cure a sick workhorse and he might not, and nobody would ever know why.

July 31: Jack went after barley with Ma's team. Pa didn't know them. I told her. She was quite bothered. It is a shame to feel to a father like I do.

It's safer, of course, for Imogene to feel anger toward her father than to recognize what is happening to his mind. She doesn't want to ask what will happen when he no longer can be left alone while her mother goes out to teach in her remote schools. Will she or one of her sisters be asked to care for him? How can she manage, and still work to support herself?

August 6: Sunday. Took another swing at the hay. Have about one day's work left I hope. Time is going & there's things I want to do & the [Fergus County] fair coming up.

August 7: I'm taking care of the kids today while the rest go to town. Have only 3 weeks left & are they full. I don't feel like I've had any vacation.

Understandable—she's been helping with haying all summer, and it still isn't all stacked.

August 9: Took off for the fair—didn't have as much time as we'd like to see things. Mary got so tired. We wanted her to see so much.

August 10: Joe got home last night—we got off late—nearly 11:00. Fan belt broke 8 mi. from Stanford but had a good wind & got a belt there.

Joe, another of my father's cousins, is home on furlough from the navy. By the summer of 1944, everyone is pretty sure that we're not going to lose this war, after all, and that someday it will end, and all the boys will come home, and life will get back to normal.

August 12: We went to finish haying. Hoped to brand the colts but Harry didn't come. Doris stayed at home. Mary doesn't feel too good.

August 13: Took Mary to the Dr. & she has impetigo. Took her to the circus. Not a bad show. It rained & going down the bottom we had to put on chains.

August 15: Rode home today. We had a time catching the horses. Jack oiled my saddle. Hope I can get $20 for it. I'll let it go if I can.

August 16: Cold—cloudy. I wrote my letters & counted the jobs I have to do & sort of planned.

August 17: Took Ma to Denton. Had car trouble at Brooks. Took all P.M. to get it fixed. Got new shoes & 2 new dresses. Got to Florence's about 6:30.

August 19: Florence told me if nothing happened to their crop they would clear out on the place. I was so glad to hear that. Kristie Lee is so sweet.

Dave and Florence have saved all the money he earned from his wartime construction work to buy a small wheat and sheep ranch in Judith Basin County, about thirty miles from my parents' ranch. For Imogene, raised on a homestead, expecting a lifetime of ranch work as normal, it must seem as though her brother and her sister are getting on with their lives while she marks time with hers.

August 20: Left 3:30. Stopped at Vaneks—nice supper—they didn't buy my saddle—but I hope to get more at a sale than I like to ask.

August 21: Mon. Had a flat & a tire ready to blow. Took cream in. Home about noon. Joe and Betty supposed to get married today.

How these names ring for me in present tense! My father's tall cousin Joe, towering over everyone else in the family, so handsome in his navy blues that my small-girl's crush on him left me embarrassed and tongue-tied in his presence. Joe's beautiful red-haired Betty is dead now, but in the pages of Imogene's diaries she's young, and Joe is young and home from the war, and they are about to get married. With what feels almost like prescience, I can move into future tense and confidently predict that Joe and Betty will live on the upriver ranch with us for several years after the war, while Joe works for my father, and that two of their children will be born during these years, for my sister and me to play with.

Does life on this obscure little Montana cattle ranch in 1944 sound idyllic? This ranch life which Imogene envied so much? Sheltered from the catastrophe of the war by mountain ranges and distance and what, to us, seems like the dead-slow pace of communications? War news came by radio, provided that somebody had bought batteries for the radio and that the batteries hadn't been run down. Or else the news came by the two- or three-day-old Lewistown newspaper, which the rural mail carrier delivered, of the Allied bombing of Europe and the liberation of France and the American bombing of Nagasaki and the discovery of concentration camps in Poland where, according to headlines a few days after Joe and Betty got married, an estimated 1.5 million Jews were thought to have been killed by the Nazis. Worse knowledge was to come, but for a little while the ranch families on the Judith River in Montana could keep their innocence.

Those ranch families had suffered, as did other Americans during World War II, from shortages and rationing. Hard to get gasoline, hard to get tires, hard to find fresh meat and fresh eggs in the stores. But in 1944 most of those ranchers were putting up their hay with teams of horses on the mowers and the buckrakes and the stackers, and they were planting gardens, as they always had done, and raising their own chickens and butchering their own meat. Most of them had never known the conveniences of electricity or refrigeration; they still pumped their water by hand and heated it on a coal stove. For bathing, a galvanized tub on the kitchen floor; for necessities, an outhouse. If they were lucky, they had a washing machine with a hand-turned agitator instead of a washboard and that same galvanized tub. Telephones? My family got one in 1949. Television? Not until I was grown and away from home, although TV had come to Montana in 1956.

Sounds like a Wendell Berry dream? That self-contained little ranch, undefiled by technology, where everybody worked hard but everybody had enough to eat, where good grass grew in those hay meadows along the river, where cattle grazed all summer long on the slopes of the South Moccasin mountains? Where entertainment, except for the huzzah and razzle-dazzle of fair time, was conversation by lamplight around the supper table? Where ranch children could grow up in innocence?

My father wanted no other life. Couldn't imagine anybody else in his right mind wanting another life, couldn't understand why some of his uncles had followed the war work to California and settled there, slaving for wages and calling another man boss. At least when a man was his own boss, he could take off a day when he wanted to (not that my father ever did, not with hay to stack between rains and cows to milk and fences to be fixed, no rest all summer long, then no rest in the early Montana winters what with teams to be harnessed to sleds and hay hauled to the cattle and horses, then in late winter and early spring the riding to look after the cattle birthing on those same open slopes of the South Moccasins, no rest all winter long). But look at Ervin, look at Dave, working construction and being paid by the hour. Why would a man want that kind of life?

There's Imogene, of course. She'll leave again, in the fall, she'll go back to teaching. But it's a little different for her, a little different for a woman. Of course she's following the teaching jobs in Washington State, for the better pay.

What if Imogene had achieved what she thought was her heart's desire and married a rancher? And had a couple of little girls of her own?

What if, instead of my mother, Imogene had cooked three meals a day on a wood stove and washed every sheet and shirt and pair of blue jeans with water she had pumped and heated on that same stove and then ironed, and what if she had fed and watered her chickens and then weeded and watered her vegetable garden (more water to be pumped and carried), and what if, then, she also had worked all day in the hay fields? What if she had been too tired to play with her little girls, or read to them, to do more than snap at them to behave themselves? Where would have been the auntie who loved the little girls and cared for them when she could? Where would have been the auntie to send five dollars for the little girls' shoes (so little cash money on a ranch, after all), to sew the pinafores and the pretty dresses?

Hard is the lot of humankind. In the sweat of thy face shalt thou eat bread, until thou return unto the ground. From the pains and pleasures of one life, the pains and pleasures of another, which would we choose?

Why did the nonfiction writer set her heart, at an early age, on escaping from that ranch, and why did she, like Imogene, think that marriage was the easy answer?

/ / /

Doris, slapping plates around the table in between jabbing at her sliced potatoes frying on top of the coal range and checking on the pan of chicken in the
oven, glances out the kitchen window and catches sight of her sister in the
shade of the box elder tree, bending down to show something to the little girls,
a grasshopper or perhaps only a leaf. Doris is thankful for her sister's company
this summer, her sister's willingness to play with the girls and keep them out
from underfoot. What with all the running back and forth between the river
ranch and the ranch on Spring Creek, Imogene and her car are a godsend,
Imogene a godsend in her willingness to buy the little luxuries, the bananas,
the shoes for the girls, the pretty pinafores. And yet—the old rivalry between
sisters dies hard—Doris doesn't know that Imogene's really happy in this life
she's chosen for herself. Money isn't everything, after all. Money can't buy
the most important things in life, and Imogene may be earning that big salary
in her fancy town school in Washington, but what has she really got?

"I haven't yet met a man who could do more for me than I can do for
myself," Imogene had remarked, earlier this summer, and Doris had paused
between one dishpan load of dirty plates and the next—"Imogene! That's no
way to think! You have to think of what you can do for *him*!"

In this late morning, watching the scanty shade of box elder leaves dapple
her daughters' silken heads as they examine Imogene's find, the grasshopper
or the leaf or whatever, squinting in the glare of sunlight on shadeless alkali
beyond the yard fence, calculating how much time she has to throw her meal
on the table and get the men fed, it occurs to Doris that Imogene may never
get married. It just may happen that Imogene never will put everybody else
ahead of herself. May—just—in spite of her generosity, her support, her willingness to lend and supply and provide presents for her nieces—may—
just—live her life putting herself first. The black absence such a thought sucks
out of the possible makes Doris close her eyes.

*August 22: Washed. Took Ma & Pa to town in the afternoon. Visited Mrs. Holt
& Mrs. Jones. Saw Dallas [Jones's] kid—he wasn't as big as I had heard he was.*

The Holts and Joneses are neighbors of Imogene's parents from homestead days. For a few years Dallas Jones paid attention to Imogene, took her to country dances and bought her supper, although he was so shy that he barely opened his mouth. Imogene liked him, though, and was crushed when he suddenly married another girl.

What if Dallas Jones had married Imogene? Always more questions than answers, as the nonfiction writer knows well. But answering all the questions is the task of the fiction writer, who, like God, must know everything there is to know, past, present, and future, about the universe of her characters.

> *August 23: Ma & I went walking in the evening, saw most of the cattle, 9 pheasants & a deer. Ma was thrilled. We took out salt too. Hope I have no car trouble.*

> *August 24: Finished my packing. Mother of God, I don't know where I'll put it when I get it there.*

> *August 25: Fri. A cold & windy day. No rain, praise be. Went up on the roof [of the old house on the homestead] & nailed on some shingles. How I hate to leave. Left after supper.*

> *August 26: Doris & I took the kids to town. She got tired——so much to do.*

> *August 27: We got up at two A.M. & drove to Moccasin. Almost ran into a skunk. Gee, how nervous I always get when going on a train.*

Apparently my parents have driven her to make train connections in the small town of Moccasin, about fifteen miles away. Why she's traveling home by train and what she has done with her car is unclear; in spite of her problems with fan belts and flat tires, she's been chauffeuring family members hither and yon right up to the time she leaves for Washington State.

August 28: We missed connections with the train to Tacoma so left at 12:30. It wasn't hard to get to Helise's. She looks so nice—believe she's lost [weight].

August 29: What a day. Started to read "Rivers of Glory." Am having a lovely visit, rest, & vacation [with Helise, at Fort Lewis]. A rare hot day.

August 30: Beastly hot. I was going to go about noon but waited till evening & it was late when I got to Tenino.

September 4: Canned 16 pts of peaches. Teachers' meeting—Think we have a much better bunch than last year. Schafer's had all of us for hambergers. Fun.

September 5: First day of school. Hot as blazes. Think our faculty is keen. No confusion at bus time. Only 29 enrolled. Expect one more. Not bad. Not bad.

The summer in Montana has been a turning point for Imogene. She expresses it subtly, she may not be completely aware of the consequences of those months of hot, sweating work in the hayfields—the grit and bits of chaff and grass that filtered down her shirt and itched and festered until she was ready to tear her clothes off, the dust that clogged her throat and turned her eyes red, until she longed for a cool drink of water and a bath, but of course no bathtub or even a shower at the ranch, only the galvanized tub on the kitchen floor—and the risk, the fear of the work, where at any moment a workhorse can startle and shy and stampede with mower and driver and sickles that grin in the sun like teeth, where at any moment a rope or a wire can snap on the stacker and fling a bolt or a wrench at somebody's head, where a rattlesnake is likely to be caught in the stacker along with the hay and be lifted, writhing and furious—*We put up a lot of hay today,* she had written on July 24, and added, *I'm scared of rattlesnakes.*

Yes, she's seen and done a lot. She's had an intimate view of her sister Doris's life on the ranch this summer, she's helped as much as she can, and in diary entries over the next few weeks she'll often note how much she misses her little nieces.

Finally, though, she's glad to be home, home in Tenino.

15

/ / /

Tenino. Anyone detouring off Interstate 5 on Washington state highway 507 today can turn her back on the spectacular scenery of the Cascade range and follow the Shookumchuck River north through urban sprawl until the river bends away from the road, which continues through sun-warmed meadows full of grass and daisies that stretch toward low timbered hills. For a few minutes it is as though the physical landscape and the landscape of the mind are finally one; time doesn't exist; any of us can wander through those meadows of memory at will. It is this dissolving of time that creative nonfiction offers as a chief pleasure. I don't think that fiction ever quite approaches this sudden sense of simultaneously experiencing the past and the present with the authority of nonfiction.

Meanwhile Imogene begins another school year. She's thirty-five years old this September, she's an experienced and savvy teacher, and she's feeling secure on her own ground.

September 6: Got one more pupil this P.M. Makes an even 30 for me. They are much better than last year. Short, snappy teacher's meeting. We are going to sell stamps.

September 7: Found a pupil had promoted herself from 1 to 3rd grade. Enjoyed P.T.A. Ex[ecutive] Com[mittee]. Ate at the Jiffy—a huge meal— Saw Grace English.

September 8: Put the little Funkhouser girl back & she wept. I expect will see Mama. It was very hot. I am so tired I just ate supper & no more.

September 11: Mr. Stuart came in & told me we might as well start the play-[ground] program & I get $1 an hour—at least $4 a week. It will buy my clothes.

September 12: Got my hair fixed. Ate at the Jiffy. Saw Miss [Mabel] Jones. Asked her up—gave her a cigarette—had a little talk. She seems nice.

This is Imogene's first reference to cigarette-smoking. I don't know when she began, but by the time the war was over, she was a heavy smoker, and she smoked until she was in her late seventies, when a doctor finally got her to quit for the sake of her high blood pressure. Of course, everyone in our family was just horrified at her habit. Dave and Jack and Ervin all smoked, but that was different; men smoked, but not nice women, not my grandmother's daughters or granddaughters. But now here's Imogene! Smoking cigarettes! At their disapproval, she laughed and lit up. It was her form of rebellion, she told me, her flirtation with the dark side.

She liked to smoke Pall Mall kings, but to smoke only half a cigarette before she stubbed it out. Aunt Mable, whose sense of thrift apparently triumphed over her moral indignation at Imogene's filthy habit, used to count the butts in her ashtray and scold her for the half-cigarettes she was wasting. And when Dave and Jack and Ervin all quit smoking in the 1970s, my grandmother would lament. "If Dave can quit, and Jack can quit, and Ervin can quit, why can't Imogene quit?"

When I look back, I wonder how Imogene stood it. Not just the constant family carping about her smoking, but the easy assumption that we were all entitled to mind each other's business, indeed entitled to set each other's standards for behavior, right down to the half-cigarette. I wish I knew what she was thinking; I only know that she listened to the barrage of criticism, laughed and lit up.

As another year in the teacher's life begins, the tone of Imogene's diary entries suggests that she is contented to be home, and gathering the familiar strands of lessons, friends, shopping, reading, knitting. She sounds as though she's relaxed and ready for a good school year.

But what is this word, *contented*? Is it just another word for *resigned*? Does it mean that she's given up on romance?

The fiction writer, who makes it her business to know everything about all her characters, might well have Daisy Lincoln raise her odd, barking voice: Imogene has let herself go! She's gained all that weight, and all she wants to do is teach her pupils and go to her meetings and then come home and put her feet up. She never wants to go out! She's taken herself right out of circulation! How does she think she'll ever get a husband if she doesn't get back in circulation?

The fiction writer has given Daisy the hectoring tone of a contemporary self-help book. Thinks she'd like to make a more complete character out of Daisy. Imagines her as a skinny woman with eyes that dart over Imogene, judging her clothes, measuring her hips, thinking it's a shame that she hides her beautiful brown eyes behind those glasses.

The nonfiction writer asks, has Imogene given up? Resigned herself to the glasses? Resigned to finding her chief pleasures from work, as she keeps telling her diary?

Or, without quite realizing it, has she gotten where she wants to be?

September 14: Stood my first trick today of playground duty of 2 hrs—made $2. Not too bad. Sylva wrote she was teaching regularly. Ha. Ha.

Oh, be charitable, Imogene. As a married woman, your sister isn't supposed to have to "work"—it's the lot of the unmarried woman to "work," as you've been working since your eighteenth birthday. But times are changing, and teachers are scarce, and Sylva's doing her bit for the war. Cut her a little slack, Imogene. But just because your married sisters think that, unmarried, you're still something of a child—like Aunt Mable in Sioux City, Iowa, boarding in another woman's house all her life—doesn't mean you can't enjoy your occasional quiet laugh in your sleeve.

September 16: Today I canned pears—painted woodwork, washed curtains, made a meatloaf, visited Mabel Jones. Really a good day's work.

The next day, Sunday, Imogene drops in to visit with Helen Cornwell, one of the hold-over Tenino teachers. Imogene spent a lot of time with Helen last year, but she never was crazy about Helen's children, and this year the friendship is starting to wane. Many of the names in these entries are new; Imogene is getting acquainted with a widening circle of new teachers.

September 17: Ironed curtains today. Never get around to study. Have as satisfactory a life as possible, single. Stopped a while at Helen's. What a pest Shirley [Helen's daughter] is.

As satisfactory a life as possible, single. Resignation? Or is she indulging in romantic daydreams?

My mother began making a dark prediction: "I don't think Imogene's ever going to get married." Then she broadened the shadow she was casting: "There's an old maid in every generation of our family. There's Aunt Mable, and now Imogene. Some people just aren't meant to get married."

What was she hinting at, I wondered, lifting my nose from my book. I was six or seven by then, and well able to read to myself from books that Imogene sent me, with romantic endings, like *Betty Zane* or *The Trail of the Lonesome*

Pine. Why weren't some people meant to get married? Who was the designated old maid in my generation? Was it me?

I was so worried that I confided in Imogene during one of her summer visits, and she put one arm around me, lit a cigarette, and did her best to comfort me. What she must have thought about a weeping seven-year-old—a seven-year-old! weeping for fear she would never get married!—or what she surmised about family gossip, she didn't say.

"Why do you think you'll never get married?" she asked.

"What if I'm not pretty enough?"

"Oh. Well." Imogene smoked and thought about that. Then she asked, "Who is the prettiest married woman you know?"

That was easy. My cousin Joe's wife, beautiful red-haired Betty.

Imogene nodded. "All right, but you'll notice that Betty's only been married once. Now, Betty's sister, Topsy—you know Topsy?—she isn't one bit pretty, but she's been married three times. So you see, getting married has nothing to do with being pretty. Anybody that wants to can get married. Even I could have gotten married, except I didn't want to marry any of the men who wanted to marry me."

I could see the logic in her argument, but I knew absolutely that being a single woman was almost as wrong as being a man who went out and worked for wages, and I also knew that I was damaged in some indefinable way that I associated with a lack of beauty. I heard a lot from my grandmother about my little cousin Kris and how beautiful she was (which my grandmother never would have told Kris, because praise to the face was open disgrace) and how beautiful my little sister was. I wasn't beautiful, I was the one who liked to read. The next summer I would learn that my ability to read could make a little boy cry. Definitely we had a problem in our family, and I was the problem; what I didn't understand was that the name of the problem was self-consciousness, and that it caught up with every child, sooner or later. Probably I got an extra, and early, dose—the writer's dose—and it was years before I realized how deeply it had divided me from family expectations, from the very landscape I grew up in, and many more years before I accepted its pains and pleasures as a blessing.

Elizabeth Hampsten has suggested that the professional woman writer is almost always an outsider: "women who write are obliged to study their regions, and those who know the country at first hand have not written. . . . Virtually no woman has written descriptively and remained where she was." I find myself both agreeing and disagreeing with Hampsten. Certainly most of the nineteenth-century western women writers whose names we recognize are outsiders, like Mary Hallock Foote, following her engineer husband from her safe Quaker haven in Milton, New York, to godforsaken places like Leadville, Colorado, and Boise, Idaho. Or Isabella Bird Johnson, or Eleanor Stuart, or Nannie Alderson, or for that matter other women artists, like the photographer Evelyn Cameron. (It's arguable that many of these women lived in the west long enough to become "insiders"—Eleanor Stuart, Nannie Alderson, Mary Hallock Foote herself—but still they wrote or drew or photographed what to their eyes was strange and wonderful and exotic and unique.)

A lot depends on whether "remained where she was" refers to a woman's geographical landscape or to the landscape of her mind. The act of writing requires several degrees of separation, the self-consciousness (the alienation, to use Hampsten's word) necessary to step back and take notes, but the twentieth century saw a wealth of women born and raised in the west, still living in the west, and writing memoirs and fiction and poetry, and the twenty-first century will see even more women writing to make sense of a region whose borders shrink and expand and blur and disappear.

How far do you have to go before you can say that you haven't remained where you were? Is the nearest university town far enough away?

September 18: My load of wood came tonight. Don Thomas helped me pile it. Then I came in & got supper. Should have gone to that meeting only it bores me.

September 20: Once this week Mr. Schafer visited school. Emalie lost her coat today but we found it for her. Made some gingerbread cupcakes.

September 21: Had a teacher's meeting—talked about P.T.A. membership. Gee, Mrs. Cornwell is sure whiny. Lion's Club is entertaining the teachers next week.

September 22: Friday at last. There's a school dance & I expect I ought to go. Have a slug of work I want to do tomorrow. Should get going on my writing & crocheting.

September 23: Slicked up my house. I do like a place of my own. Began to read Pride & Prejudice. It is humorous. So few really humorous writers. Want [Clarence] Day's trilogy.

This fall Imogene is readier to express her feelings, and succinctly: the meeting will bore her, so she doesn't go. She sure does like living in a place of her own. She wants to get at her own writing, and maybe she'll try writing humor, as there's too little of it. The stories she wrote in her old age—the only ones that have survived—are brisk and vivid and laced with humor.

September 24: A hot day—cold in the morning. How I hate to iron. Got it done at last. I'll be glad to finish Wuthering Heights. It is interesting but I don't like the characters.

September 25: Got a new pupil, keeps my enrollment to 30. Still no laundry. Nerts, I'm always so tired at night I can't work, but finished Wuthering Heights.

Always the apology for wasting time by reading books.

September 26: The Lions Club gave a dinner & reception for the teachers. It was the nicest reception I was ever at. Cigarettes are getting scarce. I'm nearly out.

October 3: Got my warrant at last. Ate at the Jiffy. Nuts, they aren't so hot. Out of cigarettes. Damn it. Ordered some Sat. but they never got in.

October 5: Tonight we had the 1st PTA of the year—about 100 people— a pot luck dinner. I liked it. We elected Mrs. Stockwell president.

I try and fail to imagine a hundred people in a town of 1,200 turning out for PTA, and I remind myself that these are pretelevision days. People attend PTA, they attend meetings of service organizations, they pay visits and ask each other to dinner. For all her upbringing on that remote prairie homestead, Imogene slides easily into the life of the community. She likes the potlucks, the gatherings, the placid comings and goings, the exchanges of books at the public library. And she would have liked the new Tenino Timberland Regional Library, a block off the main street, which I visited during the summer of 2002. She would have winked at the queue of preschoolers being led to a story hour, and she would have scanned the shelves of new books with guilty pleasure at the time she was going to waste, reading them.

Sitting at a table in the clean June sunlight that floods through the library windows, I spread out high school yearbooks and pamphlets on local history and feel as though I am returning to a place I once knew well. My aunt's diary entries may be cryptic, but I've studied them long enough that details fall in place. Amazing, really, how well I know this place. Here's the quarry, for example. Turns out that it was famous; it provided sandstone for a long list of historic buildings in Tenino and even in Olympia, beginning in 1888 until it shut down in 1926. After it was abandoned, the empty quarry was filled with water by a natural spring, which the local kids used for a swimming hole and where Daisy took Imogene swimming the first fall they taught in Tenino. *Ninety feet deep,* she noted, impressed.

Later, after World War II, the community had the quarry cleaned and fitted with rails and diving boards as a truly unique swimming pool.

Then there are the pictures in the 1946 yearbook (the earliest that the library has kept). Here's the face of Marvin Schafer, of whom I've heard so much, a middle-aged balding man in a suit and a smile. And the face of Lila Moser, rather faded and pretty, who taught math and Latin and supervised the library. And Katherine Simmons, who taught English and algebra and coached debate. And—fairly leaping off the page at me—is Imogene Welch, who in 1946 advised the seventh grade and taught physical education to the grade school girls.

I flip pages and find another photograph of her, posed with what looks like a girls' tumbling team, and this time I find my aunt as I remember her, grinning in the company of twenty little girls in floppy gym suits. She's in her element here; she also wears a gym suit, and she's braced her legs to make a comfortable base for the girl who sits atop her shoulders. Lucky little girl, triumphant and safe on Imogene's dependable shoulders.

October 6: Finally started on a diet & then after school Stuart ordered hambergers. I'll never admit I diet to the others. Hope to make 145 by Christmas. Jack Austin got licked.

October 8: Went to church. Joy & Helen both were there. Surprise. Robt. Austin shook hands with us. Wonder if they are trying to be more friendly. Darn a cold.

Can Robt. Austin be R? Or is he the father of Jack Austin, who was disciplined on October 6, and does he have a grudge against the teacher? I have no way of knowing.

October 10: No flowers this year. It has been very dry. Got Earth & High Heaven in the mail & so of course read instead of writing.

October 11: Katherine Simmons had Ethel, Mrs. Evans, & me for dinner, & then several in to sew & talk. The kind of an evening I enjoy.

So! She's finally admitting what it is she really likes to do, and it's not going out tomcatting.

Lots of new names are cropping up this fall. We don't hear about weekend trips to the ocean with Daisy and Bernita, but we do see that Imogene is widening her circle, less dependent on one or two close women friends (although Katherine Simmons and Mabel Jones will begin to appear regularly in her diary entries as Simmons and Jones), and she seems happier, even as she reports the gossip, the trivial fallings-out and long-forgotten feuds among the teachers:

October 12: Cigarettes sure are short. Had art in school. Got Jack o lantern pictures up. Stuart had Edna play for him & Helen was hurt. She makes me tired.

October 14: Went to Olympia. Left my watch. Bought an ivy. Looked for dresses. Nerts, came home & swore to lose 50 lbs—better 60.

October 15: I ought to quit taking the Sunday paper. I believe I could get lots more done if I didn't always stop to read it. I made a lemon pie.

She's clearly losing her battle with her weight. The other battle she's losing is with her reading habit. Again and again she tells herself she ought to spend less time reading and more time working, knows that reading is a waste of time—yes, the devil makes work for idle hands, and the hands that hold a book are idle ones.

It seems odd to me that my family, outwardly so secular, nevertheless held so rigidly to the old edicts. I never heard one of my parents or grandparents utter a word of prayer or saw one of them open a Bible. They didn't like to hear religion discussed; they were as embarrassed by an open display of faith as they would have been by public copulation. None of them went to church, except Imogene, and her church attendance eventually dwindled down from her Catholic-and-Methodist services every Sunday in the days when she and

Dorothy and Bernita were inseparable. And yet the edicts: no rest for the wicked, the road to hell is paved with good intentions, the devil makes work for idle hands.

My idle hands always held a book, unless the book was snatched from me by an angry mother—"She's always got her nose in a book! I can't get any work out of her! And here's this notice from the school—encourage your child to read! What would Mary be like if I encouraged her?"

October 16: New pupil—smart. Letter from Aunt Helen [in Iowa]— clippings about Glennys Eick's marriage. She had a church wedding. I hope she's happy.

October19: Letter from Pa—not bad. Stuart [the new elementary school principal] is going to hold [evaluation] conferences with each teacher. He's a good guy & trying hard. He licked 4 boys—fighting & swearing.

October 22: Went to a show tonight. Desert Song. First one I've been to this fall. Decided I really must get going next week. I could get a lot done if I'd keep at it.

A motion picture palace in 1944 would have retained much of its nineteen-thirties glamor. A lighted marquee, a glittering foyer, the heady odor of popcorn. Usherettes in tight uniforms used discreet flashlights to guide theater-goers to their upholstered seats. A rustle of expectation, a hush, and the velvet curtains rose to reveal the lighted screen and, before the previews of coming attractions and the cartoon and the main feature, there rolled the newsreel in black and white, of course (even main features are usually filmed in black and white; Technicolor is so rare as to deserve a special mention in Imogene's diary), but with plenty of flashes and flares and the charged professional over-voice to convey the atmosphere of battle. On October 22, before she saw the romantic Sigmund Romberg musical, Imogene might have watched month-old footage of planes from American carriers striking targets on Luzon, and a day or two previously she might have read in her newspaper that General MacArthur had waded ashore on Luzon. Heavily censored newsreel footage, to be sure; censored newspaper accounts, to be sure; but still, the war was a vivid presence—too vivid, perhaps, to note in her diary, except near the end, when a Tenino teacher's son is killed: *Dix Moser was killed. I feel so sorry for his mother.*

October 23: Letters from both Mother & Doris. Doris sounds moved [to the upriver ranch, where so much haying was done the previous summer]. Had a baseball game & we licked the 7th grade. More fun. Have to call an ex[ecutive committee] meeting.

Along with its mountain pastures and river meadows, my parents' new ranch held only a few weathered buildings: a slab barn and a ramshackle set of corrals, a shed, and a two-room cabin set well back against a grove of chokecherries. By October 23, when Imogene received that letter from my mother, she and my father had cleaned out the cabin for his mother, my grandmother Edna, and set up a stove and beds in the shed for themselves and Betty and me. It was an arrangement to get us through the winter, and my mother made the best of it; she pasted blue-flowered wallpaper between the raw studs of the shed and hung curtains.

In front of my grandmother's cabin was a blackened mound where a previous cabin had burned to the ground. As my parents hurried to get us under a roof for the night, I explored and found a few scorched and distorted nails, nothing more.

"Why? Why did it burn down?"

I knew there had to be a story. Sentence by sentence, I extorted something of a narrative from my busy elders. Well, it burned down because a fire got started. Why? Well, because they'd just come home from town, and the woman thought she was pouring kerosene out of a can to get her cooking fire started in a hurry, but it was gasoline in the can, and it blew up when she struck her match. Did she get burned? Yes, and so did her sister and her baby. All of them? Burned *dead*? Yes. Why? I don't know. God! Does there always have to be a why!

I wasn't quite four, and I still had the luxury of dawdling, dreaming, absorbing textures and shadows and sounds. Wood box by the stove, full of chunks still wet from the woodpile, stuck with sawdust and shredded bark. A roar inside the stove, holding the October night at bay. On the stove, water simmering in a dishpan. Drink your milk, little girl. Warm taste. Warm milk foam on my little sister's mouth. What's this in my milk, a speck in my milk, a black speck. Don't worry about it, fish it out with your finger, that's right. You girls sleepy yet?

What were their names?

Whose names? The people that got burned in the fire? I don't know their names. He worked for Uncle Theo. He was out in the barn, was why he didn't get burned to death. Now stop asking so many questions.

Did they die right away?

The sister and the baby died, but she lived for a few days. Now go to sleep!

Why, I heard my mother grumbling to my father, can't Mary just let it go? Why does she always want to have the gory details?

What must it be like, raising a ranch child intent on breaking all the old silences? A child who scratches, relentless, disturbing the peace and quiet, questioning the certainty that, no, it couldn't have happened to us. We couldn't have made that mistake, throwing the lighted match into gasoline, hearing the instant whoosh and seeing the explosion of flames as our retinas burned.

No! Never! So for God's sake, shut up about it!

October 24: I guess Helen is quite cut up about her [evaluation] conference. Bunny told me he [Mr. Stuart, the principal] just wanted to talk to two & has to call us all in. Heh——Betty & Helen.

October 25: Went to Stockwell's to ex[ecutive] com[mittee]. Had a good time but it was long. Broke up at 11:30. Had conference with Stuart after school. Poor guy.

October 26: Mrs. Major stopped me last night & said she had a kitten for me. Went to Lykan's to a party. Had a headache. Argued with Mrs. Moser about our library.

Imogene's diary entries continue through the fall, brief and inconsequential. It's possible to catch the whiff of local politics, to realize there was a campaign to elect Mrs. Stockwell president of the PTA, to note the school gossip about whose evaluations are likely to go badly, even to follow a brief thread about a kitten that Mrs. Major is giving to Imogene. We don't see Mrs. Stockwell's or Mrs. Major's faces, we don't hear their voices. We don't know from the diary how Mrs. Moser is related to the Dix Moser killed in action, although I find his name listed among the war dead from Washington State, and I learn from the records of the Thurston County *Independent* that she was indeed his mother. Imogene's diary tells us only that she and Mrs. Moser had an argument about the library on October 26, 1944, which is as close to literal truth as we are likely to find in any written document.

During the summer of 2002, a heated discussion broke out in western literary circles about a recently published memoir which contained a vivid and disturbing episode that turned out to be pure fiction.

The plaintive outcry: If we can't believe in that episode, what can we believe in?

The rejoinder: Well! We certainly can't expect to hold the nonfiction writer to a journalist's standards! Furthermore, if the memoir is beautifully crafted, if the episode is compellingly written, isn't that what matters? Isn't artistry what matters, finally?

The plaintive protest: But if it isn't true?

The rejoinder: What is truth?

A well-known novelist mused on her abortive attempt to write a memoir, which she had begun with the assertion that she had been born on a cold
day. But what, she asked herself, was a cold day? How cold? Ought she look
up the weather records for the day of her birth? And supposing that she did
look up the weather records, wouldn't *cold* be relative to the weather the day
before her birth, or the year before her birth? And if she had to document
every assertion in such a way, how many years would it take her to write her
memoir? Better to stick to writing fiction, the novelist concluded.

The interesting question is the one the novelist missed: not, how cold is
cold, but why, in the course of the on-going, never-completed, constantly-
being-revised version of her family story, was she led to believe that the day
of her birth was a cold day? What did that story tell about her family, what did
it tell about her? Because the business of the nonfiction writer is to raise such
questions, to pry into family secrets, to theorize, and to spin webs just like
the webs that the fiction writer spins, except that the nonfiction writer is
never completely sure what her web holds.

Imogene's diaries? Absolutely accurate? Pretty close. And yet there are
entries that I'm pretty sure she filled in after the fact, after several days so
hectic and demanding that she lacked even enough energy to write her line
or two at bedtime. *I think this was the day we saw the deer in the hayfield,* she
might write, in reconstruction.

Well, was it or wasn't it? And what does it matter? Surely there's an
enormous distance between writing, say, a fictional episode of violence and
wondering whether the deer were in the hayfield on a Tuesday or a Wednes-
day; yes, certainly there is a distance, but a gray one, a hazy one, and a nervous writer looking for the place to draw an absolute line between fiction and
nonfiction is likely to conclude only that for her, at least, the line is here. Or
there. Or maybe over there.

But just as a child will beg to know whether a story told to her is true—
did they burn to death? really?—so the reader longs for authenticity. A conversation heard by a four-year-old? It sounds like my mother's voice, it has

the right texture, the right rhythms, and if she didn't say precisely those words on one day, she did on another, or at least something like those words. If the reader can't get exactitude—and she can't, deep down she knows she can't— she'll accept its approximation. What she will not stand for is being lied to, which is why, when she uncovers (in an extreme case) a literary forgery, she's furious, she throws the book at the wall, and no amount of cajolery— *but, dear reader, artistry is what counts, don't you agree, and if you admired the work when you thought it was authentic, how can you admire it less just because it's been exposed for not being what it said it was?*—will redeem it in her estimation. No.

October 27: Friday—payday. We all went home early. I got my hair fixed. Pauline is leaving. I'm going to try to lose 35 lbs by Christmas.

October 28: Meant to go to Olympia but decided to lose 10 lbs & then go. I can get a 20 dress then likely. Have a notion to go to Tacoma.

October 30: Rain today. Helen's turn to do playground. The kids were supposed to go in the gym & she just went in & sat there. Party tomorrow.

October 31: Majors gave me a kitten yesterday. We had the Halloween party & program. Were the kids noisy. Guess we'll have to bear down on them.

November 2: Stuart gave me 2 day 3rd arith work books—the kind I cried so for last year. Darn my shiftless ways. Think I've got a story beginning & end.

November 4: Went to Olympia to shop for birthdays [without, presumably, losing ten pounds]. Swore it is the last time for me. The bus was crowded. I had to stand both ways.

November 7: Election, went down to vote. Gave Mrs. Angel [who lives downstairs] her plate back & some muffins. She told me there was a crazy man in town last night.

November 8: The Damn democrats won again. Gael was sure low. Went to Stitch & Chatter Club. Most were rather quiet. Last night told on them.

Gael is the new elementary school principal who doubles as the fifth- and sixth-grade basketball coach. Apparently he is a Republican, if he's "low" over the election results, as perhaps are the members of the Stitch & Chatter Club. Imogene likes Gael a lot, and mentions him often during the next few months.

November 9: One of my girls fell & broke a front tooth. I hate to have anything like that happen. Anyway I was right there. Mr. Shafer is going to report it.

November 10: One of the teachers has TB, the 2nd grade teacher, and is not coming back. Too bad, but at least her folks are not poor.

Imogene's own folks are on her mind as she writes this entry. As her father's mental condition worsens, what is going to become of her mother? She can't teach forever, she's wearing out, and anyway, Montana at this time has a mandatory retirement age of seventy-five. Without her teacher's salary, how will she pay A. P.'s bills? Is the burden going to fall on Imogene's shoulders?

The entry also may underline Imogene's preoccupation with her own health, her chronicle of headaches, colds, flu symptoms. What if she were struck with tuberculosis or polio or some other dread disease, she must be asking herself. Who would pay her bills if she couldn't work? Not her parents.

November 11: Stores all closed today [for Armistice Day] so I didn't go up town for mail even. Played the radio a lot. Cleaned house good for a change.

November 12: Hell; I'm just as far from 115 lbs now as a year ago. [On the previous November 12, she had written, "Made me a wish chart—115 lbs."] Did a lot of reading & little else. Curses. Always I begin tomorrow.

November 13: Bernita is in England, so the Denton [Montana] paper says.
In a way I envy her, not Daisy. Who'd have thot this two years ago. Life goes on.

It doesn't sound as though Imogene is in touch with Bernita. But Daisy! Where is Daisy? What is it that Imogene envies about Bernita's, but not Daisy's, life? The entry suggests that Imogene has kept in contact with her, at least knows where she is and what she's doing. Surely she's not married; surely Imogene would have noted her engagement or marriage.

Can the fiction writer find clues? Consider what we can glean about Daisy, even from Imogene's sparse notes. First and foremost, she was born and raised in southwest Washington, where her family was still living during the early years of the war. We hear of her parents, who invited Imogene and Bernita to Christmas dinner back in 1942, and of a sister and a brother. But Daisy doesn't live at home, she shares an apartment with Imogene and Bernita. For a young unmarried woman not to be living at home at that time seems odd enough to speculate further. Of course, there could be any number of reasons: large family, cramped house (Imogene does mention going house-hunting for Daisy's family, so apparently they're moving, or about to move), or perhaps the family lives too far from Napavine and then Tenino in those days of gas rationing and crowded public transportation. Another detail we know about Daisy is that she knits. She teaches Imogene to knit.

The women in Imogene's family didn't knit. My mother was taught to knit after she was married, by my grandmother on my father's side, who had learned knitting from her English mother. All these women knitted in the distinctive English style, as do I. So did Imogene. So—I deduce—did Daisy knit in English style.

Out of such fragments the fiction writer imagines a shrill young woman, alternately slovenly and exacting, who like Imogene is rebelling against a conservative family (a family in which the women knit, English style) without quite knowing that she's rebelling. A few cautious steps. The teaching job in

Napavine, the apartment with the two young women from Montana. Montana! Daisy feels a cut or two above them, socially; she condescends to them even as she depends upon them during those first heady weeks and months when they set up housekeeping, go tomcatting, rent a cabin at the beach. Imogene, who is a few years older and has lived on her own in a score of primitive teacherages, gets annoyed with both Daisy and Bernita, and they with her. But the younger women are getting their bearings, working up their courage. Bernita goes to England—what an adventure for a girl from Denton, Montana!—and Daisy goes—where?

Let's say that Daisy goes to San Francisco, to take up Bernita's old dream of wartime nursing. In San Francisco, far from her family, let's say she learns the pleasures of independence, becomes her own woman in more glittering circumstances than Imogene ever imagines. Let's give her a life out of a movie, elegant in 1940's black and white. Let's let Daisy soar.

November 17: The 5 & 6 grades went down to play baseball. We won—21-6. One of the boys was cast down because he fumbled, poor kid. Helen is all out with her assembly.

November 19: Junes came to call. One of Joys dogs got porcupine quills. I pulled 27 but they took him to the vet's. She gave me a big jar of blackberry jam.

November 21: And this year my best colt is missing. Damn & double damn.

Although she doesn't say so, Imogene has had a letter from home with bad news. Jack, riding after cattle on his new range, must have noticed that the colt wasn't with the bunch. It could have been stolen, could have been struck by lightning, could have been struck by a hunter's stray bullet and fallen, never to be found, into some brush-choked Montana coulee, Imogene will never know. And because she loves her horses, because she's hung on to her couple of mares and colts through all the difficult years, riding when she can, the loss of this colt widens the distance between herself and her past. She can't go back, she's come too far, and over the coming years her horses will graze on scorching prairie, lift their heads in the fall when the aspen leaves rustle, drift with the storms of winter as snow crusts their heavy coats. Then they will become shadows. Unremembered.

November 23: Read a book, cooked, just lazed around. Nothing I cook tastes like much. I've got lots to be thankful for—but I'm missing the thing I want most.

The one thing? Romantic love, of course.

November 24: I spend a mort of time lying around. But I don't really feel real well. Have a cold. Lack ambition. Must go to town tomorrow.

November 26: Read too much. Did get my school work done & my desk cleaned. No breakfasts next week, salad & soup for supper. Hope my cold goes.

December 1: Took the kids to a movie in tecknicolor—Buffalo Bill. It was good. I even liked it. Sunday is Jane Eyre. Guess I'll go to Centralia. Ought to go to Seattle.

December 3: Went to Jane Eyre. It was very good. Want to go to Ali Baba & the 40 Thieves. Must stop tomorrow at Schafers. I just never get any writing done.

Is she attending these movies with friends, or with her pupils, or is she going by herself? At least it's a pleasure she seems to allow herself without the guilt she feels about reading.

December 5: Went to sewing circle [which included a gift exchange, since it was the last meeting before Christmas]—Jones got the candles I brought. I got a white doily. Can use. Letters from Florence & Mother. Dave & Florence might be in [move to] Seattle.

December 8: Friday—home late—did all my school work so I can be free next week as I'm on playground. Went to Ali Baba in Technicolor.

December 11: Home late. Mrs. Funkhouser came & then I talked to Gael & then helped the kids. Letters from Pa—2. Always hate to get them.

December 12: About 7:30 Gael & Frank came along & told me PTA meeting at 8:30 at the H.S. Card from Florence saying she is in Bremerton [not Seattle, after all, not yet].

December 13: Card from Ruthie [a teacher she once roomed with in Montana]. Would have liked a letter. Got some peanuts to give my kids a shower. Two have bought bonds. Want to celebrate.

December 14: Should get my last package & my Christmas cards out. Found some coconut in the store.

The unexpected tropical treat: coconut! Probably a package of shredded coconut that somehow fell through the wartime restrictions and lasted long enough on the grocery shelf for Imogene to pounce on it. A little stale, perhaps, but it's a taste of days past and hope for days to come. The war won't last forever, and sugar will be plentiful again, and chocolate, and life will go on.

December 15: Got my little tree & put it up in a flower pot. Tomorrow I must see if I can get lights. When the war is over I'm going to get new decorations.

December 19: Thot I'd get home early but Gael came up & made coffee & we chewed the fat for an hour. I bought K[ristie] L[ee] a stuffed elephant.

December 23: Caught the 11:00 A.M. bus. Bought a house coat in Bremerton. Found K.L. as sweet as can be. Dave working. Not too cheery a season, what with the war.

December 24: We girls cooked——made candy——otherwise prepared for the morrow.

December 25: Spent the day quietly. Good dinner.

December 26: Dave, Florence & Kristie Lee went to Seattle & came home by bus. Found a water pipe had burst in my kitchen. Most of the mess was cleaned up.

Decmber 27: Washed curtains. Cleaned my cupboards——a mess. The water ran in & soaked everything in packages. Had to thro out all my puddings.

December 28: Got my curtains back up. What a difference. Wrote 6 letters. Have many more to write.

December 30: Cleaned house——shopped——got library books. Got all set to make my New Years Resolution.

December 31: Seems like my New Years Eve's have been dull. I never do anything more exciting than work on my stamp albums or make resolutions. Took my tree down.

In many ways the war seems to have faded for Imogene. The restrictions, yes; the dim-outs, the rationing and the scarcities, the difficulties of travel. But the war itself has been a presence for so long that it just is, a constant but distant process, hardly worth noting, as 1944 slides into 1945 and Imogene braces herself for the rest of the school year and what feels to her like a hum-de-dum life. Maybe she does know something of Daisy's glitter. If she's not envious, maybe she's a little depressed in a daylight life that gradually has taken the place of her dreams. It's the price, perhaps, of awakening.

16

/ / /

January 1, 1945: Ironed, waxed floor, wrote letters. Have 2350 stamps in my album now. No excitement.

The brown-eyed woman prepares for bed on New Year's Day. Creams her face and slips into her nightie, tosses back her sheet and blanket and props herself on her pillow. Takes up her diary and commences with the final year that this book will contain. *No excitement:* it's an observation that will characterize Imogene's diary entries for the first weeks of 1945. Classes begin as they always begin, chores need to be done, letters to be written. Tonight she finishes her scrawl, lays her diary aside, and turns out the lamp by her bed, so used to electricity by now that she hardly notices the convenience, hardly notices the absence of kerosene, the reflection of flame in the bowl of the lamp and the blackened streaks in the chimney. When she visits her sister Doris, Imogene will go to bed by kerosene's sparkle, and in the morning she will help to wash the lamps and trim the wicks and refill the bowls. But kerosene is not a part of her life, not any more.

Absence. What she doesn't note during these first weeks and months of 1945.

Money worries, for one. Those constant woes, back in her Montana days—*I would like to buy some more groceries but have only $2.50 left this month & two weeks*—or in Napavine—*Sure will be short in my accounts*—or that awful summer at the University of Washington—*Went to work at 5:00. I guess I can manage on $3 a day . . . Oh, I want so many clothes*—have gradually faded from her diary. She's earning enough money to live on, nowadays, and she's probably a better budgeter. If she wants to buy fabric to sew for herself or her nieces, she buys it without noting her guilt.

No more worry about her body shape. No more resolutions to lose weight, no more setting of impossible goals, no wailing that she's not thin enough to fit into her "black," only a tossed-off remark in April about new clothes and the pounds she's never lost.

No more irritation with roommates.

In fact, less irritation in general.

January 2: Started 3rd gd. X [multiplication] in arith. today. Reports due tomorrow & I need to get my calendar up.

January 8: Letter from Aunt Mary [in Iowa]. They thot I was going to get married when Pa wrote we [Imogene and Bernita—possibly in connection with Bernita's never-carried-out idea of nursing for the military in San Francisco] were going to S.F. Wish I was.

January 9: Lovely day—let the kids play outdoors. Bunny & I watched the boys play B.B. Gale tries to teach them teamwork.

January 13: Well, Daisy, Bernita & I are far apart. Who'd a thunk it two years ago. We each probably think we've the best of the deal.

January 20: Went to a PTA ex bd. meeting in Olympia. Asked for the 4th grade next year. Ate supper at Schafer's. Spilled a lot of dirt to Ethel.

January 22: Our room was so cold they evacuated my class to the main hall till recess. Got a photo of Betsy [probably my sister Betty]. She looks so old.

January 23: Floyd wrote a note & called the girls damn dopes. I scolded him & reported such to Stuart who said he'd paddle him. The girls are dopes.

January 24: Letter from Ruthie [her teacher friend in Montana]. Made me lonesome. Gael called Floyd & Clyde into the office & bawled them out but didn't whip them. Then he came & scolded my room. 3 visitors—age 5.

January 29: Helen crabby. Gael caught & paddled two of my boys. I called on Schafers.

January 30: Gael paddled Floyd today. Went to a H[igh] S[chool] B.B. game Tenino won—it was a good game. The girls had quite a scrap.

February 2: Gael paddled Josie—a 5th grader. Did me good. Pepped my kids up to win the ice cream prize at PTA. Went to a BB game. It was good.

The students of Tenino Elementary School do seem to be coming in for a lot of corporal punishment, with five, possibly six paddlings between January 17 and February 2, depending on exactly what was meted out to the hapless Floyd and Clyde. Do the paddlings reflect the disciplinary measures of Gael, compared with the departed Mr. Fox? Or are we seeing the effects of stress in general? As an end to the war becomes more and more certain, changes are also certain, but what, exactly? Nobody knows, but everybody feels it coming, and they speculate. Which teachers will leave Tenino this year? Which will stay? Will there be more jobs and better pay for teachers after the war? Or not?

Brown-eyed Miss Welch has a hard time controlling her amusement, her secret sympathy for the young culprits. She does have to keep order, and she's better at it than she was when she started teaching at eighteen, but she's got a soft spot for boys like Floyd. He's right, the girls are dopes.

February 4: Did my housework, baked cookies, ironed. Piddled around as usual. Told Joy I was glad when Monday's came.

February 6: Some one stole some money from my room —86c on up—I don't know how much. Soldiers in the park—kids crazy. Nuts.

February 9: Lord, did we gossip today. Helen let her kids invite the soldiers. Were the mamas mad. Schafer is going to talk to her—not Gael—tho he told all the kids to keep out of camp.

February 12: Went to Jones' with the makin's. We roll a terrible smoke. Said Frank's wife had tried to make him trouble. Maybe they tried to get a release.

February 16: Bluebirds organized. Ran to see Mrs. Schafer for a few minutes. Caught the 5:11 bus for Fort Lewis. Nice evening.

February 18: Got a carton of Luckies. Caught a bus [home from Fort Lewis] after dinner. Ran over to see Jones—Gael came in & we really chewed the fat.

February 21: Letter from Florence—was she blue. Dave's number comes up March 1. He may get deferred. I hope. Should go up to see her.

February 22: Most of the teachers left town & I was kind of blue. Letter from Mother. I must begin to make Summer plans.

February 23: Cleaned house. Decided to go up to see Florence she was so blue. Can go up early & come back the same day.

Dave and Florence by now are living in Seattle while Dave works in the shipyards, and Florence feels far from her mother and father, back in Denton, Montana, and ill at ease in the hurly-burly of wartime Seattle. Imogene responds as always to the needs of her family, with affection for Florence, whom she has known all her life, and for little Kristol. Over the next few months the visit to her brother and sister-in-law will become an almost weekly event, a comfort for Florence and a welcome diversion for Imogene, who, for all her enjoyment of her privacy, is finding her weekends empty.

February 24: Left at 9:00. Hard to find where the kids [Dave and Florence] lived but I did. Florence & I went downtown——I got a purse.

February 26: Last night it took me 45 minutes to get a southbound bus. All the teachers were all tired out from their vacation.

March 7: And I've blessed the day I took the third [grade]——best class I ever had. Quite a bit of fun playing marbles.

March 16: Meant to go to the prom but didn't get around to do it. Doris wrote Snip [one of Imogene's horses] was broken. Guess I'll go home this summer.

March 18: Just got my tucker [on her sewing machine] to working at last. Now to make Kristie Lee's dress. Jones came for a chat.

March 19: What a life——such a wet, sloppy day. Heard Gael's girl was lots older than he——has a 12 yr. old boy.

So Gael is engaged. Another of Imogene's unavailable men friends, he's apparently been engaged for some time, and his girl——her name is Alice—— probably has been the object of the gossip and "chats" that Imogene has been noting this winter. Although she has come to depend upon Gael, asks him for disciplinary support, meets him for coffee, plots with him over the PTA agenda, the only hint of her feelings she gives is the remark that Alice is "lots older." But note her physical response:

March 24: Developed a headache tonight. Golly I was really sick at my stomach. The sickest I've been for ages.

March 25: Sunday. Felt not too good. Jones came. She's going to move in next year. Think I'll like that.

March 27: Schafer was up & told us we were raised. $2000. No contracts. Curses. I can't wait. Ran down to see Jones & Simmons.

And then the quiet days of trivia and school gossip are interrupted by the briefest and most ominous of entries:

March 28: Letter from Mother about Pa. I have been quite disturbed. He had another spell & bothered all of Straw.

The "spell" Imogene refers to is A. P.'s disastrous caper in the moonlight. Up until now, her mother has been able to keep A. P.'s deterioration within the family, to a point, but now that he's bothered "all of Straw," something really will have to be done. But what? Imogene doesn't speculate in her diary, but the next day she catches a bus to spend Easter with Dave and Florence in Seattle. Sylva and Ervin will come down from Bremerton to make a family occasion, and surely the two sisters and their brother will discuss A. P. and what is to be done—and whose responsibility and whose fault—and perhaps when their words are spent, they will feel purged and relieved until the next bad news arrives.

March 30: We really left town—6 of us left on the 4:00 bus. Simmons spill[ed] a lot of dirt on the H[igh] S[chool] teachers.

March 31: Florence & I went downtown. She got a blue spring coat Dave likes very much. I got a hot pair of blue shoes.

April 1: Sylva & Ervin came over for dinner. K.L. enjoyed her Easter rabbit & eggs. We went up to the top of the Smith Tower [at that time the tallest building in Seattle].

April 2: Ran down to see Jones. We are all huffy over the salary situation. Heard Mrs. Woodard got a big raise. A kid broke her collar bone. One of Mrs. Blue's.

April 3: Contracts out—I got 4th & $2000. Guess they will be around with other contracts. We all kicked about Woodard's raise.

April 5: Simmons came over to chew the fat with me. I bet Jones leaves. I told Mrs. Furness I wanted the other apt. if she did.

April 8: April showers today. Ate in the Jiffy. Gael was there. We talked. He has moved my bookcase.

April 9: Last night Gael got up because his leg pained him & passed out cold. He was full of it today. Quite a letter from Doris. Pa is really out of his mind.

My mother wrote the stark facts that my grandmother may have tried to gloss over. That A. P. is given to irrational outbursts and paranoid fantasies. That no one can predict whether he'll stay in his bed or leap out of it and go running off into the night. That, of all people, he fears his wife. My mother is exact and specific. There can be no doubting the truth of what she writes, or that she cannot possibly keep A. P. at the ranch. She can't take care of him, not with her endless responsibilities, not with her two little girls.

April 10: Ran down to see Jones. She was crying. Guess she will leave. Heard there had been a lot of windows broken. Simmons came over.

April 11: Went to sewing circle at Bunny's. Her house & flowers were lovely. Their dessert was luscious. Gael has asked me to take 7th. Guess I will.

Imogene had hoped to take the fourth grade and follow her former third-graders for the coming year. Teaching the seventh grade will mean new material and new preparation for her, but also an advancement, and for the rest of her teaching career she will teach seventh- and eighth-graders. After she moves up to Port Angeles, on Washington's Olympic Peninsula, she will specialize in math, her old nemesis, and one of her seventh-grade math students will be the future poet Tess Gallagher.

April 12: Short note from Florence. They won't be down. I'm disap-pointed. Pres. Roosevelt died today. What a mess.

Does she refer to the state of the country after the president's death as the "mess," or is she thinking about her father, or about the battles being fought among the teachers of the Tenino school district?

Why is Jones crying? What is the significance of the broken windows?

How is Imogene dealing with all this stress? That much, at least, I know. She's throwing herself into activity, immersing herself in the life of the school. It's no wonder that she's glad for Mondays.

April 13: Played base ball. 3-4 boys against 6th girls. 7-8—we lost. Went to Jones & Simmons was there. She's [Simmons] sure set to fight Gael tooth & nail next year.

April 14: Cleaned house—all but my front room. Got summer school catalog. Picked out subjects I'd like to take.

April 16: Letters from both Sylva & Doris. I don't see how this summer will ever come out. I think it is a mistake to try to keep Pa at Jack's.

April 23: Helen pretty crabby. It rained all day. Bitchy weather. Wish the war would end. Accounts sound good.

April 24: Got my dress all done but the hem. Lord, how I hate to go home when I really want to go to summer school.

Here's a change! Up until now she has hated the thought of summer school, has been eager to get back to Montana, every summer and every Christmas that she can afford. But whether from working so hard at the ranch last summer, or—more likely—from the increasing tension in her family, she'd rather keep some distance, stay within these placid southwestern Washington meadows or, better yet, travel up to Bellingham with its forests and salt air and enroll at Western Washington University. Stepping off into strange territory holds no terrors for her; she knows she can live by herself and learn her way around an unfamiliar campus, and at least this time she's saved enough that she won't have to work in a box factory or a cannery and still try to study. Yes, the peace and quiet of a college campus is definitely attractive to her this year.

I hate it when my family tears me apart, reads one unexplained line in her diary.

April 25: Letter from Mother. Said she was going to try to establish a home in Lewistown. She sent for Sylva. I wonder if she [Sylva] will go.

My grandmother continues to insist that A. P. is her responsibility and no one else's, that she can make a home for him, that her iron willpower that has carried her through so much in her life—her early defiance of her father, her loss of a child, her loss of respect for her husband, her economic hardships and her wandering, endless teaching career—will see her through this new disaster. She does not know how to bend, she does not know how to give up. Not until she is confronted, finally, by all four of her grown children and her two sons-in-law will she admit that she cannot care for A. P.

April 26: Letter from Sylva. Ma asked her if she would come on a moment's notice. O, golly—have been planning clothes & the pounds I hope to lose [during her carefree summer at Western Washington University, now in jeopardy].

April 28: Met Gael this morning & had a cup of coffee with him & talked over the [junior class] play. Frisbie came to spade for me & let it out D.Y. & Bobby B. had been fighting.

Frisbie. He's just finishing the sixth grade at Tenino Elementary, and although he's one of those kids who is always in a scrape, Imogene rather likes him. She'll note his misadventures as long as she lives in Tenino. *Frisbie chewed gum. So Gael will paddle him. Poor Frisbie.*

After a year or two of Frisbie did this, Frisbie did that, she'll note that *Frisbie has quit school.* Then, *Frisbie's brother dragged him back. We'll see what he does next.*

Out of curiosity, I looked for Frisbie's picture in the 1946 Tenino high school yearbook and found him in several places, with a lock of blond hair falling over his face, grinning at that long-ago photographer. A rapscallion, no doubt about it, and Imogene must have hidden her laughter and secret enjoyment of his escapades.

May 2: Sewed on my pink dress. Went to visit Jones. Washed when I came back. Golly today was hot. Helise sent me 2 pks of cig. How welcome.

May 3: I blew up at Terry & Helen. Got Gale to call Dale R. down. Helen & her 4th grade were all sore at me because I sent a kid to the office for being noisy.

May 4: Well it's over [the operetta, which the school presents every year]. Really got a kick out of being back stage. Gael bought me a hamberger & coffee & we rehashed it. Talked with Mrs. Beam.

May 5: Got to Florences in good time. We went down town. I got a coat. When we got back I called Sylva. She leaves for Mont[ana] tonight—we went down to see her.

May 6: We went out to Alki Pt. K.L. didn't like the waves. The buses were changed. I lost an earring but Florence found it. Home & letter from Doris. Poor Ma.

May 7: Waited for the announcement of the end of the war. Gee, it was hot & I felt lousy. Visited Joy. Frank W[eketer, the high school principal] told Simmons off today.

May 8: V-E Day. School as usual. Gave tests—worked all evening on them. Golly, mine did very well. Went to a teachers meeting at the H.S.

Although the headlines on May 8 in the Seattle *Post-Intelligence* were six inches high—IT'S OVER IN EUROPE—the reaction to V-E Day throughout Washington seems to have been nearly as subdued as it was in Tenino. "The joy at the news of the German surrender was tempered for thousands of Washington families with kinfolk or friends listed as missing, or as prisoners of war, or as killed in action," writes James R. Warren in his study of the war years in Washington State. Although some of the scariest news had been kept from the public, like the May 5 death of a woman and five children in Oregon from one of the bomb-laden balloons that the Japanese had been sending across the Pacific on the wind currents, the residents of Washington were only too aware that their war, the war in the Pacific Rim, was far from over.

May 11: Caught the 4:11 bus. Gael went to town [on the same bus] & we had a chat about next year. In a way I look forward to it.

May 14: Letter from Sylva. She & Dave took Pa to a home near Deer Lodge. $75 a mo. Also heard from Aunt Mary.

The small town of Deer Lodge nestles in the shadow of mountains in Powell County, Montana, about 250 miles southwest of Denton. Somehow the family had located a private care facility in Deer Lodge, where A. P. would spend the last five years of his life. As a child, I realized only that my grandfather had been taken to Deer Lodge, and that I missed him. Reading my aunt's diaries, absorbing her scant notes, I shudder at the thought of that

250-mile drive at thirty or forty miles an hour over narrow roads, Sylva and Dave barely on speaking terms after all the arguments and recriminations over the past weeks and months, and A. P. in the back seat, probably childish, cooperative, or cantankerous by turn. They wouldn't have dared let him out of their sight. When they stopped for gasoline, Sylva would have watched him while Dave paid their bill. If A. P. needed to relieve himself, Dave would have gone with him. Did they stop for a meal? Did Sylva and Dave sit at a lunch counter with their father between them? Did they ever in their lives talk and try to ease each other's memories of that journey? Somehow I doubt it.

Imogene has avoided this dismal journey, but her turn is coming, and she knows it. As she winds up her school year, making out reports, preparing for closing exercises and the school picnic, she also is making her own travel arrangements to Montana.

May 16: Did a lot of work on my reports. Also did all my dittoing for the rest of the year.

May 22: Made ice cream all morning [for the school picnic the next day]. It was really good. We sampled it after school. Mrs. Hales just worked so hard.

And then, like a reminder that the war really is not over, the news about Dix Moser:

May 23: What a picnic. I never saw such a mob of kids in my life. I went down to the H.S. for the moving up ceremony. Dix Moser was killed. I feel so sorry for his mother.

May 24: Called on Mrs. Furness [her landlady]—paid rent till Aug. Ate quite a good supper. Kids are souveniring us to death at school.

May 25: Last day, I always hate it. Caught the 2:11 bus. Gale did too, &
we rode up to Tacoma together. I'll leave tonight on the train at 7:50.

She's on her way back to Montana now, passing at twilight through mountain scenery along the northern rail route in a ratcheting, crowded passenger
car. Perhaps she leans back against the headrest, tries to sleep. Now if Gael
were just in the next seat, they'd be having as good a visit as they had on the
bus to Tacoma last night. She has to laugh to herself, remembering some of
the jokes he told. Thinking about him, she can almost feel the warm brush of
his arm against hers. If Gael were in the seat next to her, instead of that snoring stranger, what a surprise the kids in Montana would be in for, Imogene
and Gael getting off the train together—but she stifles that fantasy before it
can bloom. Won't happen, not with Gael. He's too good a friend. Won't let
herself think further.

To distract herself, she opens her eyes in the darkened car, looks out her
window and happens to see the Glacier Park elk herd silhouetted against
the last of the light. Just a glimpse of those heavy, contained bodies of the
cows, the mighty rack of the bull, before the elk are behind her. Clackety-
clack, clackety-clack. She closes her eyes again, searches for a safe fantasy to
put herself to sleep with. A pirate out of *Wind from the Carolinas,* perhaps.
Herself in period satin, skirts billowing. It's no use. Her neck is stiff, her back
aches, headache threatens. Finally at Shelby the snoring stranger wakes up and
departs the train, and she can put her feet up on the seat and try to get comfortable. At least they're past Shelby now, and only a few more hours to go.

May 26: The train was crowded as far as Columbia Falls [in western Mon-
tana]. I got a seat then alone. At Shelby I had a double seat.

May 27: Ethel [Uncle Theo's youngest daughter] met me [possibly in
Ware, near home, but more likely in Harlowton, sixty miles to the southeast.
That Ethel is meeting Imogene's train, that nobody else can get away, is a

reminder how much spring work is going on in Montana.] It is rainy. Jack hoped to brand but it is too wet. Lots of company. I rode old Pet across the [Judith] river [probably to visit Uncle Theo's family].

May 28: Doris & I helped Jack punch cows. We caught Snip & brot him home. Lord, I hope LaFountain [a local Metis horse-breaker] finishes the horses.

May 29: Doris & Ma washed. The rest went to town to a sale. Wed. Jack wants to brand. After that I guess Ma wants to go to Deer Lodge to see Pa.

May 30: Quite a branding—110 calves—10 men—a big feed. Wonderful ice cream. Betty got a heifer calf branded [my father's form of a savings account for his daughters was to brand calves for us].

May 31: Jack went for a load of barley. Ma got to see the ranch. Her tenant is getting a crop in. Doris, Jack & I cut out the yearlings. Rode from 5-9.

The ranch Imogene refers to here is the Welch home ranch, near Denton, with that two-room frame house and attic bedroom where Imogene once slept and stored her junk until her mother rented out the place and she had to move everything to Doris's. During her teaching years in Montana, off in those sparsely furnished teacherages, this ranch was Imogene's home base, her one certain point from which she departed and returned. The house on its knoll overlooking wheatfields and blowing grass, the attic reached by climbing a ladder nailed to the kitchen wall and through a trapdoor. In the attic, her own bed, the familiar smell of her quilts, and real silence, the sound of silence best heard after a return from even a small town with its anonymous night traffic. Out here are no highways, only the two tracks of a dirt road leading out of the yard and along a barbed wire fence toward the horizon. Out here, even during wartime, the remote drone of an airplane is rare. And now there are no Welches out here to receive the silence, only the tenant and his family, whose eyes see and ears hear through a context of their own. At least the tenant will get a crop in, pay a third of the cash it brings to Imogene's mother, toward her expenses and A. P.'s. But Imogene, who called herself a homeless rat last summer, has nowhere to call hers in Montana now. She can share a bed with one of her sister's little girls. Sit at her sister's table. Or stay with her mother in a rented hotel room. Maybe the censorious voices sound in her head: *After all, she's not married! Where else would she live?*

And now she's coming in for her share of the family burden, as she knew she would. Her stark lines convey something of the twelve-hour bus trip to Deer Lodge with her mother:

> *June 1: Ma & I went to Deer Lodge. Quite a trip. I hated it but Ma couldn't rest till she saw Pa.*

> *June 2: Slept in a lobby from 2-6. Got a room. Saw Pa. Just as I thot. Ma could see she couldn't care for him.*

> *June 3: Started home by bus after 9:00 & got to Lewistown at 9. Rained all day. Saw George Swears [a friend of my father's].*

> *June 4: Killed time. Shopped. Got the kids some junk. Ma got a room for a week. I'll go to Jack's tomorrow. Rain—rain.*

> *June 5: Jack met me at Ware [she probably took the train from Lewistown, where she has been staying with her mother in a hotel]—Golly is it muddy. Poor kids—its tough on them when it is so wet.*

> *June 6: Wed. Still raining. Letter from Ruth. Nuts, I'll be glad to get started at summer school.*

> *June 7: Thurs. Fried chicken for supper. Counted Mary's books. She needs a primer & 2 1st readers.*

Until I read those lines, I had no idea that Imogene was supervising my early education. I was five years old that summer, and dying to be read to, and none of the grownups had the time or the inclination to sit down and read to me, and I remember my frustration and boredom and the knowledge that currents of incomprehensible emotions were swirling over my head, that my mother and my aunts and my grandmother were disturbed and angry—with themselves, with each other, with me? I didn't know. I sulked and kicked at things and teased my toddler sister until my mother beat my bottom with her clothes brush, and finally I shambled off and hid in the chokecherry grove below the cabin, where one trail led to the chicken house and another to an ancient, unused outhouse from the time of the house that burned.

By June the chokecherry blossoms had fallen and the hard green cherries had set on, growing in clusters like miniature grapes. I picked the cherries and pretended that I was an Indian maiden, the last of my kind, and then I gathered last year's rosehips from the wild roses, broke them open, and tried grinding their seeds between two rocks. Stole my mother's paring knife and carved my way deeper into the brush. Pulled grass and made myself a nest among the thorns, where no one could find me, and I could feel sorry for myself or ponder dark thoughts, about the women who had burned to death, or my grandfather's fugitive mind, or where I would go and what I would do when I was grown and could get away from this place.

The next summer, in just such a mood, I would seize my father's old geography book—*Our Little Neighbors at Work and Play,* filled with accounts of children's lives in wonderful, faraway places like China or the Philippines—which I had been badgering somebody, anybody, to read to me, and I would carry it off to one of my hiding places and try reading it to myself. By then I was six, and I could read, after a fashion, recognizing individual words and stringing them together, but it wasn't an easy process, it wasn't pleasant, it had none of the lulling, out-of-body transportation to another time and place that came with being read to. On that particular day, however, I bore down on *Our Little Neighbors at Work and Play,* one word to the next, one line after another, and then somehow I was floating in a current, absorbing the book as the chokecherry leaves absorbed sunlight. Thought or effort had nothing to do with what I was experiencing, which was a way of being, a kind of transcendence, and I knew I would never go back to what I was.

Meanwhile, my aunt feels bored, frustrated, hemmed in by family. While I dream of the world beyond our Montana river bottoms and dry hills, she notes the trivial days and doings between her and her own life:

June 9: Spent the evening at Theo Jr. A nice supper but I did not relish the trip home. Betty really "My, my" when we went into the river [in the wagon, behind a team of horses].

June 10: A wet day. Everyone sleeping & taking it easy. I'll be glad to get on with my summers work.

June 11: We went to town. I got the kids books & bananas. How they like them. Got Ma a hat for her birthday.

June 13: Jack fenced. They have so much to do but someday they will have a real place here.

June 14: Jack took me to the train. Just caught it. Looked like rain. Had to ride to Ware for my coat. Dave wrote the meanest letter to us.

June 15: Had a headache—not bad. Hard to leave Mother—but at least she feels better. This has been a tough spring for her.

June 16: Oh, me. How I loathe traveling on a train. My 20th trip across the Rockies. Wonder if I'll go home next summer.

After the war, she will buy an airline ticket and fly over the Rockies. It will be the end of another era: the end of cheap and available rail connections throughout the Rocky Mountain west. For Imogene it is another transition. For the first time, she's wondering if she really wants to make this trip every summer. Until now, it has been homesickness that she writes about, her longing for Montana and for her family, and how she is scraping together the money and studying the rail schedules to find a way home. Home will always be in Montana, but increasingly Montana will be where she's from. She lives in Washington, now. Washington is where she'll put down her roots, and eventually home, real home, will be her own house and rampant garden overlooking the Strait of Juan de Fuca.

June 18: Finished registering [for the summer term at Western Washington University in Bellingham]. Wrote to Mother & Doris. I am so lonely for Betty & Mary.

June 19: First day over & all going well. Washed my hair & some hose. Wish I could buy more hose. Nice lunches at Eden Hall.

June 22: Bought a pair of nonrationed play shoes—white. Hot cha. Now I can get a pair of rationed oxfords & still have my Aug. stamps.

June 26: Tuesday. I enjoy my music class the most. Mr. Boson is quite a card. Took a test this A.M. Got my hair done.

June 28: Salmon bake tonight. It was delicious. Bumped into Bobbie Wilson [who taught at Napavine, the first year Imogene was there, and then moved to Vancouver]. Can you imagine that.

July 3: Letter from Sylva. Holiday tomorrow—nowhere to go. Wish I had a date. It's a long time since I had a real Hell raisin' 4th.

July 4: Ma at Jack's, Pa in a home—I guess I should not crab. Had a good dinner to the tune of $1.57.

July 6: Lordy, I'll be glad for school to start this fall. Summer school is not much fun. Kind of had the feel last spring for it but Pa sort of took the edge off.

July 10: Went swimming this P.M. Enjoyed it very much & believe I'll be able to do a quarter of a mile by the end of the summer. Hope to get a swan & jackknife.

July 11: My period again. Feel punk. My panel in T[eaching] T[echniques] is rotten, I think. Nuts to all T. T. A bunch of old mossbacks.

July 17: Went swimming. Did 6 lengths. Want to get a good backstroke—breast, crawl, front, swan, & jackknife. And do a 1/4 mile.

July 18: Like my classes much better—had swimming, archery. Saw Gael & had a short chat with him.

July 30: Mon. Curses—they closed the pool on account of polio. Does that irk me. Bet it won't get opened all summer.

August 1: Wed. Play pingpong instead of swim. It's fun—but not so much as swimming & I did want to work on diving.

August 6: Letter from Bunny. Said Gael might be in grade school! Damn if he is. Mother writes she would like me to go in with her & buy & fix up a house next summer.

Especially after A. P.'s removal to the nursing home, my grandmother dreamed of making a home for her unmarried daughter, who in her eyes was never quite an adult. Given her strong sense of duty, Imogene must have felt torn between the obedient daughter she always had been and the grown woman she had become. But just as her diary entries earlier in the summer hint, she's coming to understand that she can love her family, she can help her family, she can write and visit and chauffeur and support, she can punch cows, cook and wash dishes and help with branding, and she can round up reading material for her bookworm of a niece, but to be her own woman she must always say goodbye, board the train or get behind the wheel of her own car, face west again, and pick up the threads she's weaving into a life she never imagined but somehow finds satisfying. If she no longer dreams of a ranch and a cowboy husband like her sister Doris's, her dreams now are within her reach. A house of her own, a garden, a job in a pleasant town that's far enough from Montana that she can shed the half-life of her mother's unmarried daughter, her sisters' understudy, her nieces' favorite auntie. To her pupils she's Miss Welch, to her friends she becomes Gene, or Genie, and always she has her pets, her books, her sewing.

A few days remain of summer school in Bellingham, a few more days before the war is over and life begins again as postwar:

August 8: Hot dog. I took second place in an archery contest—5 ends— have 32. Made one 40. Letter from Aunt Clara [in Idaho]. They had been to see Pa. Wonder what Dave thinks.

August 9: Took 3rd in archery today—but my days average was good. Got an invitation to Gael's wedding.

August 11: Got a book for K.L. She's 3 next Friday. Hot cha—only a week more. Looks like the war is on its way out.

August 12: Sunday. Spent the day wondering if peace would be declared. Some people aren't at all excited.

August 13: Monday—still waiting for the news that war is over.

August 14: At last. The whistles blew at 4:00. We were in Math class so we got out. Cora & I watched the parade & crowds.

The next day would be V-J Day and the official end of the war.

CONCLUSION

How to write a conclusion to Imogene's account of her war years? And what conclusions to write for Bernita, or for Daisy?

"No one can help you here. An ending takes an act of inspiration," writes Rick DeMarinis.

Creative writing classes always used to teach that fiction, in its concluding moments, contains an epiphany, or moment of revelation, during which the central character suddenly feels, or understands, a previously obscured mystery or hidden truth. Norman Maclean's father teaches him to hear the words under the current of the river that runs through all things. Gabriel Conroy hears the snow falling faintly through the universe. The Alpha and the Omega. Ripeness is all. The rest is silence.

No such certain agreement exists in the "how-to" circles today. "[The epiphany] is a minor but pernicious lie of literature, that at times like these, after significant or disappointing divulgences, at arrivals or departures of obvious importance, when touchdowns are scored, knock-outs recorded, loved ones buried, orgasms notched, that at such times we are any of us altogether in an emotion, that we are within ourselves and not able to detect other emotions we might also be feeling, or be about to feel, or prefer to feel," complains Richard Ford's character Frank Bascombe in *The Sportswriter*. "If it's literature's job to tell the truth about these moments, it usually fails, in my opinion, and it's the writer's fault for falling into such conventions."

"I don't believe a character's experiences in a story have to be validated by a conclusive insight or a brilliant visionary stop-time movement," writes Charles Baxter, in *Burning Down the House: Essays on Fiction*. He adds, "One other trouble with epiphanic endings is that they have become a tic, a habit, among writers (and editors) of literary fiction."

If advice for concluding fiction tends to be negative (avoid the "suddenly I realized" cliche) or the easy-to-give, hard-to-follow (read and note well the conclusions drawn by other writers), where can the writer of nonfiction turn for advice? How does she end a road trip through a dimensionless map?

Pondering this question, remembering the anxieties of writing students (I'm afraid I've got an epiphany in this story! or, I hate writing nonfiction, I feel so out of control of the conclusion!), I riffled through a dozen or so handbooks on creative writing, the kind of complementary handbooks that presses send to professors in hopes that they will require their students to buy them. These handbooks tend to fall into two categories, the didactic and the romantic. Those that focus on craft, like Robie Macauley's *Techniques in Fiction*, will assume that writing can be learned and will explain, for example, the difference between an omniscient and a limited point of view. Those that focus on sensitivity, like Natalie Goldberg's *Writing Down the Bones: Freeing the Writer Within*, will assume that writing is plumbed from the depths of the writer and will offer exercises to facilitate the overflow. Neither category is without usefulness, especially for beginning writing students, although most emphasize the writing of fiction over the writing of nonfiction. My surprising discovery, however, in my hurried riffling through tables of contents and indexes, was that, while both categories are ripe with advice on getting started, with whole sections on freewriting prompts, and effective first lines, and the pros and cons of opening with dialogue, say, or with a general observation, or with scene-setting, most have nothing at all to say about conclusions. Even Rick DeMarinis, who includes a four-page section entitled "Endings," speaks mainly about the difficulty of conclusions, or points to examples in poetry and fiction.

What does this mean? Why such an absence? Do the writers of creative writing handbooks assume that everyone searches for a beginning, but that no one will get around to finishing? Or that conclusions will take care of themselves? Or perhaps, especially in nonfiction, there are no conclusions? The closest I could find to a nonfiction equivalent of an epiphany, complete with the potential for the reflexive tic of a cliche, was in Philip Gerard's *Creative Nonfiction: Researching and Crafting Stories of Real Life:* "An ending derives from all that has gone before. . . . It is often useful to end on a resonant image, one that will bring back the rest of the piece."

What closure, then, to bring to Imogene's diaries? What happened next? What happened to Bernita, in postwar England, with her violin and her gaudy engagement ring, given to her by faceless Jake? What of Daisy, with her embroidered tablecloths and placemats, gathering her homemade lares and penates around her in postwar San Francisco? "A story," writes Charles Baxter, "can be a series of clues but not a solution, an enfolding of a mystery instead of a revelation."

So:

After her brief elation over the war's end, Imogene finished summer school and returned to Tenino to teach for another year. But she didn't stay in Tenino long. The war had given her the opportunity, and she seized it. Accumulating credits during the summers, she completed her baccalaureate degree at Western Washington University and took the position in Port Angeles, up on the Olympic Peninsula, teaching junior high math and breathing salt air. For a few years my mother's letters would be addressed to her at 319 ½ East

6th Street in Port Angeles, which she rented from a Mr. and Mrs. Harrison. The Harrisons remained her friends for the rest of their lives, but Imogene lived in their apartment only until she saved enough money to buy a lot north of town, large enough for berry bushes and fruit trees and flowerbeds and a vegetable garden. Here, with financing from Aunt Mable, and with her brother-in-law Ervin as contractor, she built her dream house with windows that looked out across the Strait of Juan de Fuca toward the distant lights of Victoria, British Columbia. She remained a dutiful daughter, and when my grandmother finally retired from teaching and bought her five-acre chicken ranch near Seattle, Imogene made the long drive and ferry crossing at least once a month to lend a hand with whatever needed to be done. Every summer she came to Montana for a few weeks and lent a hand at the ranch, and she lent my sister and me her sympathetic ear and her wisdom. Her birthday checks and Christmas checks bought us some of the skirts and sweaters that we thought we had to have, to fit in with the girls in town, and her sturdiness buoyed us. We were the most fortunate of nieces.

But always she left us after those few weeks during the summers, left us and drove back toward that other life that we knew so little about. Back to her cats and her garden, to catch up with her weeding before she began another school term with its endless stream of seventh-graders and classroom routines and friendships and fallings-out and gossip and potlucks. She never married— in her seventies, she groused about friends who had tried to fix her up— "With an *alcoholic,* and why at my time of life they'd think an alcoholic husband would be better than none!"—but her diaries gradually reflect her contentment with what she once called her "own vine and fig tree," until, at last, her mind wavers, dissolves, and the diaries come to an end.

Or this:

West of the spectacular scenery of the Cascade mountains, but still a long way from the ocean, inland Washington State spreads into serene meadows in the shelter of low hills. Subdivisions sprawling down from Olympia have taken over many of these meadows, and auto repair shops and fertilizer dealer-ships in brightly colored aluminum siding are open for business along the two-lane highway that angles northeast from Interstate Five. Yet there are moments when June sunlight on ripening grass, the soft shape of firs along the sur-rounding hills, cattle sleeping in pastures, and the white faces of daisies in the borrow pits suggest to me that this is a road my aunt may have driven toward a new teaching job in 1943.

Because in her later years my aunt had a habit of beginning sentences with, "When I lived in Tenino—" and, in part, because I cannot remember how she ended those sentences, I have turned off I-5 this morning to follow this narrow highway through pastures and meadows toward a town where I have never been.

All roads lead somewhere, but I am beginning to wonder if this one really leads to Tenino. I have seen no markers since I turned off the interstate, and when I pass a roadside grocery offering beer and ice and propane for campers, I tell myself that I should have stopped and asked. But my own lifetime habit has been to press on, around just one more bend in the road, over one more hill to see what lies beyond. It is a habit which has too often led me miles in the wrong direction, not to speak of hanging on to relationships—jobs, mar-riages—for years longer than I should have. I wonder if this is what my daugh-ters will remember about me, years from now: *for my mother, it always had to be one more bend in the road, one more hilltop, even when she worried it was the wrong direction.*

My youngest daughter, Rachel, is nineteen. Today she rides beside me on what I hope is the road to Tenino, observing the passing scenery, making no requests, expressing no opinions. Rachel and I are pretending that she has come with me on this road trip to help with the driving, but we both know it is because she is afraid to stay home alone. It has been over a year since her last bad episode, when she was hospitalized for depression for over a month, but now her phantom fears are back, the omens only she perceives, the universal connections only she draws. I'm staking a lot on her recent change in medication, which has left her less weepy, if more perplexed.

To me it sometimes feels as though Rachel has reverted to a younger self who used to ride beside me, hugging her Cabbage Patch doll, watching for signs of McDonald's Golden Arches, and asking strange questions. "What are you, Mom?" It's as though she's learning about the world all over again, from this side of a divide, and I think, hope, it's just possible that my investigation into the earlier life of the woman she remembers only as white-haired, blank-eyed Auntie in the final years of senile dementia will offer Rachel a connection she can trust.

I had begun reading my aunt's diaries after her death, trying to learn something about my own life from the way she had lived hers. I had the idea of writing a book based on her entries during World War II, which had been a time of great transition for her, and I got as far as a first draft. But the book resisted me, as though it did not want to be written, and now I'm driving miles out of my way to Tenino, Washington, where my aunt taught school during most of the war years, to get a sense of this place and what it may reveal.

My aunt had left Tenino and gone to teach in Port Angeles, on the Olympic Peninsula, by the time I was old enough to visit her, and now, driving through this quiet countryside, I'm beginning to realize how much I've always associated her life in Washington with long ferry rides through the smell of salt and tar and those spectacular peninsula vistas of mountains and ocean. Perhaps that's why I feel unsettled by this easy, inland highway. It's not taking me where I expected to be.

And of course, reading and rereading my aunt's diaries have been no help to me at all in imagining landscape. She notes the trivia of her life, the doings of her school children—*September 7, 1944: Found a pupil had promoted herself from 1 to 3rd grade*—the difficulties the war is causing her—*October 12, 1944: Cigarettes sure are short*—the arcane and long-forgotten politics of the faculty—

November 27, 1944: Simmons was mad—said she was the only teacher they didn't invite last year—but she never describes the town, never writes a word about the surrounding fields and hills, never assumes a reader who might long for context or connections. Of course she doesn't explain what she already knows. She makes the occasional remark that I pause on—*Bob Wilson taped a kid's mouth shut today. I had to laugh*—but any beginning is arbitrary, any closure years ahead. Open a diary where I will, I'm always in midstream.

Also, in reading her diaries, I am living in my aunt's present tense. Although she writes in past tense—*December 1, 1944: Took the kids to a movie in teckni-color—Buffalo Bill. It was good. I even liked it*—she is writing in her own moment, at a time when Technicolor is an innovation. As I read, I feel as though I'm living within a memory like my own, which explores and abandons and redis-covers the trails of a dimensionless map, roused perhaps from some chance remark of Rachel's, who even now turns from her contemplation of the scenery and asks,

"Mom, how do trees decide what color they're going to be?"

I'm nonplussed for a moment. "What do you mean?"

"I just saw a purple tree."

"A what—oh—that was a red maple. It's got to do with chlorophyll—I don't know, I don't remember how—I suppose I once learned how trees process sunlight—high school biology—but it's not as though they actually *decide*, the color depends on their genus and species—"

"They're born with it, can't change it?"

"I guess."

"I don't like hearing that," she says, and then I remember her anxieties about determinism and wonder what else I could have said.

To look at Rachel is to see her father, who died when she was seven. She barely remembers him, but she has his eyes, shading from blue to green depending on light and background and mood, the long shape of his bones, the angles of his face, and even the honey-blonde hair which, this summer, has grown almost to her waist in a tangle of curls. I don't know where these genes come from. Rachel's father was the only fair-haired child his parents had, of five. Does Rachel carry his compulsion toward risk and high stakes, and is she brain-damaged from Ecstasy, as he was, eventually, by oxygen deprivation and disease? We have no way of knowing, but I can't wonder that Rachel worries about fate.

I, on the other hand, look like my mother and my aunt and my grandmother, women who believed that the way to overcome any obstacle was to grit their teeth and try harder. Consider how my aunt, limping on crutches from that June horse-and-mowing machine accident that nearly severed her right foot, loaded such of her belongings as she could fit into her Ford sedan and left family and friends and all that was familiar in Denton, Montana, to drive for three twelve-hour days through late summer heat to this part of Washington State, where she had managed to locate a teaching job. I read between the lines of her diary and try to imagine that brown-haired, round-faced young woman after those three days, during which she averaged about 25 miles an hour and spent her nights in campgrounds because she could not afford lodging, arriving in that strange town, parking her car on a residential street and reaching for her crutch. Stepping out on gravel and trying not to put weight on a foot so swollen that it cannot bear a shoe while she looks up at the stairs she's going to have to climb to her new apartment.

Mrs. Curtis helped me carry my things upstairs. Seems nice.

Two days later, that young woman was teaching a combined class of 39 third- and fourth-graders. Do I carry the genes for even a faint imprint of her spine? Does Rachel? I sure hope so.

My aunt mentions the war very little in her diaries, which is one of the reasons why I've had trouble writing the book I originally envisioned. After an initial outburst—*I say little about the war. It shadows every day*—she seems concerned mainly with scarcities or inconveniences—*Out of cigarettes. Damn it. Ordered some Sat. but they never got in,* or, *Was able to get a box of marshmallows, the first in a year, thot they would make a nice treat for the Bluebirds.* She is saddened by the death of a local boy, Dix Moser, and occasionally she notes a really dramatic event, as on June 6, 1944, on her way home to Montana with her sister: *D-Day—invasion—we got in on the middle of a broadcast.* But even then she adds, *Had a fairly good day. Made Cheney. Paid $3 for a cabin.*

Because for my aunt in 1943 and 1944, the war just is. It goes on and on, it sometimes seems as though it never will be over, but meanwhile she goes about her life, teaching and gossiping and shopping for treats for her Bluebirds and dealing with her own small crises.

Guess what. Mice. I got 2 traps.

What counts as a crisis, after all? And what did I care about world events the night I coaxed a shivering, white-faced Rachel into my car and drove her to the emergency room, where an on-call doctor asked her if she had had thoughts of harming herself.

"I'm not going to tell you that," murmured Rachel, barely audible.

"I have to take that as a yes," said the doctor, as angrily as though she thought her logic should have jolted Rachel into reality.

But no, only another silence, and only the nervous movement of Rachel's eyes indicating that she had heard the doctor, that somewhere in the tangle of her mind she was processing the doctor's words, searching them for a loophole and escape.

"I have a professional duty not to allow you to harm yourself."

Silence.

"Either you can agree voluntarily to commit yourself, or we'll have to do it the hard way and call the judge and have you committed. Which is it going to be?"

Silence for what seems forever, and then—"Okay," whispers Rachel.

"You'll sign?"

"Yes," she whispers.

What did I note at that time of world events, when even the immediate background was a blur of lights and noise, faces appearing and reappearing around the blue curtain where my daughter sat numb on a hospital bed—no the psychologist hasn't answered, it's a weekend—yes, she's finally answered, she's on her way—yes, the best place for your daughter is St. Joe's in Lewiston—no, not St. Joe's after all, but the facility up in Coeur d'Alene. Someone's phoning to see if they have a bed available for her. Yes, they have a bed. Can you get your daughter there tonight?

"Yes," I said. "I'll get her there."

What was on my mind at that moment was the eighty-mile drive in the dark to Coeur d'Alene. Did I have enough gas in my car? Would I have to stop? Rachel looked docile enough, almost catatonic, but what if she tried to make a break and run off into the night, as my grandfather once did?

What counts as a crisis? On June 6, 1944, when my aunt heard that radio broadcast about D-Day and noted the cost of her night's lodging, she was on her way to Montana to help assess my grandfather, whose mind was hardening into the delusion that my grandmother was trying to kill him.

Much of what I know about Tenino comes from my aunt's postcard photograph of its main street, probably taken in the late 1930s. Perhaps the town was more of a market center when my aunt lived there than now, when its residents can take I-5 to shop in Olympia or even Seattle in a fraction of the time it would have taken in those days of bumpy roads and gas rationing.

Went to Olympia to shop for birthdays. Swore it is the last time for me. The bus was crowded. I had to stand both ways.

In the postcard photograph, Tenino's main street looks self-contained and hurried. Anything you really needed you could find along those two or three business blocks of single-story buildings of brick facades over dressed sandstone. A Model A truck is parked beside the Tenino Feed Store, a few more cars beside Puget Sound Power & Light and the barber shop and the drug store and Campbell & Campbell, which offers dry goods, shoes, and hardware. Farther down the street I can make out a cafe sign, but not whether it's the Jiffy, where my aunt so often ate dinner or met friends.

Ate in the Jiffy. . . . Met Gael this morning & had a cup of coffee with him &
talked over the [junior class] play.

Suddenly the highway ahead looks more promising; from the 35 MPH sign,
we must be nearing a town, and yes, there's another sign, *Entering Tenino,* and
next is a Lions Club emblem, and I remember a diary entry of my aunt's—
The Lion's Club gave a dinner & reception for the teachers. It was the nicest reception
I was ever at. I have time to wonder whether the Lions still hold receptions for
the local teachers every fall, and then the highway slows into a street which
bends, and with no warning I'm looking down the main street of Tenino, the
same main street in the postcard photograph that I've studied for so long, and
I catch my breath, because it's like driving through a veil into the past.

I glance at Rachel, but of course she doesn't see what I'm seeing, and of
course the street is not the same. The businesses have changed. There's a cafe,
but it's not the Jiffy, and there's an espresso bar, and a couple of antique
shops, and a quilting shop, all very contemporary. What is unchanged is the
street itself, the sunny pavement and the sandstone buildings in the same
places they were fifty years ago, and yes, carved into one long sandstone
facade is Campbell & Campbell, long closed now, but where in 1944 my aunt
noted that sheets could be purchased on sale for $2.50.

I should park my car and walk up and down this street, taking my time. But
time is what I don't have. I'm due in Portland, Oregon, this afternoon, and I
still have to locate the Tenino branch of the Timberland Regional Library and
see what they've got of local history. So I drive around the corner, past the old
sandstone city hall, wait for a crocodile of preschoolers between two teachers to cross the street, spot the library and turn into the parking lot. Obedient as one of the preschoolers, Rachel gets out of the car with me, waits while
I lock it, and follows me into the library.

Through these modern glass doors is no haunted past, but lots of ordinary
light falling through enormous windows on the clean surfaces of pale wood
tables and chairs and the tidy free-standing shelves of recent fiction and

nonfiction in plastic jackets. But the helpful woman at the circulation desk knows just where to find the material I need. She pulls out a slim paperbacked local history written in the 1970s, together with a few pamphlets and a couple of school yearbooks, and I thank her and settle with my notepad at one of the tables.

Rachel finds herself a seat at another table and looks out the window, uncomplaining but apparently uninterested in her surroundings even when the crocodile of preschoolers arrives, to be shushed and shooed into a corner for story hour. What is on Rachel's mind, what thoughts so deep? In the flood of light from the windows her face looks soft, her eyes untroubled by the storms that used to rise at any provocation from me, at any suggestion of mine so outrageous, for instance, that she should sit and wait while I read.

What is on my mind: not Tenino, not the book I am writing, but the plate glass doors of the locked facility in north Idaho and the light that falls down the corridor on the other side. The attendant who comes to answer my ring and let me into the library-like hush. Quiet children sit on plastic chairs along that corridor, surprisingly young children, one of them only four years old, Rachel tells me in the privacy of a conference room for the thirty minutes we are allowed to spend together once a week.

"A four-year-old? What could a four-year-old do, to be committed here?"

Rachel shrugs. "I don't really know. We aren't allowed to talk to each other."

Rachel looks pale and gaunt in her institutional gray sweats and shirt. It has taken weeks for her to be able to carry on a conversation more complicated than a whispered *yes* or *no* to direct questions. Weeks before she has consented to drug therapy for the depression that the therapists and the psychiatrist believe is related to unresolved feelings about her father's death. (Another source for worry. Does she carry the genes for the depression that runs like a polluted river through both sides of her family?)

I should not be surprised if she's angry with me, the psychiatrist has warned. Anger is an indication that she is beginning to recover. But she hasn't been angry, not with me, not that I can see. "Why haven't you given up on me?" she whispers, on one visit, and "Thank you for coming," at the end of another.

Is this a bad sign?

How ironic that I now worry about Rachel's docility, when only a few years ago it was her anger and defiance that kept me awake at night, wondering where I had gone wrong and what I should try next. I still don't know what I should try next. But I don't want her to catch me watching her, and so I drag my attention back to the little book on Tenino's history, and the next thing I know, I'm being reabsorbed into the past.

The forgotten politics of a past age. Tenino began as an accidental outcome of a dispute in the state capitol, Olympia, over the placement of a railroad line. Its very name may have to do with its location on the line: Ten-Nine-Oh. A rail spur ran out to the sandstone quarry, the very one my aunt noted on September 19, 1943: *Daisy [and I] went to the quarry & picked blackberries. It's a good swimming hole.* The quarry dates from 1888. It supplied much of the building materials not only for Tenino but for the public buildings of Olympia. In 1926 the quarrying operations ceased and a natural spring filled the old pit. *Daisy & I went swimming [again] in the old quarry 90 ft. deep,* my aunt notes on September 24, 1943, and adds, *So hot this afternoon.*

I come across more trivia as I read. Here's the outbreak of scarlet fever. From March 23 to April 3, 1944, the Tenino schools were closed to help avert an epidemic.

> *March 21, 1944: Nurse was out late tonight—they may close school for 2 weeks—how I hope—what a vacation—I could get caught up with everything.*

> *March 22, 1944: Nerts—a nurse checked the kids & sent 4 home for a week. I sure could use a vacation. It rained horrid. Bluebirds had to play inside.*

March 23, 1944: Hot dog! School out till April 3. Ten whole days of vacation. Isn't it wonderful. I'm going to catch up on all my odd jobs.

Trivia is what has caused so many problems for me with this book I've been writing. Who cares, I ask myself, about a stone quarry used as a swimming hole in southwest Washington State, or about a scarlet fever epidemic in 1944 that a young teacher welcomed so fervently because it gave her a ten-day vacation from classes? And yet, when I look up from the book of local history and see the library filled with light, the preschoolers in their corner where their story is being read aloud, Rachel with her hands folded, gazing patiently out the window, I feel a curious elation, as though I've discovered details that matter. At this moment, in this spinning light, I feel buoyant enough to float.

Is this sensation a testament to the power of close reading, or is it a testament to the habit of writing, however mundane, that not only connects the dots of local history but transcends history? It seems to me that, if only for the length of a sentence, Rachel and I and the preschoolers and the librarian and everyone in this small town have been freed from the inexorability of past tense. I can open one of my aunt's diaries at any page and experience her simultaneity of past and present; and in a kind of dramatic irony, I often can draw upon my memory and my research to foretell her future. Each of us, even the preschoolers, live in the present and contain the past, and we cannot describe the future until it, too, becomes the past. All else is illusory, no matter how hard I try to see around the next bend in the road or over the next hill or anticipate what will happen to Rachel.

It's time we were leaving the library. I want to make one more stop, at the office of the weekly newspaper, to see if by chance they've kept their files for the 1940s. I close the little volume of local history as Rachel turns from the window and I see, like one transparency layered upon another, my baby, my toddler, my angry adolescent, and now this heartbreakingly obedient nineteen-year-old.

"Would you like me to drive to Portland?" she asks, and I answer, "Yes, I'd like that."

And at this tiny evidence of her returning confidence, my heart leaps.

Now—months after our visit to Tenino, a *now* encrusted with more layers of the remembered past, and with a new draft of a book that has completely changed direction, I hand these final pages to Rachel and ask her to read.

"Ought I show it to anyone else?" I ask, as she finishes.

"Yes," she says.

"It doesn't seem to you an invasion of your privacy?"

"No."

Despite her one-word answers, Rachel really is much better than she was in early summer. She wasn't able to finish her semester of college, but she has found a job and kept it, and she has been doing the cooking for the two of us, and she has learned to play Scrabble well enough that occasionally she can beat me. I want more for her, though; and I want more *from* her, and so I press.

"What do you remember about Tenino?"

I've told her about Auntie and her life and her diaries. Now I wait as Rachel ponders.

"The dandelion in the sidewalk," she finally answers.

"A dandelion?"

"It was growing in a crack in the sidewalk outside the library. Nobody had picked it. It was just—there. You don't remember that?"

"No."

She shakes her head at this lapse in my memory. "Do you want to play Scrabble tonight?"

"Sure. But what if I were to publish these pages?"

"I think you should," she says.

NOTES

INTRODUCTION

I have quoted from page 3 of Will Baker's *Mountain Blood* (New York: Simon & Schuster, 1986); referred to Norman Maclean's *A River Runs Through It and Other Stories* (Chicago: Univ. of Chicago Press, 1976); and quoted from page 16 of Linda M. Hasselstrom's *Between Grass and Sky: Where I Live and Work* (Reno: Univ. of Nevada Press, 2002). Regarding postmodernist readings of diaries and letters, I have found Jennifer Sinor's *The Extraordinary Work of Ordinary Writing: Annie Ray's Diary* particularly useful for Sinor's review of the past twenty years of diary scholarship and for her thoughtful examination of the ways in which we may read alternative texts.

CHAPTER 1

In "Creating a Mythic Past: Spanish-style Architecture in Montana," *Montana the Magazine of Western History* 51, 3 (Autumn 2001), 46–59, Hipolito Rafael Chacon discusses the Fergus County courthouse along with several other historic buildings in Lewistown. Chacon's article is a delight to lose oneself in, particularly for those of us who grew up in Lewistown and can appreciate the clarity he brings to the familiar. In a letter to the editor of the Spring 2002 issue of *Montana the Magazine of Western History,* an elderly cousin of mine notes that Chacon's article awoke a recollection of her childhood pleasure in running up and down the courthouse's marble staircase and pretending she was a princess.

For the history of rural schools in Montana, I have relied heavily on the revised edition of *Montana: A History of Two Centuries,* by Michael P. Malone, Richard B. Roeder, and William Lang (Seattle: Univ. of Washington Press, 1991).

CHAPTER 4

The letters from David Welch and Florence Welch from which I quote in several chapters are part of my private collection, as is Imogene's undated poem in typescript, "The Scent of Wild Roses."

CHAPTER 6

For information regarding the reportage of World War II, especially in Seattle newspapers, I am greatly indebted to James R. Warren's *The War Years: A Chronicle of Washington State in World War II* (Seattle and London: History Ink, in association with the Univ. of Washington Press: 2000). In this chapter I quote from pages 8–11. A brief overview of the Japanese invasion of the Aleutian Islands during World War II can be found in *The Aleutians,* vol. 7, no. 3 (Anchorage, Alaska, and Edmunds, Washington: Alaska Geographic Society, 1980), 133–37.

CHAPTER 7

I have quoted from page 226 of Elizabeth Hampsten's *Read This Only to Yourself: The Private Writings of Midwestern Women, 1880–1910* (Bloomington, Ind.: Indiana Univ. Press, 1982). Although Hampsten considers diaries and letters that were written at least thirty years before World War II, I have found her insights an excellent foundation for understanding the nuances of texts like Imogene's diaries.

Hampsten argues (and Jennifer Sinor, two decades later, agrees) that one of the reasons nineteenth-century women wrote of trivia was to assure themselves that they were living in a tranquil domestic circle where nothing important was happening, otherwise their circle wouldn't be tranquil. This conclusion is only partly true of Imogene's diaries, which do note the weather and list routine chores, but less to foreground the trivia than to assure Imogene that she's in control of her days (or that she can get control if she just tries harder). Also, no one could possibly read her diaries and believe that nothing important is happening.

Like the family letters quoted throughout this book, Warren's letter is part of my private collection.

I have quoted from page 21, volume I, of Ellen Gordon Fletcher's *A Bride on the Bozeman Trail: The Letters and Diary of Ellen Gordon Fletcher 1866,* ed. Francis D. Haines (Medford, Oreg.: Gandee Printing Center, 1970), cited by Susan Badger Doyle in *Journeys to the Land of Gold: Emigrant Diaries from the Bozeman Trail: 1863–1866* (Helena: Montana Historical Society Press, 2000).

CHAPTER 9

I have quoted from page 56 of Jennifer Sinor's *The Extraordinary Work of Ordinary Writing,* and I refer to Marz Harper's *Solitary Travelers: Nineteenth Century Women's Travel Narratives and the Scientific Vocation* (Rutherford, N.J.: Fairleigh Dickinson Univ. Press, 2001). Harper found that the women who wrote these narratives suffered periodically from severe depression, perhaps because they felt torn between social expectations and their own ambitions; although they predate Imogene by nearly a century, like her they are breaking away from their families and testing their independence, but at a price.

I have quoted from pages 39 and 41, and following, in Warren's *The War Years.*

CHAPTER 11

I have quoted from Elizabeth Hampsten's *Read This Only to Yourself,* page 261, and from Art Dwelly's *Tenino: The First Hundred Years* (Tenino, Wash., 1971), pages unnumbered.

CHAPTER 13

I have quoted from Sinor's *The Extraordinary Work of Ordinary Writing,* page 197. In connection with Imogene's use of slang, I am indebted to the insights of Melody Graulich. I also have quoted from Hampsten's *Read This Only To Yourself,* page 226.

CHAPTER 15

Dix Moser's death is noted on page 245 of Warren's *The War Years.* His obituary appeared in the *Thurston County Independent* of May 25, 1945, page 1.

CONCLUSION

I have quoted from Rick DeMarinis's *The Art and Craft of the Short Story* (Cincinnati, Ohio: Story Press, 2000), page 40; from Richard Ford's *The Sportswriter* (New York: Random House, 1986), page 119; from Charles Baxter's "Against Epiphanies," *Burning Down the House: Essays on Fiction* (St. Paul, Minn.: Graywolf Press, 1997), pages 66–68; and from Philip Gerard's *Creative Nonfiction: Researching and Crafting Stories of Real Life* (Cincinnati, Ohio: Story Press, 1996), page 124.